THE Radical Write

a FRESH APPROACH to

Journalistic Writing for Students

BOBBY HAWTHORNE

TAYLOR
PUBLISHING COMPANY

Dedicated to my wife Mary and my daughter Sarah and to the memory of James F. Paschal, my mentor and friend.

International Standard Book Number 0-87833-101-8

Printed in the United States of America.

THANKS Y'ALL

I OWE a great debt of gratitude to the following people, who helped define, shape, organize, clarify, proof and edit this book:

• Howard Spanogle, whose perfectionism and professionalism saved me from many embarrassing mistakes and misjudgments. In addition, his wisdom and vast knowledge helped shape every page.

I am grateful to the following people for their contributions, suggestions and support: John Bowen, Lakewood, Ohio; Bob Button, Grosse Point, Michigan; Kem Brossman, Houston, Texas; Nan Cayton, Fairmont, West Virginia; Hope Carroll, Monroe, Louisiana; Lorene Denney, Austin, Texas; and H. L. Hall, Kirkwood, Missouri.

Also, David Knight, Lancaster, South Carolina; Jack Kennedy, Iowa City, Iowa; Dr. Terri LeClercq, Austin, Texas; Terry Nelson, Muncie, Indiana; Sandy Hall-Chiles, Dallas, Texas; Candace Perkins, St. Charles, Illinois; Mary Pulliam, Duncanville, Texas; Rob Thomas, Los Angeles, California; Rob Melton, Portland, Oregon; Laura Schaub, Norman, Oklahoma; Earl Straight, Morgantown, West Virginia; and George Taylor, Tamaqua, Pennsylvania.

I also am indebted to Barbara Calaway, Nelly Valadez, Rachel Seewald, Pat Wisdom, Trisha Ardiana and David Trussell.

I APPRECIATE the many newspapers that granted permission to reprint stories or portions of stories: the *Austin American-Statesman*, the *San Antonio Light*, *The New York Times*, the Associated Press and the *Boston Globe*. In particular, I appreciate the *Dallas Morning News* for its many contributions to this text. I also am indebted to the American Society of Newspaper Editors for its contributions.

I also am grateful to the following student publications (listed in no particular order):

• *Panther Prints*, Duncanville (Texas) High School.
• *The Tiger Rag*, Irving (Texas) High School.
• *Jackets Journal*, Arlington Heights (Texas) High School, Fort Worth.
• *The Rambler*, Temple (Texas) High School.
• *The Lion*, Lyons Township High School, LaGrange, Illinois.
• *The Tower*, Grosse Point South High School, Grosse Point, Michigan.
• *The Talon '80*, Eisenhower High School, Lawton, Oklahoma.
• *The Echo*, Glenbard East High School, Lombard, Illinois.
• *The Little Hawk*, City High School, Iowa City, Iowa.
• *Serif*, Tarpon Springs (Florida) High School.
• *The Arrow*, Utica (Michigan) High School.
• *The Torch*, Sharpstown High School, Houston, Texas.
• *The Regit*, Spring Woods High School, Houston, Texas.
• *Lone Star Dispatch*, James Bowie High School, Austin, Texas.
• *Cat's Tale*, Sulphur Springs (Texas) High School.
• *Featherduster*, Westlake (Texas) High School
• *Excelsior*, Stillwater (Oklahoma) High School.
• *The Regit*, Spring Woods High School, Houston, Texas.
• *The Lion's Tale*, R. L. Turner High School, Carrollton, Texas
• *Mohigan*, Morgantown (West Virginia) High School.
• *Episode*, Yorktown (Indiana) High School.
• *Maple Leaves*, Fairmont Sr. (West Virginia) High School.
• *The Eagle*, Labay Jr. High School, Houston, Texas.
• *The Searchlight*, Eastlake North (Ohio) High School
• *Lyncean*, Winona (Texas) High School.
• *Campus Corral*, Central High School, San Angelo Texas.
• *The Searchlight*, Eastlake (Ohio) North High School.
• *The Lance*, West Springfield (Virginia) High School.
• *North Winds*, Northside High School, Roanoke, Virginia.
• *Inklings*, Staples High School, Westport, Connecticut

MANY OF the examples are from Texas publications. While countless others may have been used from publications throughout the nation, I opted to use the examples with which I was most familiar and comfortable.

I owe much to Rick Hill for his advice, technical assistance and friendship.

And of most importance, I am indebted to the hundreds of students and advisers at workshops and conventions, whose enthusiasm for this style of reporting and writing convinced me that young readers want more from their publications than data.

Cover design and art, and interior art by Barbara Tyler

Interior design by Bobby Hawthorne.

Edited by Howard Spanogle.

Production assistance by Bradley Wilson and Leigh-Ellen Clark.

DO SOMETHING NEW

Do you really read your high school newspaper? Does the content make you laugh? Does it make you cry? Has a story ever moved you to write a letter to the editor? To slam your fist on your desk? Has a story ever been the subject of a big argument between you and your friends?

Probably not—unless you're one of the lucky students who receive a newspaper that is leading the way to good reading. Most likely, your high-school newspaper tells you what happened, what's happening or what will happen—safe stuff you already knew or don't care about. It doesn't grab you by the throat. It doesn't get in your face. It's not written to be read.

And that's a shame because for many, high school is the ultimate experience, the precise moment when hormones, money and freedom intersect, when teenagers get their first taste of what it is to be an adult. It's exciting and dangerous, a ripe topic for writers with imagination and verve.

But while the teenage experience is described vividly in thousands of movies and books, high-school publications too often convince us that it is nothing more than an endless series of club meetings, athletic events and popularity contests. All the life is squeezed out of the stories so they can answer who, what, when, where, why and how.

"Hi. My name is Brenda. I am a member of the pep squad, the band and the yearbook staff. My favorite food is pizza, and I love my family, school and country. I have no problems, fears or concerns."

Brenda's thinking about suicide, but that really doesn't fit any of our pre-existing formulas.

But I have never met Brenda. So how do I know this? Because for almost all of my professional career, I've judged hundreds of high-school newspapers and yearbooks for at least 15 state and national press associations, and I've begged other people to judge them for me.

In fact, I was driving down the road and saw this guy holding a sign that said, "Will work for food."

When I pulled over and asked him if he'd be interested in judging a few high-school newspapers, he replied, "I'm not that hungry."

Then, I recognized the guy. He judged for me the year before and admitted he had to take a handful of No-Doze to finish the job.

My point is this: high-school publications should be more interested in capturing, describing, analyzing and interpreting the emotional roller-coaster ride that is high school than in telling the reader who's on the volleyball team or honor roll.

So I decided to write a book.

I realize the last thing the world needs is another book on reporting and writing, but this book is different. First, I don't assume that students will read the newspaper. You have to make them read the newspaper. You have to make the stories so interesting, so colorful, so dramatic, so compelling that they'd come to school sick rather than miss a single issue. I'm not kidding.

Second, I don't think you can do this by following all of the old rules. The old rules got us in this mess in the first place. While television, books, movies, music videos and electronic videos have exploded with graphic intensity, newspapers have satisfied themselves by running spot color over boring stories. It's stupid, and it doesn't work.

Let's do something new. It's time to take a radical look at all high-school publications and student newspapers in particular. I want you to forget everything that you think you know about newspapers. Forget the inverted pyramid. Forget objectivity. Forget the 5Ws and H.

Focus first and foremost on message: Which stories do I want to tell? To whom do I want to tell them? What is the best voice and tone for me to use as I tell them?

Remember that you bring a wealth of information and opinion to every story you write. That doesn't mean that you should write an editorial instead of a story. It means that you should have the freedom to frame the story in terms of your own experiences.

Journalists gather information with a sense of their individual writing styles in mind and then write based on the information they've gathered.

Sadly, this message is sometimes lost on student journalists, who are force-fed the inverted pyramid and its subliminal message that this form is more important than the function of a student newspaper, which is to inform, to interpret and to entertain.

The stories making up a large percentage of our student newspapers accomplish little. Having judged these publications over the years, I found it difficult to criticize reporters whose stories may have satisfied the criteria for news writing as outlined in a textbook or the association's evaluation guide but completely failed to take into consideration the needs and expectations of their readers.

This isn't to suggest that I didn't criticize them. I did. But I felt guilty about it so I decided to write a book that would better explain the standard against which their publication was being evaluated—by this judge at least.

Before I proceed, let me say that I realize the style of writing I propose is by no means the only successful strategy journalists can employ. Journalism will always have a place for summary and quote leads and other traditional news and feature approaches. We haven't seen the last startling statement lead.

In particular, I'm not promoting the demise of the inverted pyramid. I agree with Linda Jones, an associate professor of journalism at Roosevelt University in Chicago, who wrote in the January, 1993 issue of J•Communique, "The inverted pyramid style of writing is good discipline for beginners. It emphasizes conciseness, which is so important to news writing, and it can be used as a reporting guideline for novices who otherwise might forget some crucial elements of a story. Most importantly, the inverted pyramid provides a fall-back structure for beginners, whose reporting and writing may need emphasis over organization."

However, the inverted pyramid should be reserved for what the old-schoolers call "hard news," those timely stories that inform more than entertain. Given that student newspapers are published, on the average, once or twice a month, the opportunities for hard news are few and far between. And considering the impact of CNN and Headline News, I'm not certain what qualifies as "hard news" for daily newspapers anymore, except for those stories that the newspapers themselves break.

Furthermore, I believe you enjoy reporting and writing more if you imitate the network television reporters. And how do they present news? They tell the story of an event in terms of the people involved and affected. This approach allows readers to literally see how events—the economy, the response to a medical crisis, hurricanes, earthquakes, famines, floods, war, whatever— change the lives of real people who aren't so much different from themselves.

Telling the story of a 14-year-old sophomore who quit school to get a minimum wage so he could help pay his family's bills says more about dropout rates than any statistics released by the Education Department.

I am convinced students would read a story reported in these terms before they would read a story that recited mountains of numbers of facts.

Though I've heard that students today don't and won't read, I disagree. I spend much of my time in workshops reading to students, and they seem to enjoy it. I doubt it has anything to do with my mesmerizing storytelling abilities. It's the power of the stories themselves and the abilities of the reporters to tell them. And then I give them similar stories for them to read on their own, and they do because the examples I give them are informative and entertaining.

While I am unwilling to concede that students cannot or will not read, I'm convinced that they will not read formula stories that ignore the humanity of a story or boil it down to nothing more than the 5Ws and H.

I hope this book brings about a radical change in your writing, its power and its ability to speak with conviction and passion. I also hope this book radically changes your publication. Then your readers will treasure every issue of the newspaper and every volume of the yearbook you produce. And I'm not kidding.

THE WRITING PROCESS: HOW A BOOK HAPPENS

If you think writing one of those 10-page research papers is tough, try writing a book some time. It's a pain.

Another person might have cranked this out in six weeks, but it took me four years. I thought I was finished with it until I mailed a copy of the manuscript to Howard Spanogle. I figured he'd drop me a "looks good" note. Instead, he wore out a dozen red pens on it, and all of his comments were on target so half of this laborious process has been editing. Keep that in mind when you read the chapter on editing.

So why did I put myself through it? Ego. Students and teachers who had heard my lectures at workshops or conventions on writing for student newspapers wanted to know where they could find a textbook that provided more information on this particular style of reporting and writing.

While I assume that texts are available, I know of no book that forcefully targets this topic. I began by transcribing my notes. Then I added chapters here and there so I had to find ways to state more convictions about writing. I've tried as best possible and advisable to maintain the same voice I use in my lectures.

While it has an edge, it is never my intention to belittle student efforts. My respect for young reporters and editors is boundless.

Many of the examples and points made in this book began as recommendations that I had made to staffs whose newspapers I was judging for one of the scholastic press associations.

Other chapters evolved from articles that I'd written for professional journals or from sessions that I conducted at scholastic press association conventions. Chapter 3 evolved from a session I conducted at the Columbia Scholastic Press Association spring convention in New York City. Later, I adopted the ideas for an article that appeared in CSPA's Student Press Review.

Other portions may have been columns or portions of columns that I've written for The Leaguer, the official publication of the organization for which I've worked as director of journalism since 1979.

No chapter, however, is self-contained. Each must be read in the context of the entire book. The chapter on angle cannot be fully understood without understanding the chapter on theme. The chapter on interpretation must be considered in relation to the chapter on objectivity.

It is also important that you read the examples. I've chosen them, particularly those labeled "Showcase," because they are a good read. Don't simply skim through them. They're the best this book has to offer.

Learn from them.

CONTENTS

CHAPTER ONE

FIND A READER

Student journalists have plenty to write about and a receptive audience to write for. What is needed now is the understanding that they're writing for other students, not for a teacher or for another adult.

The problem with most high school newspapers is that they're not read.

They're scanned. Students thumb through them in search of their names or the names of friends. Being mentioned in the newspaper implies a person has achieved status within the school, regardless of the subject or the context of the story. Joe is a member of the football team. Susan was named a master debater. Mrs. Hunter won a teaching award. Thus, the newspaper serves as a monthly "who's who," the school's social register.

But does that mean the newspaper is being read?

No. At a session of the Columbia Scholastic Press Association in New York City, I asked students how many of them read the *Wall Street Journal*. Out of a class of 100, one or two hands went up. Most students looked at me as though I were nuts. Why should they read it? It contains little information interesting or relevant to them.

But would you read it, I asked, if once a week your names were printed in the paper. A few more hands rose.

"You're lying," I said. "You'd scan it for your name. But you wouldn't read it."

That's what "readers" do with school newspapers.

And why not? Stories are not written to be read but rather to fill a space on a page, to complete an assignment, or to satisfy a

source's demand for publicity—a kind of "I don't care what you say about me so long as you say something and spell my name correctly" request. The reader is the last consideration in the formulation of news, despite most staff's stated intentions to publish newspapers that inform and entertain. Most high school newspapers rehash old news or restate the obvious with all the clarity and style of a lawnmower manual.

So there. Get mad. Take offense. Huff and puff.

It's true.

Although high schools rarely publish weekly or even bi-weekly, many staffs still treat all news questions as equals, mulching them together to conform to the traditional inverted pyramid formula so the focus of many student news or feature stories is most likely to be "who, what, when or where" even though the subject concerns an event that occurred three weeks earlier.

It matters not that readers have long since forgotten or ceased to care—if indeed they ever cared—about the event. Reporters cover events because they happened, and the thrust of the news coverage is just that: they happened.

Homecoming and student council elections are good examples. Although the election took place three weeks earlier, the newspaper staff focuses on who won what, when and where. High school journalists seldom explore reactions and/or ramifications, if there are any, and fail to consider that if there are not, then perhaps this really isn't all that newsworthy a story after all.

Sports leads also provide excellent examples of the "too little, too late" coverage. Few readers need to be told or wish to be reminded the team won or lost a game played 14 days ago. They certainly don't need to be insulted with leads such as, "With the first chill of autumn air comes football season. The Fighting Vikings take to the field next Friday against Mercerville. Members of the team are . . . ."

DATA DOMINATES STUDENT PRESS

However this approach to coverage and writing dominates the student press. It's fact/data oriented. The Pep Squad did this. The Debate Team did that. The Chess Club will do something else. When asked about it, the club president said, "blah, blah, blah."

Do readers care? Yes and no. Readers don't care where the Spanish Club went for its annual Cinco de Mayo lunch, but they may be interested in the Spanish Club's efforts to raise money for a fellow member who is undergoing chemotherapy. Readers may not be interested in the Academic Bowl officer election, but they may be interested in a story that captures the anxiety of the last competition. Readers may not care that the Student Council will hold a blood drive in the school cafeteria, but they may be interested in a story that reveals students' unfounded fears that they may contract AIDS by donating blood.

So it's a balancing act: These facts should be contained in the paper, albeit in sidebar lists, graphs, summaries and other reader-friendly graphic elements. But the majority of the paper should be reserved for "stories."

For some reason, though, newspaper staffs believe that if they provide details about an issue or event, then somehow readers will

care enough about the issues or events to read the stories. Not true. Because of the way information is presented, readers look at a newspaper whose contents consist of nothing more than mind-numbing data. It reads with all the zest of a geometry textbook.

You disagree? Too harsh an indictment, you argue. Fine. Conduct a readership survey at your school. Distribute the paper to a study hall. Give students 30 minutes to read it, if they choose to spend that much time with it. At the end of the half hour, give them a pop quiz on its contents. Ask data-based questions. When is the Drama Club production? Who are the leading performers? When will the ACT test be held? Where will the Speech Club compete this weekend? What is the National Honor Society planning? Who scored the third touchdown in the football team's 36-7 win?

Chances are, students won't have a clue. And why should they? They'll see the stories, give them a cursory glance for names, and then zip on through the remainder of the page.

Maybe this is too scientific a procedure for you. Try this: count the number of papers that are left in desks, in wastecans or on the floor during the same class period they're handed out.

If you want to produce a newspaper that is informative and entertaining—and I think we all do—then you must rethink coverage, reporting and writing. We can begin by debunking one of the oldest myths in journalism education—that names are news.

THEY ARE NOT!

If names alone were news, we'd wake up each morning, smack down a bowl of Sugar Crisps and read the phone book. We don't. Why? Because nothing is less newsworthy, less interesting than a list of names, unless the story states something such as "students who'll be kicked out of school for no apparent reason today include . . . ." Perhaps then names are news. But this is rarely the case. More often, stories will state something along the lines of, "Well, it's volleyball season again, and the girls are bumping, setting and spiking their way toward a state championship. Members of the team are . . . ."

It reminds me of a newspaper I found a few years back. The banner headline in the first issue, which was published on Oct. 1, screamed, "School Begins." This must have come as quite a shock to the students who'd been in class for four or five weeks. To make matters worse, the story stated something along the lines of:

THE LAZY DAYS of summer are now over, and students are back in class. No more lounging around the pool, sleeping late, and watching soap operas. It's time to crack the books and start studying.

Students attending school this year are . . . . ★

Is it news to anyone?

The so-called news story then listed the names of all students enrolled. Persons not listed, I assume, were free to leave. "What do you mean I don't have to be here? That's news to me!" But was it news to anyone else? No. It's data. Certainly, a focus on people is the key to readership, but we must use names to hook readers into stories of real interest. That's the key point. To create interest in "news," the writer must interlink, three elements:

• **Message**—the information readers should know. This consists of the news questions who, what, when, where, why and how.
• **Audience**—the people you want to get the message, such as students, teachers, parents, members of the community, alumni, people who wait in doctors' offices.
• **Interest**—the motivation needed to turn people into readers. In other words, why would a person read this story? What are the needs and expectations of the reader?

What is it about the student newspaper that attracts readers? Can a factor or factors

be isolated, refined and developed to consistently—story after story, page after page—match the expectations and satisfy the needs of the reader of a student newspaper?

Not to give away the big punch line which I promise to reveal, bit by bit, but the answer is "YES, YES, GOOD GOLLY MISS MOLLY, YES!"

So why aren't they? Why do we have stories in high-school papers like this:

AS PART OF AN EFFORT to make philosophical principles more relevant to social concerns, the philosophy department at Concorde State College will sponsor a series of lectures and discussions entitled, "Persons, Responsibility and the Law," beginning in February and continuing until April.

The free series will feature outstanding philosophers from the United States and England addressing topics of pressing social and legal concern. Each lecture will be followed by a panel discussion involving representatives of community organizations co-sponsoring the series.

Major funds for the series were provided by the National Endowment for the Arts and the Texas Committee for the Humanities: All lectures will begin at 4:30 p.m. in the Gardner Lecture Center on the Concorde campus.

Among the speakers will be Herbert Charles Laughton of Kings College, Cambridge University. He will lead a panel discussion entitled, "Changing Paradigms in the wake of the Los Angeles Riots." ★

Somehow, I just can't picture a throng of 16-year-old boys busting a gut to get into Gardner Hall so they can hear Herbert Charles discuss changing paradigms, but there it is, running front and center on the high school newspaper.

Why?

Because, students claim:
• There's nothing else to write about.
• Even if there were, it would be old news by the time the paper is published.
• We want to cover controversial subjects, but our cranky old administrators won't let us.

SURVIVING IN THE WORLD OF INSTANT MEDIA

Covering the 1960 Democratic National Convention, syndicated columnist Liz Carpenter learned of the maneuvers behind the nomination of John F. Kennedy and was prepared to write a story when, to her horror, she was scooped by TV.

As I wrote my exclusive story of political intrigue . . . suddenly to my horror, I saw on the TV screen Mr. Sam (Rayburn, Speaker of the House) and his glower addressing the Texas caucus. The announcer was telling people in Austin, and as far as the cable reached, the very things I was writing for them to read the next morning. From one of those curtained panels, where I had peeked in, there had been a camera peeking in, too. My story, stolen!

Dejected, I rolled my story out of the typewriter, tossed it in the wastepaper basket, put another piece of paper in the typewriter and began again —not writing WHAT had happened but HOW and WHY.

And that was the way it was to be forevermore for newspaper reporters. Analyzing, interpreting, yes, dancing around the story with what the cameras didn't have time to show.

- But heck, who are we kidding. Even if we did, no one would read it because our students are so dumb and lazy.
- So as you can see, it's not our fault.

YOU MAY NOT EXCUSE YOURSELF!

Let's examine these excuses one at a time.

- *There's nothing to write about.*

Is it possible to cram several hundred teenagers into a building, eight hours a day, five days a week, some weekends, and not have anything to write about? I don't think so, unless these kids are roboclones, incapable of thought or action, possessing no dreams, desires, fears, anxieties, anger or joy. In addition, they neither affect nor are affected by the world outside the classroom. The Berlin Wall comes down. They shrug. Public education crumbles around them. They yawn. Their SAT scores top the state. They flip the page. They are oblivious to all forces of commerce, culture, history, politics, the arts. They are mindless, faceless automatons.

Is this our youth?

Are you kidding?

Teenagers today may not know as much as adults would like them to, but they sure feel. They are hopeful, afraid, in need of love and attention, occasionally desperate. Many are children, lost and scared, even if they look grown up. And they look so grown up. They primp and posture, imitating MTV heroes. They work to perfect an attitude, to create a shell. Why? Because they face problems that the Baby Boomers could never have imagined.

For the first time in our nation's history, students cannot expect to achieve a higher standard of living than their parents. They face environmental pollution, a deteriorating infrastructure, empty homes, the threat of cancer and AIDS, racism and intolerance, soaring divorce rates and a widening gap between the haves and the have nots. They may not know what the national debt means —who does?—but they probably know that it is already a trillion dollars and climbing, and no one does anything about it.

In the face of all of this, how can a newspaper staff suggest that it has nothing better to write about than a rehash of who won homecoming queen, of what happened at the prom and of Judy Smith's win as student council president three weeks ago.

Of course, many staffs will respond, "We had to cover these things because nothing else happened."

Sure, you must cover prom, but must coverage assume no one attended or knew anything about it?

Certainly not. Bright reporters would search for angles that provide a thoughtful preview of the event instead of rehashing the obvious.

And about the comment, "because nothing else happened . . . ."

What do you want? A tornado to wipe out the school so you can interview the survivors?

THE LAZY DAYS of summer are now over, and students are back in class. No more lounging around the pool, sleeping late and watching soap operas. It's time to crack the books and start studying. But wait. A tornado hit the school last week.

Students no longer attending school this year are . . . . ★

> Is it possible to cram several hundred teenagers into a building, eight hours a day, five days a week, some weekends, and not have anything to write about?
> Seems doubtful.
>
> • • • • • •

So what are your other excuses?

• *Look, we tried to write about a big drug bust at our school, but by the time our paper came out, the whole thing was over.*

Doesn't wash. The problem here lies not in what you're covering but in how you're covering it. Rather than concentrating on what happened, examine instead the effects of the event. What are people saying about it? What new issues are generated? Search for reactions and response. Find a local source who can give you a fresh angle on the story. Ask more analytical questions such as "Why did it happen when it did?" and "Why was the policy changed?" Find out who is involved that people here know. Talk to administrators. Don't focus on the bust. Focus on the aftermath of the bust?

Tell readers something they don't already know. News is not static. It changes rapidly. Ted Turner's Headline News has shown us that. Updated every 30 minutes, the newscasts evolve quickly. The election of Bill Clinton provides a perfect example. The news changed quickly from reports of his victory, to reactions by world leaders, to implications for the Republican Party, to an analysis of how the demographic shift and economic realities converged to forge new political times.

• *Look, we know our stories are boring. We want to write about interesting stuff, but our administrators won't let us.*

No doubt, prior review and restraint are realistic problems, but they're not impenetrable barriers to superior content. In fact, working to present real quality materials is one of the best ways to combat these difficulties. Many staffs want to cover controversial issues for the sake of covering controversial issues. The best example of this I can remember was in a tiny Texas Panhandle town, where the students wrote about gay rights. Was it a local, timely issue? No. Why was it covered? Because the staff thought it was so juicy that it would appeal to the more ignoble

instincts of teenage boys and girls.

Student journalists have tried to cover all the controversial topics for no better reason than to say they did. The big three are substance abuse, teen sexuality and delinquent behavior.

• *"We had a story about Satanism in our paper."*

Oh yeah. What did it say?

• *Well, we wrote all about it, how some students are worshipping the devil and kidnapping children and doing all sorts of creepy things.*

Has this happened in your school or community?

• *No.*

Are your students engaged in these activities?

• *No, not that we know of.*

Well, if it isn't a problem here, if school and police authorities claim it isn't an issue, then why write about it, given the availability of so many local, timely and relevant issues?

• *Well, we wrote about it because it was controversial and we thought our students would like to read about it. And we thought the newspaper judges would be impressed that we're covering controversial issues like this.*

Where did you get your information?

• *From* Time *and* Newsweek. *And we talked to some students.*

What did the students say?

• *That Satanism is pretty yucky and that they're against it.*

And that's it?

• *Yeah. That's pretty much how it went.*

And so it goes. All coverage must be timely, relevant and local; otherwise, it is bad journalism, pure and simple. But it is particularly offensive for staffs to cover issues simply in an attempt to appeal to prurient interests.

• *Okay then, if we can't write about controversial topics, then we might as well shut*

THE "WHY" LEAD —The motive or cause of an event sometimes is the most important feature. Musician Shawn Phillips may not have had high school journalism in mind when he said, "Whether you're 14 or 114, one always needs to question the 'why' and the 'how' because otherwise you have died inside." But he makes a lot of sense.

In an effort to teach Shakespeare to sophomores, English teacher Gina Hatley and science teacher Phil Barnes reenacted the love scene between Romeo and Juliet. "It's the only thing I thought they'd understand," Ms. Hatley said.

THE "HOW" LEAD— The method by which something is accomplished.

By flunking every course, missing 62 days of class and assaulting two teachers, Bubba Snively gravely endangered his eligibility for high school basketball.

GET A GRIP. The trick to a successful publication is to engage the reader on an intellectual and emotional level. To that end, take a step back and start looking for the humor in high school. Capture those special moments that will bring a smile to the reader's face. *Photo by Joel Simon, Westlake HS (Austin, TX).*

down because our readers are dumb and lazy anyway.

I'll grant this: readers are lazy. Not just high-school readers. All readers. Give them half-an-excuse to quit reading and most will take it. It is possible that a few persons who started reading this book quit at some point prior to here because my prose didn't fully captivate them. Chances are, they're now reading a supermarket tabloid. I can accept that.

Still, the challenge of reporting for a high school newspaper—or for any other medium—is to engage the reader on intellectual and/or emotional levels.

The purpose of this book is to teach you how to engage the reader. Today's students may read less passionately than did their

parents and grandparents, but they do read and they are still passionate.

I'm amazed at the number of high-school students I saw toting *Jurassic Park*, the novel, even though most had seen the movie. Their attraction to that book suggests that teenagers are capable of getting as big a jolt from the written word as they are from Steven Spielberg's technological wizardry.

How and what they read are not the same, and their motivations for reading are different as well. Most high-school students can and do read, if provided compelling reading material. Stephen King has no problem attracting young readers.

Therein lies the trick: to write journalistically in a compelling, dynamic manner so readers will have no choice but to read. That's what this book is all about.

However, I must caution you. This method of reporting and writing is time consuming and difficult.

Students can babble off the top of their

heads about drug abuse or rehash material already printed in a weekly news magazine about teen pregnancy. As the American writer Truman Capote said of beat writer Jack Kerovac, "This isn't writing. It's typing."

Typing is easy. Reporting—that's the difficult part. Even in this age of desktop publishing, with its graphic bells and whistles, the heart and soul of the student newspaper rests in its news reporting. Without substantive information collection, you may have a student publication—but it isn't a newspaper. It isn't journalism.

The bottom line

In the final judgment, the student newspaper should be journalistic. Within that criteria, staffs have tremendous latitude in determining what to cover and how to cover it. Some will prefer a straight news approach, others will lean toward news/ feature or personality profile coverage, and still others will emphasize in-depth news coverage. These decisions are based on many factors: reader needs and expectations, staff talents and interests, publication format, and the availability of issues and events to be covered, to name a few.

Regardless of the path chosen, the final product should be journalistically sound. In terms of news reporting and writing, this means:

• The story has news value.
• Journalistic values—clarity, accuracy, brevity, relevance, attribution, fairness, balance, identification, objectivity and truth —are observed.
• All news questions are answered in the story but not necessarily given equal prominence in the lead.
• Information is attributed to a source.
• Direct and indirect quotes provide information rather than clichés and are structured effectively.
• Stylebook rules are followed religiously.

• All news stories contain one or more news elements.
• Elements of news—timeliness, currency, proximity, consequence, prominence, oddity, conflict and human interest—are included.

Facts over expressive writing

More and more staffs have allowed expressive writing to creep into their publications. No wonder why—it's easy. Students can sit at the desk and crank this stuff out, whether they are pontificating on the latest rap song or the threat of nuclear annihilation.

These essays, posing as journalism, are labeled "features." They are not. They may be term papers, research essays, or stream-of-consciousness mental tumbling exercises. But they are not journalism.

Journalism requires that reporters research, interview, observe and listen—then write because journalism always has informational value. Expressive writing requires only that the reporters have an opinion. Facts are nice but an unnecessary luxury.

The task of reporting involves the collection of facts from a wide variety of sources and then the painful realization that most of them can't and won't be used. Only the most important information, the most compelling anecdotes, the most interesting and thought-provoking quotes will be used. One of the toughest jobs a reporter faces is not determining what facts to collect but rather deciding which ones are worth using in the story.

Consider the following stories involving the winter holiday season. The first represents the expressive writing mode, common to secondary language arts classes.

"SILENT NIGHT, holy night.
"All is calm, all is bright."
Is all really calm in the 1990s? Or has Christmas gone from desired to dreaded? Some would think so. The peacefulness of Christmases past seems to have disintegrated in the hustle and

NEWS LEADS WE'VE SEEN FAR TOO OFTEN

The following leads may be effective for briefs but are not recommended for longer news and feature stories.

The "who" lead—If the "who" is a well-known person place or thing, it is usually the feature of the lead. The name alone attracts attention. Unless one of the other elements is particularly outstanding, the "big name" comes first. For example:

Coach Randy Fowler, who led Pine Valley to four consecutive district football championships, announced his retirement in order to sell used cars and whole-life insurance.

The "what" lead— Concerning an event, result, trend or policy.

A truce was declared last week between the mother of a student and the Pine Valley cheerleaders. Mrs. Tammi Lynn Bouffant agreed to stop tossing water balloons at the cheerleaders if her daughter, Nikki Sue, is allowed to cheer with the team every other road game.

bustle of commercialized shopping. The expenses of Christmas often discourages its sole purpose of holding a place on the calendar.

What is the purpose of Christmas? What does it really mean? Is it merely a holiday that takes place on Dec. 25 just because there is nothing else going on? Even a small child could tell you the answer—no!

Some would say that it is simply a holiday set aside to spend time with family and friends while others feel its main purpose is for the distributing of gifts. This idea would support the ever-famous myth of Ol' Saint Nick (although I think there's a little bit of love for Santa in everyone's heart). And still others believe that it is a celebration of Christ's birthday. This is certainly the most popular dogma. I, being a Christian, thoroughly support this belief.

Whatever your idea of Christmas, it is a happy time of celebration—a time of giving thanks and appreciation for all that has been given to you. These theories seemed to have disappeared over the years.

With presents to buy and no money to buy them with, people have become overly concerned with the disbursing of gifts. Where will I get the money? What will I buy family and friends? Thus, the joys of Christmas are hidden with all of the worry and fret. If Santa Claus were real, would he approve of this abuse of this custom of giving? Let's make this Christmas unforgettable and get back to the true meaning behind it all.

". . . Sleep in heavenly peace,
Sleep in heavenly peace." ★

A nice thought but hardly journalistic. Such stories appear in the news and feature columns as often as on the editorial pages of high school newspapers.

Here's another typical story:

CHRISTMASTIME MEANS many things to different people, but they all have one thing in common—traditions. Each family has its own traditions that it cherishes for years to come. The traditions range from putting up the tree to writing letters to Santa Claus.

The Christmas tree itself is the object of many traditions. Families go out in search of the perfect tree whether it may be in a tree lot or the woods. Some families put their trees up on the day after Thanksgiving while others put theirs up on Christmas Eve.

Traveling is also an important tradition. Families travel to visit grandparents' houses and exchange gifts among relatives. Many people attend church services on Christmas Eve. Some prefer to go to the evening service while others go to the midnight service.

Groups of people can be found shopping, caroling or enjoying Christmas parties.

For the kids, the traditions may be watching the Christmas parade, writing letters to Santa Claus or staying up as late as they can in hopes of getting a glimpse of jolly ole St. Nick eating the cookies they left for him.

Christmastime means decorating and putting up lights on the outside of the house for others to look at.

Sending Christmas cards and baking treats for others to enjoy are a few more traditions on a never-ending list.

Many individuals have traditions that bring smiles whenever they think of Christmas. ★

Did either of these stories tell the average reader anything new? It is possible that exchange students from Outer Bedpania may be unfamilar with holiday traditions, but who else stands to learn much? While these articles offer sweet and safe sentiments, they are journalistic duds.

REPORT FIRST, THEN WRITE

Report! Find news. Research. Interview. Observe. Listen for dialogue. Interview some more. Then make that news into a news story.

Compare the earlier stories to this one.

SHOWCASE

By ANNA HARRIS
Irving High School, Irving, Texas

THIS IS NOT YOUR average Christmas story, but all the elements are there. It includes the typical family that seems to have nothing but bad luck. Their money is tight—almost nonexistent. The father had an on-the-job accident which may cause him to lose his job. The mother was involved in a car wreck. The hospital bills pour in. Christmas doesn't look very promising.

Sound like a typical Christmas human interest story? Maybe so, but there's a difference. The family found help. Someone reached out to them.

For the second year in a row, Irving High School homerooms are "adopting" children for Christmas. The youngest child in the above mentioned family will be one of the adopted children. Her name is Cindy Jones, and she is a first grader at John R. Good Elementary School. A few weeks ago, Cindy brought home an information sheet about the Adopt-A-Child Program.

Her mother, Ms. Barbara Jones, explains how she felt: "I was embarrassed a little, at first, but Cindy doesn't understand the money situation right now. She wanted to be in the program. Then, it made me feel good."

Cindy's first reaction after receiving her parents' permission to be in the program was to make out a "wish list."

Its simple contents included a Mon Chi Chi stuffed animal and a Tippee Toes Doll. Before the adoption program, Cindy had not bothered to make out a list.

"This year, Christmas would not have been anything. Just us being together," Ms. Jones said.

Since money is not available for buying Christmas presents, the Joneses must rely on their own talents for Christmas gifts. Both Mr. and Mrs. Jones are taking a jewelry-making class. Ms. Jones also enjoys sewing clothes for her children. Besides Cindy, the Jones have two other children who both go to Austin Junior High School. Surprisingly, Cindy's brother and sister showed no jealousy toward Cindy's being in the program. In fact, they were happy that she, at least, would have a nice Christmas.

Ms. Jones said that she and Mr. Jones have always tried to teach their children to share with each other. "All the children are extra good about sharing," she said.

Added Patty Jones, Cindy's sister: "I like the program. I think it will help her with Christmas. I was excited when I heard about it."

Cindy is looking forward to making some new friends at the Adopt-A-Child Party, scheduled for next Friday. However, she said she is a little apprehensive about talking to so many people.

To encourage Cindy, Patty said, "Cindy may be nervous at the party, but after she brings the stuff home, she'll be happy."

All of Cindy's Christmas presents will come from IHS. Since most children will receive their presents on Christmas Day, it seems likely that Cindy would be let down on Christmas morning. Cindy's mother thinks otherwise.

"It's just a part of Christmas to her," she said. "She'll just be tickled to death to get something. Time won't make much difference. Usually, she has a second-hand Christmas.

"I am very glad that Cindy will have this opportunity," Cindy's mother added. "It's something we can't give her. We need help right now, and I'm not going to turn it down. This party will be something she can remember and say that help was there when she needed it. It lets her know that she does have friends and that people do care." ★

This story is about a real person who is benefitting from a real program. It says far more about the meaning of Christmas than either of the former articles because it's not a pie-in-the-sky lecture or rehash of the obvious.

A key to the success of this story is that it deals with a single person rather than with a general population of needy persons. Most high-school reporters make the mistake of writing about the program itself, basing the story on quotes from adults, supervisors or instructors rather than from the perspective of the recipient of the goodwill gesture—in this case, Cindy.

Telling the story from the child's point of view brings to life and makes concrete the rather abstract notion of public service. The story allows Irving High School students to say, "Perhaps we couldn't help all needy persons in the season of giving, but we brought happiness to this one child. Maybe we can change the world, one 5-year-old at a time."

What more appropriate testimony to the spirit of the season? Granted, this approach requires empathetic and sensitive reporting. Recipients of charity often prefer to avoid publicity, and it would be ethically and possibly legally wrong to place under the

MORE NEWS LEADS WE SEE TOO OFTEN

THE "WHERE" LEAD— Avoid "where" leads, especially "at WHS next week. . ." On rare occasions, the "where" is significant enough to over-shadow the other Ws, such as in the following example:

In the living room of his mobile home, Principal Gerald Skinner stood in front of his prized velvet painting of Elvis Presley and renewed his recommen-dation that courses in the study of "the King" be required in order to graduate from Pine Valley schools.

THE "WHEN" LEAD— Rarely is the time of an event the most interesting feature. However, circum-stances may make it significant. For instance:

When football coaches gather to talk about the team these days, their cocktail of choice may be Maalox. As they debate how to fire up a team that hasn't won a game in three years, one outcome is virtually certain: something good better happen quickly or they'll all be looking for new jobs next year.

spotlight those who would rather remain anonymous. In that case, seek alternatives.

The following article achieves the same but in a touchingly humorous way:

BY ERIK NICHOLSON
Grosse Point South High School,
Grosse Point, Michigan

SHOWCASE

LISTENING TO YOUNG voices sing "Jingle Bells," a group of National Honor Society students stands outside a Richard kindergarten classroom.

As they enter the room, the song ends, and pairs of eyes turn to stare at those "big kids." Mrs. Marian Lamb, the kindergarten teacher, comes over and announces, "Boys and girls, these are the South students who have come to help you write letters to Santa. Now, who is ready to start writing?"

Of course, every little hand shoots up, for what 5- or 6-year-old doesn't want to tell Santa Claus what he or she wants for Christmas? Every kindergartener rushes over to one of the "big people" and places his small hand into his new friend's. They walk over to get a piece of paper and pencil and sit down at a munchkin-size table, with a munchkin-size chair to match, and begin to write what is probably a child's most important letter all year.

Part of National Honor Society's function at South is to volunteer its services and time to the school system and the Grosse Pointe community. For several years now, NHS has helped Richard kindergarteners write their letters to Santa and then return a letter to them from "Old St. Nick himself."

The beginning journalism classes and some of the beginning typing classes write replies to other young children in the school district.

As the children sit down to write their letters, the new "big" friend begins to ask them questions. Whether they begin their letters with "Dear Santa" or "Dear Santa Claus" or "Dear Santa and Mrs. Claus" doesn't matter for many of the kindergarteners wishing to rush right into their long list of "I wants."

Of course, some of the shy ones need prompting, but not many. Television commercials have helped program their little minds. Most run off a long list quite easily.

The popular toy this year must be a thing called a "Smurf," for the majority of letters included such things as "I want a Smurfette (a female Smurf?)" and "I would like a Dr. Smurf," a "super Smurf," and the "Smurf Hall." But of course, the traditional Barbie dolls, teddy bears, trucks, space ships and play dishes make the list too.

Many children's letters, however, when completed, are not filled with just "I wants." Many said, for example, "I will leave some apples for the reindeer and some cookies and milk for you, Santa."

And others wrote, "I wish Mrs. Claus a happy Christmas. And Rudolph too!"

Children, too, even at a young age, seem to have learned that Christmas is a season not just for taking, but for giving.

Five-year-old Joni Brown said, "I like when I wake up and see the lights on the tree and presents. I'm so glad when Santa eats all my cookies I gave him."

Asked what she liked best about Christmas, young Casey Collins said, "I like best when Santa Claus comes."

But for some kindergarteners, Santa Claus is not the first thing that comes to mind when asked what is important about Christmas.

Stevie Boocher said "Jesus" is most important, but he said he didn't know why.

So classmate Elizabeth Brasseur explained, "Because he was borned on Christmas." ★

THINK ABOUT YOUR READERS

To summarize, student journalists have plenty to write about and a receptive audience to write for. However, young readers can spot quickly a story bulging with cold data, written to fulfill the requirements for a grade or to please a teacher rather than to tell an interesting story or communicate to students on their own level and in their own language.

Often, students believe they are the last considerations in any decision the school bureaucracy cranks out. Student readers don't want and don't deserve to be second-class citizens in their own newspaper as well. Intelligent editors and reporters will make sure that doesn't happen.

CHAPTER TWO

FOCUS ON REPORTING

While it's easy to dress up newspapers with squiggles and with reverse type that stretches across the page, the success of the publication as a news medium hinges on the power of its reporting.

When desktop publishing burst upon the scene in the mid-1980s, many student journalists embraced the Macintosh in hopes that all the fancy typefaces, screens, clip art and other assorted bells and whistles would save their publications. Alas, no magic results. Even now, the journalists spend too much time contemplating what the computer can do and not enough time thinking about what the reporter should do. Without persistence, no amount of fancy packaging will rescue weak coverage.

In other words, you can't turn a Minnie Mouse newspaper into a Madonna simply by packing on a few more layers of eye-shadow.

In fact, sometimes writing teachers can't decide whether the Macintosh is a blessing or a curse.

Some believe Macs encourage creativity, boost productivity and enhance the learning process. Others argue that the computer, with its assorted graphic doo-dads, leads to both mechanical and intellectual sloppiness in composition.

Marcia Peoples Halio, the assistant director of the writing program at the University of Delaware, suggested in an article, "Student Writing: Can the Machine Maim the Message?" published in *Academic Computing*, that students who used Macintosh computers wrote at the intellectual equivalent of a music video while students using IBM computers dealt with meatier issues with more sophistication.

She then asked, perhaps rhetorically, "Can a technology be too easy to use? Can such a technology arrest their writing at a less mature stage of development?"

She may as well have asked the Kuwaitis if they minded while Iraq invaded. Mac-fans, who came out of the woodwork, accused Halio of all sorts of graduate-school type errors and probably called her a few names to boot.

While neither side has claimed its findings are definitive, both are working furiously to debunk the other. And so the furor rages on.

This debate is fairly meaningless on the high school level. Most English and journalism teachers would agree the comma splice and run-on sentence came along light years before the PowerMac, and I'd agree. From where I sit, I'd have to concede the Macintosh has been a godsend, like other stunning inventions, such as the cordless iron. I'm not sure how I survived without it.

Similarly, desktop publishing has revolutionized student publications, at least from a production, design and graphics perspective. However, the same cannot be said for its impact on content or copy.

Undoubtedly, the Mac has simplified writing and editing. Students may now compose, splice and revise with unbelievable ease and then send their copy through a program that catches misspelled words.

"I began using computers with an Apple II," said George Taylor, who advised the student newspaper at Tamaqua, Pennsylvania. The Apple II computer was a forerunner of the Macintosh.

"All of our staff had training on the Apple II, and all copy was submitted on disk. Editors read and made suggestions right on the copy. The disk was returned for revision. The computer has made revision far less painful and therefore more likely to happen."

But there's a down side. Student publications have shown a tendency to imitate microwave food. Pop them in the machine and seconds later, out comes something totally indistinguishable from everything else.

I'm not ready to place the blame squarely on the Macintosh, but the content of student publications has plunged in the past decade. However, the slippage has nothing to do with censorship or a shortage of funds or curriculum changes. It boils down to this: reporting is becoming a lost art.

Publications are full of essays, reviews, opinion columns, infographics, fiction—even poetry. Some of this writing is quite good, but good writing is not necessarily good reporting, and student newspapers are woefully short of good reporting.

Reporting is hard work. You have to get up out of your chair, interview people you might otherwise never talk to, go places you'd rather not go, spend time watching and listening to something other than the television. Reporting requires a commitment that extends beyond a hit-and-run interview.

Furthermore, reporting is a process. It has a before and an after, a beginning, a middle and an end—with each step in the process defining and being defined by the other steps individually and collectively. Reporting requires planning, contemplation and, most importantly, footwork.

Sadly, student publications crank out lots of copy but exhibit little evidence of solid reporting. Whether the Macintosh can be blamed for this, I can't say, other than to note that the use of screens and stretched type has become something of an art form.

More than the sum of its parts

In this day of instant gratification, students and advisers want a quick and easy critique of their writing. Are we writing about the right topics? Does the lead work? Is it long enough? Are there enough quotes?

Unfortunately, the answers are never cut and dried. Perhaps students are writing about the right topic, but what have they said? How have they approached the topic to make it meaningful and interesting to a young audience? Why did they emphasize this news question over that one, or more likely, why did they treat all news questions as equals? Who did they quote and why? Why did they choose to tell the story in this particular tone or voice? Have they told anyone anything not already known, and if so, have they told it in such a way to make readers want to know more?

Students are rarely prepared to respond to such a rigorous examination of their stories. More often than not, students have taken a "path-of-least-resistance" philosophy in writing so the results are a stillborn product. Stories are approached in the same ways, time after time, with the same sources asked the same questions, resulting in interchangeable, fill-in-the-blank copy.

It need not be so. While it is dangerous to reduce reporting or writing to a series of steps, the following criteria at least force students to see each story as a living organism that is more than the mere sum of its 12 individual parts:

❑ theme	❑ research
❑ angle	❑ focus
❑ clarity	❑ order
❑ transition	❑ word choice
❑ description	❑ interpretation

❑ accuracy   ❑ unity

These standards interlink with one another. We will look at them briefly here and in greater depth later in the book.

❑ THEME

Too many stories fail because they're not about anything. Yearbook club coverage is the perfect example. Copy blocks rarely tell readers anything they didn't know or couldn't figure out on their own. For example, "The purpose of the Future Teachers of America is to teach students about careers in education. This year, students in FTA visited area schools. Members of the club included . . . ."

This approach is taken for all stories—short item and in-depth alike. Take, for example, the personality profile. It is often little more than biographical sketches, a rehash of the resumé. Genuine attempts to develop the personality are rare, partially because writing about a person requires establishing a special rapport between the reporter and subject. Consequently, a story about a retiring teacher will consist of when the person started teaching, where, what subjects and for how long. It'll end with an obligatory "I'll miss the kids" quote.

Having read the story, readers know no more about the teacher now than they did before. So the story really isn't about a person: the teacher. It's about a thing: a retirement.

People, particularly young people, don't want to read about things. When you ask yourself, "What is this story about?" the answer had better be "a person."

For example, a story on homeless teenagers should focus on one teen and allow that teen's story to represent a greater truth. I am not suggesting that you can't talk to several, but the story should center on one person. The reader wants to know that person, to care about him or her. Otherwise, the reader doesn't know any of the people in this story, and consequently, can't really care about any

individual.

The same is true of longer, in-depth stories—the so-called controversial topics. Too often, the stories read like research papers written for social studies teachers. Facts are piled atop facts, data on top of data, most or all of which is pulled from national magazines rather than local sources. The result is a collection of details that leaves the reader in a fog.

For example, a staff devotes an issue of its newspaper to covering crime. How did it choose to do so? By crunching numbers. There were "X" number of crimes committed, costing taxpayers "X" amount of dollars. "X" percent were solved. "X" percent of the criminals went to jail, serving "X" amount of time. "X" percent of the offenders were female. "X" percent were males. "X" percent were teens. "X" percent of victims knew the offender. And finally, the staff tacked on safety tips to prevent being victimized and guidelines for using crime stoppers.

I'm not certain for whom the stories were written, but I'm confident they were not written for a teenage reader because no high-school student I've ever met would have been interested in wading through such tripe.

Not only must reporters know what they're writing about, but they must also ask, "For whom am I writing?" Once determined, the reporter then asks other questions, including:

• What does the reader expect and need?
• How much will the reader already know about this topic, if anything?
• How can I make certain the story remains timely?
• How can I localize and personalize the story?
• Who are my primary and secondary sources?

The answers to these questions will determine the reporter's strategy for collecting information. For seasoned reporters, the process is an unconscious one, an almost

MORE NEWS LEADS WE SEE TOO OFTEN

• LABEL LEADS—A label lead generally begins with the name of a club, class, team, or person. For example:

The Pine Valley High School Chess Club will . . . .

Another form of label lead begins with a prepositional phrase answering the news question "when" (such as, *"On Tuesday, the Pep Squad . . . ."*).

The story should begin with the most interesting and most important information. Label leads never provide this information.

automatic assessment of their readerships. "News judgment," it's called, and it's an occupational by-product. Unfortunately, most students haven't been on the job long enough to develop that kind of judgment so it's useful to rely on criteria such as change, conflict, impact, proximity and timeliness.

Now, let's go back to the example regarding crime. Are readers likely to be more interested in a lot of numbers or this story?

SHOWCASE

BY LESLIE COURTNEY
Arlington Heights High School
Fort Worth, Texas

NATHAN SHAFFER thought about his friends, closed his eyes, and tried to imagine what it would be like to die.

Sept. 8 was just another normal day for Shaffer while he checked out customers in the express lane at Thrift Mart on Camp Bowie until two masked men with guns walked in and told everyone to get on the floor. One of the robbers told the 17-year-old Heights senior to put the money from the register in the bag. Shaffer complied. Then the robber asked, "What's under the register drawer?"

"Nothing," Shaffer said.

"Take the drawer out," the robber said.

Under the drawer, Shaffer found more money. The robber then pointed a gun a foot from Shaffer's face and said, "Now you're going to die."

"I felt like running to someone for security, but no one was there to run to. My only security was the floor."

Nothing in his life had prepared Shaffer for this experience, he said. And the trauma left emotional scars that will probably never heal.

"It makes me wonder every time I go to work whether it will happen again," Shaffer said.

One moment everything is routine—dull. Then seconds later you are fighting just to live.

"I was working in the express lane. I was checking out a customer. I didn't see the two men come in, but I heard them yell, 'Get down on the ground.' At first I thought it was some of my friends," Shaffer said.

Everyone in the store immediately got on the floor, he said. One man jumped over the counter into the office. The other one came over to Shaffer's register.

"When the robber said I was going to die, what mostly went through my head was all the time I spent with my friends," Shaffer said.

"I started to think about what it would be like to be shot. I wondered if I would just die, or if I would see the people around me slowly fade away," Shaffer said.

As suddenly as the robber decided to shoot Shaffer, he changed his mind. He grabbed the money bag and ran out the door, Shaffer said.

The first thing Shaffer did after the robbers left was run to the back of the store and throw up, he said. The trauma left him weak and shaken.

Linda Allen was working in the office when the other robber came into the office with a gun and told her to open the vault.

"This was the first time I had been in a robbery, and I was scared. I thought he was going to shoot me. I thought this was the end," Allen said.

"After the men left, I went into a state of shock. I was told I went to the hospital, but I don't remember any of it—only pieces."

Shaffer was scheduled to get off work at 9 that night, but was told to stay, clean up and keep working until 11, he said.

Mr. Bill Kiker, the manager of Thrift Mart, said he told Shaffer to continue working because one of the workers had been taken to the hospital. Kiker said there were four other workers left to continue running the store, but he felt Shaffer should stay.

He would not comment on the fact that Shaffer was the only worker left who had had a gun pointed at him moments earlier.

Shaffer said one of the most traumatic parts of the evening was having to walk home at 11 p.m. He said the police had agreed to give him a ride but had left before he was allowed to leave work.

"It was dark and scary. I was so afraid," Shaffer said.

About two weeks later, Shaffer was called by the police to try to identify a suspect in a line up.

"I had never been to a police station until the police called me in for a line up. I was nervous," Shaffer said.

"I was behind a two-way mirror looking at the line up. When I walked in, I turned around and hid my face. It felt like the men in the line up could see right through the mirror," Shaffer said.

"I went up to the glass, and I picked out the

man that held me up. When I pointed him out, he was looking right at me through the mirror. When I moved, his eyes followed me," Shaffer said.

After the line up Shaffer went back to school. "When I got into the classroom, I couldn't concentrate. The line up kept running through my mind," Shaffer said.

Shaffer went to his vice principal and asked to be excused. Shaffer was physically ill the rest of the day, he said.

Alfred Arredondo was charged with aggravated robbery after Shaffer identified him as the robber. Arredondo pleaded guilty and was sentenced to 30 years, Detective John McCaskill, with the Fort Worth Police Department, said.

A positive identification has not been made on the other suspect, McCaskill said.

"I am glad they caught a suspect so fast. I didn't really think they would catch anyone with the description I gave the police," Shaffer said. "I didn't want to be like these people who are afraid to press charges because they might be harassed."

He added, "If it ever happened to me again, I can't say what I would do.

"I'd just pray I would live through it." ★

❏ RESEARCH

Too often, students interpret research as plagiarism. They copy information verbatim from already published sources and offer it as their own. How often have you read stories that were based on information—news facts, statistics, direct quotes—taken directly from teen or news magazines?

Granted, student reporters must do their library research, but, as Jeff Currie, adviser of the Oak Park-River Forest *Trapeze*, said, "The objective is to gain information and understanding, not to 'lift' already published materials. The materials gained from research only form the base or the general context of the story."

Professional reporters might refer to this as deep background: data that is used to set the context of the story, to provide the reporter with an understanding of the issue. However, it is assumed this information will not appear in the story, except perhaps to establish a context. A story worth printing

and reading should be comprised of locally generated direct quotes and personal observation.

This is true for news or features. Suppose the school board announces the district will lose $6 million because voters defeated a bond package. The reporter must search—research, if you will—beyond the minutes of the school board meeting to show the impact that such a loss of funds will have. Rather than dwelling on the results of the election or the pronouncements of the board members, the student reporter should ask, "What are the repercussions. What are people saying about it? What specifically would it mean for the school to lose $6 million?"

A lead like this would be much more compelling:

"THEY WANT US TO TEACH driver's ed, but all they give us are these Model Ts to drive," computer teacher Cheryl Ford said.

She was talking about the state of the school's computers, mostly first generation Apples and IBMs, all of which are long outdated. Plans to purchase new Macintosh computers for the computer classes are on hold now that the $6 million bond failed.

"The state's school funding situation is a mess, and no one knows what will happen there," said Bobby Reynolds, communications specialist. "Locally, we must have some relief if we are expected to do a credible job. People say they value education for their kids, but they sure don't act like it."

For example, several buildings at Andress need to be air-conditioned.

"We were supposed to be moved out of the East Wing so that air conditioning could be put in, but that's now off," said history teacher Janet Elkins. "You can't imagine how hot it gets down here some times. Students simply cannot concentrate in such an environment." ★

Because you are writing for a student publication, you should focus on the part of the story that will most interest and affect students. Students cannot be expected to understand the full repercussions of a loss of a bond package. But they can understand all

MORE NEWS LEADS WE SEE TOO OFTEN

• QUOTE LEADS—A quote lead begins with a direct quote. It is a lazy way out. Almost always original writing makes a stronger lead.

Intersperse quotes throughout your news briefs, but make certain the quotes add substantially to the story. In too many cases, the quote either repeats other information or echoes the obvious. For example: The art teacher is planning a trip to France. Too often, the quote will read, "I'm really looking forward to it," she said.

Big deal. Avoid quotes that provide facts. The quote should state an opinion about facts.

Thus, a better quote would be: "Although they have a reputation as terrible hosts, I've always found the French to be warm, friendly and engaging. And Paris is my favorite city in the world."

too well what it means to sit in hot and sticky classrooms.

❏ ANGLE

Now, let's assume the reporter has interviewed, observed, listened and researched. The next task is to use the information to grab readers and invite them to read the story.

The task begins with the selection of the subject for the lead, your intention being to engage readers in a drama or narrative.

Once reporters have gathered facts, they must decide through whose eyes, in what voice and tone, and in what order to tell the story. It is the most difficult step in writing.

Imagine, for a moment, that you've been assigned to write a story about the newspaper staff itself. The immediate tendency might be to write, "The newspaper is busy at work, putting out another issue. Students work after school to produce a publication that they hope will be popular." And so on.

MEMBERS OF THE Bobcat Blab staff are working hard to publish a newspaper that the students will appreciate. Newspaper staff members spend long, hard hours after school interviewing, writing and designing pages.

"We take our work seriously because freedom of the press is important to Americans," said Cynthia Claborn, editor. "We hope you enjoy the paper." ★

Such bland reporting isn't likely to cause anyone to take the staff seriously, no matter how hard the staff is working.

Instead, it would be more effective to pinpoint a single situation that symbolizes the nuances, both the joys and the frustrations of being a member of the staff. We must become competent storytellers. The following story generates both empathy and understanding.

HUGS. Don't write about clubs. Write about club members. Focus on the activities that make membership in an organization special. *Photo by Taylor Jones, Westlake High School, Austin, Texas.*

THE HEADLINE WOULD not fit.

Try as she may, Jana Jackson could not manipulate the two-line head into the too-short space. So she exercised her editorial judgment.

"Oh well, we can save this story for the next issue," she reasoned, tossing it into a folder labeled "December." Such is the stuff of high level, journalistic decision-making on the campus newspaper staff.

"Sometimes, you have to go with what fits and what's available," Jackson said. "We'd like to include stories of every club on campus and give everyone as much publicity as they'd like, but it's impossible. So we do the best we can and hope people will enjoy what they read."

Like football players and musicians, the school's journalists spend most of their time preparing for the big game. And that is the day the bi-weekly newspaper hits the halls.

"Most people think the newspaper just pops out of thin air," Jackson said. "They don't understand the work behind each story, every headline and every photo. Students will criticize in 30 seconds what it takes you two weeks to produce." ★

Notice that one practical and ethical question comes to represent a more universal dilemma.

Reporters' success often lies in their ability to identify, isolate and develop verbally and visually a complex situation or problem. Thomas French, a reporter for the *St. Petersburg Times* and author of *South of Heaven*, a book about students at a South Florida High School, told Iowa student journalists, "The inverted pyramid must die as far as I'm concerned. We tell ourselves that people don't have the time or the desire to read so we hedge our bets with an archaic writing formula that tells the story backwards and sabotages any possible pleasures once associated with reading."

French called for a fresh, unabashed writing style that grabs readers and coaxes them to continue past the headline, and that will mean abandoning many of the old rules associated with journalistic writing.

"What kills me is that readers hate these stupid rules even more than I do," he said. "They want something different and something more. They're dying for it. And if we give it to them, they will read and read and read. All of them, even the ones who supposedly don't even know how to read."

He added, "They want to be challenged, seduced, cajoled, tickled, slapped, even bullied into picking up our paper. They are just waiting for us to wake up and make the first move."

❏ Focus

Again, young reporters are under the wrong assumption that all information collected must be used. Because diligent reporters collect two or three times the information needed, the most difficult aspect of the job is to decide which information to use and which to discard. Of course, reporters must answer all news questions: who, what, when, where, why, and how, and so it becomes a matter of deciding which supporting evidence—direct quotes, anecdotes, examples—to choose.

How do you choose? Well, return to your theme, and ask yourself, "What is this story about?" Any piece of information that does not carry forward the theme should be torpedoed.

If the story deals with the success of the senior play, maintaining a clear focus means the reporter will not use the following quote from the play's director:

"I would like to thank each member of the troupe for all their hard work and Mr. Burns for letting us use his lumber and Mayor Parks for reserving the city library auditorium for our rehearsals and Suelynn for being an absolute darling," said Dudley-Lawrence Montadale. "If I have forgotten to thank anyone, I apologize, but I think I thanked everyone who deserved to be thanked, I think. And now, fans, I'm off to London!"

❏ Order

The typical fiction novel is told in chronological order. The same is true for movies. This is not to suggest that either begins at the beginning and ends at the end. However, a good book or movie follows a logical sequence of events. It doesn't bounce around from past to present to future. We've all seen movies in which the action takes place in flash-back form, and we're never quite sure whether the action is taking place then or now.

The same goes for news copy. Whether reporters choose to start at the beginning, middle or end, they should then present the stories in a logical if not chronological order.

Consider the following approach, in which the reporter begins in the present, then works her way through the story, and concludes again in the present. Although the action takes place over a fairly long period of time, the reader never loses track of the action.

MORE NEWS LEADS WE SEE TOO OFTEN

• BABY STEPS LEADS—They waddle into the story. For example:

Riverside's tennis team competed in the Pine Valley Tournament last weekend. Capturing the boys' singles title was Brad Gunter.

A much better lead would have been:

Using a booming serve, Brad Gunter whipped Jefferson's David Jones, 6-3, 6-2, to capture the Pine Valley Tennis Tournament singles title Saturday.

The results are the news—not that there was a competition. In the same space, the second lead gives far more information than the first. Notice how the lead of this story answers "how."

Never lead with a statement of the obvious, such as "Football season is here again" or "The purpose of the Student Council is . . . ."

Also, avoid leading with dictionary definitions. They are a sure sign that the writer has made no effort to use an interesting lead.

BY LISA KASBERG
Temple HS, Temple, Texas

SHOWCASE

EACH MORNING SHE looks to her sister's empty bed. Stuffed bears and other animals are piled by the headboard.

It has been two months since she's last seen Angelica, her 11-year-old sister.

Laura often walks down Houston St., where her sister was reported being last seen, and wonders about what happened there. During these times she recalls the day her family realized Angelica was missing.

Mornings are one of the worst parts of the day, for senior Laura Gandara remembers all the mornings her sister Angelica was by her side preparing for school. Angelica failed to return home to her North Temple residence July 14 after visiting her grandmother.

Police believe Angelica was kidnapped.

"It was Sunday; I had gotten back from church at 4 p.m. My parents left, and I thought she was going with them because she left about the same time. Around 7, my parents came back.

"When I got home at 8, my mom was wondering where she was. By that time my mom had already called my grandmother, friends and relatives. She was hoping she would be with me.

"She made it to my grandmother's house and left around 5. She said she was going home, but she never made it home.

"We called the police, and everyone went searching in parks, alleys and streets. We looked all night, and nobody slept," Gandara said, "We didn't sleep for the first three days. Later, some slept outside waiting for her."

The Gandara family reported to the police that Sunday, but a search was not made until Tuesday.

"I talked to Sergeant Flippo and Officer Rubik, and they apologized and said that the police force should have started right away because a child was involved," Gandara said.

Although Gandara realizes everything is being done by the Texas Rangers, she seeks the day when a national organization would be searching. "I wish that there were an organization, a team that would go around the U.S. searching and looking for clues. Right now they're just doing it in this area."

"One thing about the first day of school that made it real hard was that we would always be in a hurry to get ready," Laura said and paused, reflecting on past years.

"I was thinking today she would have started to Lamar," Laura said. "She was excited about starting middle school where she would be able to change classes and have different teachers. I think she would have liked it."

The return for her senior year was a hard decision for Gandara. "For a while I was thinking about whether to go back to school. I wanted to, but I didn't know how I would feel."

"I only go three periods; I stay home most of the time in case someone calls, like Missing Children, Child Find or even Angelica," Gandara said.

Gandara said she feels the need to remain strong for her family since both parents have great difficulty in speaking English.

"I have to be stronger because I have to talk to the news press and the police, but I don't mind because the main thing is letting people know. If they know, they'll keep interested," Gandara said.

Keeping people interested is just what Gandara intends to do. With the help of local merchants and the community, a $5,000 reward has been donated for anyone with information leading to the location of her sister.

"People have been sponsoring dances and ways to raise money. A lot of out-of-towners have come by and gotten posters to go out of state," Gandara said. "Teenagers always wonder how they could help and believe that they can't in any way, but high school students have cars and we could give them posters. If they travel, maybe others would see and remember."

One of the biggest aids to Gandara and her family this past summer was her teachers.

"During the summer they'd call and really encourage me to not give up hope. I've received cards from some. They all said if I needed to talk, I could count on them," Gandara said.

Although teachers have been a big help, she often feels uneasy at school.

"When I go to school, I feel like people are afraid to ask anything. I don't mind if they ask questions. It seems like everyone has to be so cautious."

The Gandaras look toward their religious beliefs for strength. "I believe God is protecting her wherever she is," Gandara said. The family's Catholic faith is evident because of the many religious pictures and crosses which adorn the walls of the Gandara living room.

Laura's and Angelica's room remains the same as before. The stuffed bears and other animals piled by the headboard will be left intact in hopes of Angelica's return. ★

❑ CLARITY

Readers expect reporters to be the experts, not only about the subject matter but also about its delivery. Their job is to communicate in such a way as to inform, explain, persuade, and entertain. It is no simple task. It requires not only that they know almost as much as their sources but also that they present the information more clearly, more precisely and more logically than the sources ever could. Several years ago, I came across a news story, produced by a university information service for Texas newspapers, large and small, daily and weekly. I can only imagine the expression on the face of Ma and Pa Editor of the *Hickville Gazette* when they read:

THE MOST urgent task now facing humanists is to transcend the pluralism that has been the foundation of American culture and strive for a synthesis to bring a sense of order and community to the American experience. ★

The story concerned a meeting in which history professors at The University of Texas at Austin talked about government funding of the humanities, but you had to read the press release two or three times to figure it out.

Similarly, would you rather read about computers in a company manual or in a newspaper column? Most would say the latter. The manual is likely to be filled with arcane jargon, decipherable only by computer junkies, while the newspaper column would be written for the average reader.

Which of the two examples is more likely to appeal to a teenage audience?

• Dr. Thomas elucidated on the actualization of adolescent aspirations before concluding his colloquy with a primal caterwaul.

• With a hoop and a holler, Dr. Thomas told seniors to get to work if they wanted to achieve any degree of success in their lives.

Clarity is often dependent upon the use of everyday, simple-to-understand words and upon the meticulous attention to transitions so sentences and paragraphs are linked together in a logical order.

❑ TRANSITION

Transition words, sentences and paragraphs hold the story together. Transitions introduce a general situation or fact and are followed by specifics that clarify or amplify. Transitions are usually short sentences or indirect quotes, whose purpose is to provide the reader with verbal as well as visual signs along the winding path of the narrative.

❑ WORD CHOICE

It is not an accident that the English language has more than 500,000 words. Part of the purpose of journalism as a language arts course is to help students differentiate the nuances among words.

Without getting into a long discussion of diction, it is enough to remember that slang, jargon and clichés should be avoided.

Likewise, when a sentence states action, an action verb should be used. For example: "The pass by Tim Newton was caught by junior flanker Rod Smith" could be more effectively worded, "Rod Smith caught Tim Newton's pass."

Ask, "Who is the actor in this sentence?" Then, place the noun at the beginning of the sentence, followed by the active verb, followed by the object or recipient of the action.

The micro-computer can do marvelous things. But it never has been nor will it ever be a substitute for a reporter with a pencil, a pad and a healthy dose of skepticism and curiosity.

• • • • • •

MORE NEWS LEADS WE SEE TOO OFTEN

• CHATTY LEADS— More often than not, these result in editorializing. For example:

"One of the fastest growing as well as friendliest clubs in school is the Young Historians Club."

It is not the job of the reporter to assign labels (good or bad) to organizations or persons. Report the news and be done with it. Another example:

There is a new organization here at school. It's SAVE (Students Against Violating the Earth). Just what is SAVE, you ask? Well, it's a youth organization whose primary purpose is to get students involved in improving the environment.

Three points to be made here: Short item news should remain third person—never first or second.

Sentences should be direct statements—not chatty statements or questions.

"Blah words," such as "there is/was/are," take up space and add nothing. They rob reporters of chances to use more powerful verbs.

Another rule: Any time you have a choice between words, always choose the one with the narrower meaning. For example:

WEAK: "The new principal wore an expensive watch and a colorful shirt."

BETTER: "The new principal wore a Rolex and a Hawaiian shirt." Selecting the more precise word eliminates the need for adjectives.

Notice how the word choice in the lead of a story by Chris Smith, Lyons Township High School, LaGrange, Illinois, is critical to the success of the story:

HE TRUDGES ALONG in the darkness, a solitary figure on a path illuminated by street lamps. In his hand, he carries a sack lunch; over his shoulder is a backpack full of books.

At 5:45 A.M. he checks into the station, unburdens himself, and begins to choose albums.

His partner arrives a few minutes later, bleary eyed and carrying a load of books. At exactly 6 a.m., they flip on the controls and play a two-minute John Belushi comedy bit. Then Blondie. Then the Rolling Stones.

Later they sit on opposite sides of a glass panel, each equipped with a microphone, reading news and chatting. "If you've got to be somewhere by 6:30," one cajoles, "you're already late."

Such a line may sound irritating to someone who is groping for, swatting at, a bedroom alarm clock, but for juniors Phil Schrock and Ted Slowik, it's just part of their job.

For nearly two months, the pair have been the voices within the clock radio, by voluntarily beginning the WLTL broadcasting day each school morning.

"It had to be done," Ted said later. "Seven a.m. was just too late to start. And because the morning show hosts switched each two weeks, the format was always changing. There was no consistency in the music or listeners."

Ted, who gets up at 4:30 A.M. and walks one and a half miles to school, has not yet missed a show. "Sometimes my alarm goes off, and I'll have been up late the night before, and I think that I'd pay any amount of money to just roll over and sleep until 7 like everyone else," he said. "But it really adds to my day, and I look forward to it most of the time."

The format used on the morning show is different from WLTL's regular format. "At night, the format is most comparable to WXRT's because of the variety of music," Ted said. "But in the morning, we switch to a Top-40 style show, alternating between two popular songs and a promo, news or conversation." ★

Not only can we picture the two as they trudge (what a great verb!) along the dark, empty streets, but we can almost feel a chill from the morning air. We sense the reporter was there, too, on the street and in the studio with Phil and Ted that morning, probably as bleary-eyed as they.

❏ DESCRIPTION

Because description is dependent upon either observation or scene recreation, it's a rarity in student publications. Too many stories are as flat as an airport runway. They merely attempt to transact data, and often they are told in terms so vague and general that the stories could appear in any issue of any student communication—newspaper, yearbook, bathroom wall.

"Emphasize observation—direct reporting," said Jack Kennedy, adviser of the newspaper at City High School in Iowa City, Iowa. "One of my pet peeves is the story that has filtered through two sources when we could have been there."

While metropolitan newspapers have embraced visual reporting as a means of competing with television news, the scholastic media has been slow to follow. Our stories may consist of quote after quote, statistic upon statistic, reams of data piled atop reams of data. But they rarely attempt to place the reader in the middle of action.

Here's an example. Many high schools participate in academic decathlon or other current events competitions, and certainly these activities are worthy of coverage. But this coverage too often comes in this form:

LAST WEEK, Mrs. Joyce Cripe's senior government classes participated in the Citizen

Bee contest. According to Mrs. Cripe, the purpose of Citizen Bee is to help students understand world issues and events.

"We learned a lot about what's going on around the globe and how events in one part of the world affect us here," junior Lance Brinson said. ★

The subsequent paragraphs pretty much rake the same ground. The story fails to capture the excitement and drama of Citizen Bee. A better approach would be to describe the anxiety of the moment. The following story contains information and meaning that the earlier story lacks. It places the reader in the middle of the action.

JENNIFER SCROGGINS couldn't believe the question: Who was the mayor of Berlin at the time the wall was built?

"Who cares," she thought. Seconds earlier, her opponent had received what she thought was an easy question: Who was Richard Nixon's Secretary of State.

"Why didn't I get that one?" she asked herself, hoping all the while that the correct answer to her question would pop into her head.

It didn't. And so another student advanced in the Academic Club competition.

"I guess the most frustrating thing is that you never know what they're going to ask, and there's so much history that you can't learn everything," Jennifer said. But that hasn't stopped her from competing in the meets.

"I'm a big Jeopardy fan, and this is my way of playing Jeopardy," Samantha Haney said. "It's nerve-wracking, but I love it." ★

❑ **INTERPRETATION**
Student reporters often fail to place their stories into a context, to explain the meaning behind behavior. The action—if any action exists—in most stories seemingly takes place in a vacuum. Things happen, without rhyme or reason, beyond cause and effect.

Interpretation is rare because student reporters have failed to get close to the subjects of their stories. They've answered the five W's and one H and tossed in a quote just to say they have one. But the story lacks any

personal involvement. Consider the beginning-of-the-school-year stories about new teachers. Most state something along the lines of, "The school has 10 new faculty members. They are . . . ., and here's a brief bio sketch about each."

In comparison, the *Dallas Morning News* ran a story by Mark McDonald, titled, "New Kid In Class." (See complete story, page 175).

IT'S THE SMALLEST of sounds, a door clicking shut. But two weeks from today, for new teachers all over Dallas, that sound might prove to be the most frightening thing they'll ever hear.

Their training is over, the degrees have been earned and the theories digested. And when that classroom door swings shut for the first time, The Student of Teaching will suddenly become The Teacher, and there will be those 25 young faces— 25 chances for hope and joy and reward, 25 potential stab wounds in the new teacher's heart.

"In that first year, you just get the feelings that you're all by yourself and you're all alone," says Laura Corman, a former teacher at Dunbar Elementary in South Dallas. "You're just out there, without any support."

"It's a very lonely experience," says Julie Bangle, a teacher at Rosemont Elementary School in Oak Cliff. "Each person has to go in and reinvent the wheel because you're in there with the kids all by yourself.

All by yourself. That is how many teachers will feel during their first year in the Dallas Independent School District. Here's the classroom, there are the kids, now get in there and teach.

Almost none of them know what they are getting into.

"College doesn't teach you what you need to know," says Brent Vidrine, 25, who spent his first year of teaching at Rusk Middle School last year. "You can learn about Freud and dogs salivating and all that, but it doesn't mean anything. You've got to reach that certain place in each kid. It's there. You just have to find it." ★

The reporter didn't say this is good or bad, merely that *it is*. There's no bias, no attempt to editorialize—merely an effort to place action into a setting. Again, this is just the first nine or 10 inches of the story. The rest goes on to fully develop the theme.

❏ ACCURACY.

Are all facts—names, times, dates and places—correct. Are all direct and indirect quotes correct?

As importantly, do voice and tone of the story match the content? Serious topics are treated with an appropriate amount of seriousness, light topics with humor or a clever touch. Several years ago, a major beer brewer named the University of Texas at Austin as the nation's number one beer drinking university in America. If ever a story demanded a feature lead, this was it. Instead, the story was reported as though the brewer had announced all beer consumed at UT had been laced with rat poison. Which lead do you think would have been more appropriate?

THE UNIVERSITY of Texas at Austin is the number one beer-consuming campus in America, a spokesman for a major brewer announced here yesterday. ★

or

THE FOOTBALL TEAM lost to Oklahoma and A & M. Academic standards are sliding downhill.

Because of a computer snafu, fall registration was a mess.

No wonder UT students are drinking so much. And they are. Yesterday, a major brewer crowned The University as the nation's top beer-drinking school. ★

While this odd story should not be written as seriously as an industrial accident, it still must be 100-percent accurate.

By the way, the example above is used merely to make a point. I'm not promoting alcohol consumption. In fact, I quite discourage it among high school students.

❏ UNITY

Whether news or feature, an article is unified when all the individual elements—theme, angle, focus and the rest—work together to tell a concise, complete and coherent story.

SUMMARY

In too many schools, student journalists have lost sight of the ultimate purpose of school publications—to report the events and issues affecting their classmates. Of course, it isn't fair to blame the students. It is instead an adviser problem. "The whole point of education is to get kids going in the right direction," Jack Kennedy said. "That's the adviser's job."

Up-to-date advisers are abandoning teaching methods and materials that have more in common with the 1950s than they do with the 1990s. Metropolitan daily newspapers represent the finest in American journalism today, and they are dramatically different than they were 10 years ago. Unless students study contemporary reporting and writing strategies, their papers will never fulfill their stated goals: to inform, to interpret and to entertain.

We need to integrate the best of words and images into our publications. You can have one or the other—but the best publications combine them both.

While it's easy to dress up publications with squiggles and gray squares, with reverse type that stretches or rolls across the page, the success of the publication as a news medium and an educational tool hinges on the power of its reporting. The computer can do marvelous things. But it never has been, nor will it ever be, a substitute for a reporter with a pencil, a pad and a healthy dose of skepticism and curiosity.

COMPARE & contrast

THE TYPICAL STORY

February is Black History Month, and the school will again participate in a wide variety of activities commemorating the many contributions blacks have made to the United States and to the world.

Activities already scheduled include guest speakers, assemblies, film strips, videotapes and a gala.

The chairman of Black History Month is history teacher and coach Dennis Sims.

"The main theme of Black History Month is to celebrate the past and define the future," Sims said. "This year, we will have a number of student projects, but we also plan to have a gala in which citizens are invited to experience firsthand the African-American culture."

The African-American gala will be Friday, Feb. 7. The gala will include poetry recitals, films, guest speakers and fashion displays of various ethnic clothing and jewelry. Booths serving African-American foods will also be set up.

Sims said students are currently involved in planning an ethnic awareness assembly.

"The purpose of the assembly is to look at the contributions to science, business, education and other fields made by African-Americans," Sims said.

"Many people fail to understand the many contributions that blacks have made here in the United States," he added. "We want to educate them on these many achievements." ★

THE CREATIVE ANGLE

History teacher and coach Dennis Sims remembers his high school days all too well, and the memories aren't particularly good ones.

"Although I lived only a mile from school, I was forced to travel 10 miles out in the country to attend an all-black school," he said. "We weren't allowed to mingle with the white kids even though I'd played with many of them all my life."

He said he remembers how members of his family were denied basic rights such as voting and recalls the night a band of thugs lynched a young black man for talking to a white girl.

"I grew up in a segregated community that treated us harshly," he said. "Thank God that's all changed."

As evidence, the school will again participate in February's Black History Month, and Sims will be in charge of the annual event.

"I don't want this to be something kids feel like they have to do or is forced on them," Sims said. "I want all students to be excited about learning about African-Americans in our society because we must come to understand and appreciate each other in order to live in peace together."

Sims said the Rodney King verdict and the Los Angeles riots that followed it confirmed his belief in the importance of Black History Month.

"We must begin to appreciate the things that make us unique," he said, "and those things that are common to us all if we are to survive." ★

MORE FUNNY RULES ABOUT USING QUOTES!

• Avoid quote fragments or partial quotes. If the speaker's words are clear and concise, use the complete quote.

• Never use part of a quote out of context. Have you ever noticed how movie ads showcase words that may have been taken out of context from the whole review. For example: "The movie is a monumental flop." The ad might herald, "Monumental!"

• Don't use quotation marks to report a speaker's words if the words are factual information. Use quotes to provide opinion or explanation about the fact.

WEAK: *"The meeting will be at 7 P.M.," John said. "It will be a zoo."*
BETTER: *The meeting will be at 7 P.M. "It will be a zoo," John said.*

• Remember: The period and the comma always go within the quotation marks.

WHERE DO YOU FIND THE STORY?

The goal: look beneath the facts for the real stories. Quality coverage begins when reporters take that additional step from merely telling what's going on to showing how students are changing their communities, in these cases, for the better.

FRENCH CLUB

The French Club recently elected its officers for the 1994-95 school year. They are Jennifer O'Neill, president; James Borders, vice president; Shelly Bryant, secretary; Stephanie Bonita, treasurer; and Tawanna Kemp, parliamentarian.

The club had participated in a toy drive with the speech department for the Salvation Army. Toys were collected and delivered to the Salvation Army headquarters, where they were distributed to needy families.

Take a photo of a club member handing a toy to a four-year-old. A story that led with a scene recreation of the toy give-away and captured the emotion of the moment would have debunked the myth of the apathetic teenager.

FUTURE HOMEMAKERS

During the holiday season, FHA is reaching out to help local needy people by collecting food and toys. Many of the FHA students are volunteering at the Salvation Army by separating toys into groups for different ages. Others are delivering food to needy families. If you would like to contribute in any way, please contact the Salvation Army or talk to a FHA student.

Again, assign a photo of students collecting food for needy families. Talk to the students and, if possible, to the families receiving help. What are their thoughts on this? Be sure to treat them with dignity.

POLITICAL AWARENESS CLUB

The PAC would like to wish everyone a Merry Christmas. If you drink over the holidays and need a designated driver, you can call a PAC member who will arrange for two students to drive you home. For more information, talk to Mr. Johnson, who started the "Dial-A-Ride" program for high school students two years ago.

Does Mr. Johnson have a first name? Talk to him. Why did he start this program? Talk to students who performed this service last year. What were their experiences? Can you recreate a scene?

NATIONAL HONOR SOCIETY

The National Honor Society met Tuesday, Dec. 5 to discuss several topics. Tutoring assignments were given to those who volunteered. NHS members are tutoring junior-high students as part of an effort to lower the school's drop-out rate.

Also, NHS chose to produce and perform a skit for the Students Against Drunk Drivers (SADD) campaign, held Dec. 11-15.

Focus the story on one student who is tutoring an at-risk junior high student. Tell their story. Describe a scene that includes dialogue. Show the special relationship between the two, but don't editorialize.

SPANISH CLUB

The Spanish Club met Nov. 22 and 29. At both meetings, trips and fundraisers were discussed. Nov. 21, the Spanish Club officers were on the morning show, "High School Happenings," and they talked about the club and what it has been doing this year.

The first trip that the Spanish Club has taken was to Casa Bonita on Nov. 30. Other trips for the club have not been decided and fund-raising has not been decided either, but for Christmas, Spanish Club has a few projects. They have planned to make food baskets for the families in town. They are also planning on helping the Salvation Army by ringing bells and helping sort clothes and toys for the bags given to needy families.

FUTURE BUSINESS LEADERS

Future Business Leaders of America (FBLA) have been busy this year volunteering. FBLA President Missy Jones helps handicapped children at the "A-Leg-Up" riding center. FBLA supported this organization by donating $100. FBLA also participates in "Project Ask," a foundation for the study of children with cancer, and is planning a trip to the Ronald McDonald House in Memphis over the holidays.

DISTRIBUTIVE EDUCATION

Distributive Education Clubs of America (DECA) students participated in a Bowl-A-Thon on Dec. 9. The purpose of the project was to raise money for the Big Brothers/Big Sisters program. Students recruited sponsors on an individual basis to pledge money per pin. DECA raised $750 through its efforts. The funds will help support volunteer recruitment efforts to screen adult volunteers who will work with children and to provide professional staff monitor matches in the community. DECA sponsor Jim Dancey is the local chairman for Big Brothers/Big Sisters.

Because so many clubs are involved in the "High School Happenings," a feature story on the show might be appropriate. Write a descriptive feature on the program. Do not dwell on what a club is not doing. Instead, concentrate on what its members are doing. For example: focus on the satisfaction of making food baskets or on the courage needed to stand outside department stores and ring bells.

If ever a student deserved to be the subject of a feature story, Missy Jones does. What stories does she have to tell? Have her describe relationships she's formed with these children. And while you're at it, get a photo of Missy assisting a handicapped child. Who are the students involved in Project Ask? Such a powerful and emotional issue begs for coverage.

Again, take a human interest photo of a senior Big Brother and his little brother at the bowling alley. Isolate one special relationship, and show how this project helps needy children. Dialogue and scene development are essential to the writing of a story to do justice to such a dramatic issue.

LOOK FOR THE STORY BEHIND THE FACTS.

I'm constantly frustrated by staffs complaining about a lack of story possibilities. "There's nothing going on," they whine. Then, I thumb through their papers and find one great story idea after another.

The stories are out there if you know where to look for them. Here are a few more ideas:

✔ *Beyond an event lies a broader, more significant story. What is the probable cause of the event? Is the cause likely to create similar effects in other places? If so, where?*

✔ *Does the story pertain to a common location, a shared cause or experience, a particular class of people, or similar institutions or places?*

✔ *Is the event a single, concrete event or a part of a more subtle trend? If so, can we anticipate the next move?*

✔ *Can we tell the story through the eyes of someone who can provide a unique perspective? Or are we interviewing the same people as always?*

COMPARE & contrast

FOCUS ON THE EVENT

On Sunday, Monday June 6, Americans across the nation celebrated the 50th anniversary of D-Day, the Allied invasion of France that led to the defeat of Adolf Hitler's Nazi Germany during World War II.

Hundreds of veterans of the Allied forces who defeated Nazi Germany have invaded Normandy again to gaze upon the beaches they stormed, walk the sunken roads they fought over, mourn at the military cemeteries, but most of all, celebrate their triumph.

Among those who traveled to France to pay homage in Europe was President Bill Clinton and former principal Douglas Starks, who was accompanied by his wife, Helen, and their sons, David and Robert.

They arrived on June 2 in London where they met with members of the U. S. 1st Infantry Division, which was made famous by the movie "The Big Red One." Then, the Starks flew to Paris on June 4 in order to be in France for the June 6 ceremonies.

"It brought back a lot of memories," Mr. Starks said. "And it was wonderful to see so many old friends."

After the war, Starks returned to Alabama to finish his college work. He earned a degree in history and became a teacher and a football coach. He was head football coach here from 1955-1962 and principal from 1963-1976. He retired in 1976. His youngest son, David, is an assistant principal at the middle school. ★

FOCUS ON A PERSON

"We saw the dawn before we landed. At first, everything seemed to be going pretty well: we had good smoke and fog cover."

That's how former principal Douglas Starks remembers the beginning of D-Day, the Allied invasion that led to the defeat of Nazi Germany during World War II.

It's far from how he remembers the rest of that day.

"As soon as we hit the beach, we came under heavy fire from a battle-hardened field division—the German 352nd Division," said Starks, who like thousands of D-Day veterans traveled to Normandy for the 50th anniversary of the historic invasion.

"We were in a very bad position," said Starks, a former teacher, coach and principal here. "We were pinned down on the beach with a German division in front of us and the ocean behind us. We had no where to hide. There were people falling all around us. You'd go into the water, but the water was washing bodies in and out. Bodies, heads, flesh, intestines; that's what Omaha Beach was."

Starks said it was his duty and honor to return to Normandy where so many of his friends died.

"I wanted my sons to experience this so that they can tell their children about it," he said. "I didn't do this because I wanted them to think that I am a hero. I wasn't then and I'm not now. I was in the U. S. infantry, and we had a job. I was just doing my job." ★

CHAPTER THREE

TELL A STORY

To sell anything in America, even an idea, it helps to have a human face to make it real. The problem with too many high-school students is they're so busy looking for facts they cannot find a story.

Interviewed in *Rolling Stone* magazine, Don Hewitt, executive producer of CBS's "60 Minutes," said, "A producer came to me one day and said, 'Why don't we do a story about acid rain?' I said, 'Acid rain isn't a story. It's a subject. Tell me a story about somebody whose life was ruined by acid rain, or about a community trying to do something about acid rain, but don't tell me about acid rain.' "

Hewitt said that the number one rule of "60 Minutes" is that they don't cover issues; they cover stories. The second rule is that every story must feature a captivating central character or two, and he or she must speak clear English.

He added that most "60 Minutes" stories rely on the classic dramatic structure of conflict, struggle, resolution. "Little morality plays," he called them.

This is precisely the formula high-school journalists must adopt to produce lively, compelling copy.

Let's begin with this premise: We're not collecting data. We want to tell stories.

How is this accomplished? By subjecting any story idea to a rigorous and demanding criteria, all with the intention of determining the most interesting and informative way to tell the most interesting and informative story.

It begins when an editor or reporter asks the fundamental question, "What is this story really about?"

Whether it is ever identified and developed, every story has a theme. The theme is the essential truth of the story from which all information sprouts. Anything that fails to develop the theme should be discarded.

Remember: the worst four-letter word in journalism is data. We are not interested in collecting data. We want to tell a story. So let's look at the following story possibility. The school's sociology class is involved in an out-reach program for elderly citizens. Your job is to write an article about this program. The novice reporter will interview the sociology teacher and perhaps one or two students. With this data collected, he or she will write a story that sounds something like this.

A NEW PROGRAM has been started by sociology students at the school. The program is called "Telephone Buddies," and its purpose is to contact and reassure elderly citizens.

"I am proud to take part in the program because it is serving a real need in the community," senior Jeff Smith said. ★

While this story may satisfy all the demands of textbook journalism, it isn't going to win many readers. Given that the story ultimately deals with the fears and loneliness of elderly citizens, it is pitifully bare of heart and soul.

Compare it to the story on the following page:

ONE RING. Then another and five more after that. Finally . . . .

"Hello," answers the wheezy and somewhat perplexed voice of the 86-year-old widow, who obviously isn't accustomed to receiving many telephone calls.

"Mrs. Worsham," a young woman chirps. "It's me, Karen Couch. How are you doing today?"

"Well, not so good, I'm afraid . . . ."

And so the conversation begins. For the next 20 minutes, while her friends and thousands of other teenagers roam the malls, watch television or just hang out, Karen discusses arthritis, poor eyesight and, most importantly, loneliness with one of society's forgotten souls.

"It's tough," Karen admits. "Most of these people don't keep up with current events. All they really have to talk about is their physical pain, their families and their loneliness. I hate to admit it, but sometimes I'm bored to death."

But not bored enough to abandon her six-weeks sociology project, volunteering for Telephone Buddies, a program designed to contact and reassure elderly citizens. ★

TELL A STORY IN HUMAN TERMS

The first story attempts only to transact data. The second attempts to tell a story in human terms. The theme of the story is "Students are trying to help lonely people," and the story places a name and a face with that loneliness.

In the next example, the reporter collects a few sketchy facts but in no way captures the essence of the event.

WOW! LOOK at the presents! Do you know what it's like to see 22 kids with a big Christmas twinkle in their eye?

Fifty-five National Honor Society members discovered this thrill when they traveled to the Stepping Stone Day-Care Center for their yearly Christmas visit. Club members furnished presents and refreshments for 3-, 4- and 5-year-olds. Santa was one of the main attractions for the kids. This year's jolly old man was portrayed by senior Randy Jones. The club left Wednesday morning for their short sojourn to Birmingham and returned that afternoon.

Everyone had a great time! ★

WHAT IS THE FUNDAMENTAL TRUTH?

Remember, the essence of the event is the theme. What is the fundamental truth? What bit of information, what emotion, what image should the reader retain after finishing the story? What does the reader want and need to know? Who are the players in this story, and what specifically did they do to become players?

In the case of the National Honor Society's Christmas visit, it is not enough to simply state what happened. To succeed, the story must use specific anecdotes and narrative to show the consequences of members' actions. For example:

SHY AT FIRST, the 4-year-old tottered from behind the protective shield of his teacher's khaki trousers, past the baby dolls, the record players and the musical toys to the lime-green stuffed alligator. A quick tug and flash later, again behind the khaki trousers, he was hugging his new friend.

Meanwhile, two brothers—a 4-year-old and a 3-year-old—fought over Barney. The tussle ceased when the 4-year-old ripped off Barney's head. Horrified and covered with stuffing, the younger brother began a slow wail that continued, even after his older brother had, in an attempt to pacify him, tossed him the headless purple dinosaur.

And Santa—in the guise of senior Randy Jones—wasn't getting away without a few minor bruises as well. A persistent 3-year-old insisted on pulling St. Nick's beard, which though a powdered white imitation, was glued tightly to his face.

"I thought the kid was going to pull my lips off," Santa admitted.

Through it all, Stepping Stone officials called the day a rousing success, even if Santa and some 3-year-old may beg to differ. ★

YOU CAN MAKE ANY STORY INTERESTING

See the difference? Even a story as predictable as a club visit to a day-care center can be made entertaining and informative. In fact, you can make any story interesting. If it involves people, you can make it interesting.

In teaching workshops, I often ask, "How

many of you are interested in working conditions in meatpacking houses?"

Not many raise their hands.

"How many of you think you could be interested in such a topic?"

Again, few hands appear.

Then, I read them the lead of this story by William Glaberson of *The New York Times* (to read the complete story, turn to page 171). Whereas business reporting is sometimes stuffy and full of jargon, this is dramatic and compelling.

SIOUX FALLS, S.D.—Mary Tvedt had learned to live with the dirt and the danger of a meatpacking house. So she did not think much of it when the huge blade jammed in the bacon slicer where she was working. She turned off the power, opened the machine and began clearing out chunks of bacon the way she had a hundred times before in her years at John Morrell & Company's plant here.

After a minute or two, a co-worker thought the cleaning was finished. From where he was standing he could not see that Mary Tvedt was still working. Morrell had not supplied the most rudimentary of safety devices, a lock to keep the power supply off. He hit the switch. The four fingers of Mary Tvedt's right hand came off in one swift turn of the big blade.

It is 81 years since Upton Sinclair's *The Jungle* described the brutal working conditions of the Chicago slaughterhouses. But here in Sioux Falls —and in places like it throughout the Midwest— history is quietly repeating itself.

Modern machinery has changed the look and the sound of a packing house. But the meatpacking industry, which employs about 100,000 people, remains today the most hazardous industry in America. Meatpackers work in extreme heat or refrigerated cold, often standing shoulder to shoulder, wielding honed knives and power saws. Grease and blood make the floors and the tools slippery. Occasionally, an overpowering stench from open bladders and stomachs fills the air.

The workers cut themselves. They cut each other. They wear out their insides doing repetitive-motion jobs. They are sliced and crushed by machines that were not even imagined when Sinclair published his book in 1906.

At one end of the plant are the yards teeming with livestock. At the other, boxed and processed meats emerge ready for market. In between, a chain carries hanging carcasses past workers who dismember the meat with a series of cuts, each person performing the same motion over and over, sometimes a thousand times an hour, tens of thousands of times a week.

A meatpacking house has always been a grisly place to work. But after years of improvements, life in the packing house has been getting worse again. Several forces have combined to make life tougher for meatpackers: weaker health and safety regulation, automation, intense competition in the industry and unions weakened by a fight for survival.

After her accident, Mary Tvedt went home, by way of the Mayo Clinic, to adapt to life with her mangled hand. The Occupational Safety and Health Administration cited Morrell because it had not supplied a lock to keep the power off. ★

A CHICKEN OR EGG PROPOSITION

This story, as evident by the first 10 inches of a 68-inch feature, shows how a reporter combines scene re-creation, interpretation and a little bit of outrage to tell a compelling story and also present a moral argument of people wronged by a negligent, greedy and cruel system.

Selecting a theme is a "chicken or egg" proposition. Do reporters report first and then determine the theme? Or do they collect information to satisfy the needs of a preconceived theme?

Most likely, neither and both. In the case of the meatpackers, the reporter probably received information about the working conditions in the plant and then went searching for a face and a story.

While it may sound insidious to say that a reporter left the office in pursuit of a story with preconceived notions about what to write, in reality this occurs almost without fail. Reporters know, in general, what happened, and they seek names and faces to show the consequences of the action.

Of course, the nature of news for a high-school newspaper is far different than it is for a daily metropolitan. But the approach in

(to read the complete story, turn to page 171)

WHAT ARE STUDENTS SAYING ABOUT YOUR PAPER?

Criticizing the media is a great American pastime. Because your newspaper is part of the media, it, too, may be a frequent target of student criticism.

At some point, you must ask whether the criticism is valid. What are your students saying about the newspaper? Is it:

• Too soft? Does the staff avoid complex or controversial topics?

• Too hard? Does the staff report every story as though the survival of civilization rested in the balance? Does the staff ever look for the humor and joy in life? It should.

• Published too infrequently? It is published every major holiday or war?

• Published too frequently? Some staffs lose perspective, and the deadline becomes the end-all.

Covering the news is more important than meeting deadlines for the sake of meeting deadlines.

WHICH STORY WOULD STUDENTS RATHER READ?

MANY NORTH LAKE students are looking forward to seeing their peers at Patriot Stadium once again for the Rockfest '95, which will be held May 12.

In its ninth year, Rockfest is a service project that helps raise money for a number of clubs, including Beta Club and Key Club.

This year, 23 area bands have agreed to play, said Eileen Schmidt, Beta Club president and coordinator of the event.

"We held tryouts, and all bands were required to submit a demo tape," she said. "A lot of local bands said they would but didn't. Still, I think it's going to be the best ever."

Among the featured bands will be the Caskets, the Dirge Monkeys and North Lake's own Reckless Drivers.

The show will begin at 4 P.M. and last until midnight. Admission to Rockfest will be $4 in advance and $5 at the door. Tickets are available from any Beta Club member.

"I hope everyone comes," Schmidt said. ★

THE REHEARSALS at Trey Parker's house have been long and hard. Lead singer of the Reckless Drivers, Trey said he wants to make certain the group is ready for next month's Rockfest '95.

"We're trying to get as much exposure as possible, and doing well here would be a big boom for us," Parker said. "We're putting in a lot of overtime. I've neglected my studies lately, but this means a lot to us."

Twenty-three bands from throughout the area will perform, with proceeds benefiting school service clubs. But the reason most bands participate has less to do with charity than with promotion.

"All the musicians are young and hungry, and fans can expect one wild afternoon," Parker said. "I know we're going to put on one heck of a show." ★

> **ROCKFEST '95**
> **May 12**
> **4 P.M.-midnight**
> **Patriot Stadium**
> **Tickets: $5**

---

covering the news need not be radically different. Reporters for both must balance the needs of the audience versus the constraints of their publishing realities.

When did the event occur? Who will know about it? How much do they know? How can we capture the most compelling, provocative elements of the story?

Rather than writing about conditions in meatpacking houses, high-school reporters are more likely to cover club projects, class activities, personalities, teen issues and traditional school events. Still, the formula holds true. Unfortunately, stories are too often written in a "fill-in-the-blank" manner, regardless of the content. Too often, any given story in a high-school publication will read something like this:

(Name) received (honor) last Monday. When asked what the honor means to him/her, he/she said, "This is an honor that I will always cherish," he/she said. "I was thrilled to receive this award, and I promise to uphold its honor. I'm so thrilled, I just can't stand it."

(Name) is a member of (list clubs). He/she received the (list other honors won). ★

This isn't a recipe for success unless your goal is to sell journalism like eye-glasses or pizza. Formula copy shouts:
• News in about an hour.
• Hot news in 30 minutes or less.

Of course, we know that it won't take even a marginally bright student 30 minutes to consume a newspaper that contains content like this. Chances are, it can be had in five minutes or less.

So if your goal is to make certain readers can skim through the paper, search for a few familiar names and faces and be finished with it in five minutes or less, then there's no need to read on.

Take a Literary Approach

Which would you rather read: a Stephen King short story or a typical wire service news story?

For most teenagers, this is an easy question. They'd choose the short story, hands down, regardless of the topic of the news story. Why? Because they know enough about Stephen King to predict that he's going to give them a good ride. Unfortunately, they know enough about typical newspaper reporting to predict that the wire service story will be formula driven.

It's time to change all that. Let's move away from the stilted inverted pyramid to a compelling writing model that stresses the more human elements of the story. Rather than thinking about stories in terms of who, what, when, where, why and how, consider them in terms of drama, character development, conflict, dialogue, organization, anticipation, climax and resolution.

Consider each:

DRAMA—The portrayal of events involving intense conflicts results in strong emotional reactions, whether serious or humorous. This isn't to imply that every story is a life-and-death struggle against evil enemies. The drama behind a story about the annual blood drive might deal with efforts to overcome fear of transmission of AIDS. The drama behind the story about the annual Battle of the Bands might deal with attempts by local students to win the adoration of fans. You must isolate and develop the drama in each story.

CHARACTER DEVELOPMENT—Stories that deal with generalities are doomed to failure. To succeed, the story must showcase specific characters, giving the readers a reason to care whether these people succeed or fail. Let's again use the blood drive as an example. Rather than writing about a "thing" (the blood drive), frame the story in terms of a specific person for whom the success or failure of the blood drive is crucial.

Perhaps you have a student in your school who is a hemophiliac. Perhaps a student was involved in a horrific automobile accident and required mass quantities of blood to survive. Perhaps a tenacious student has taken it upon herself to make this the most successful blood drive ever.

Build your story around a real person and fully develop that person's character. Give the readers a reason to cheer for or against the people embroiled in the drama.

CONFLICT—Conflict is the struggle between opposing forces. Sometimes, this conflict is internal. For example, you have a student who is struggling against drug abuse or anorexia nervosa. The choice is to submit to the urge or to overcome it.

Sometimes, the conflict exists between human beings and nature. For example, the baseball team has been unable to practice because of two weeks of continuous rain. How has the team coped?

The conflict may exist between man and powerful outside forces. For example, a teacher may want to teach curriculum that the school board or state education agency forbids. In Texas, a teacher was suspended for introducing creationism into her science class. In another state, a teacher was fired for giving too many students failing grades. The conflict in both cases was between the individual and a bureaucracy.

Even in an article about the academic bowl, the story could be framed in terms of the conflict between student and curriculum. Each spring, I direct a series of current issues and events contests, and I witness the conflict between students and the test. Students' preparation for the contest is no less rigorous than that for a sporting event. The battle between student and test is no less competitive than an athletic event.

Finally, the conflict may be between individuals. The typical student council election story provides virtually no evidence that the race is anything other than a popu-

DRAMA— A series of events arousing intense emotions about serious problems or humorous situations.

CHARACTER DEVELOPMENT— Unlike the fiction writer who must create and develop a character, the journalists need only develop the character. This is done by describing the person physically, by examining their traits, by describing their personality and by exposing their actions.

CONFLICT—The struggle between opposing forces.

DIALOGUE— Dialogue is a conversation between characters.

ORGANIZATION—The order in which a story is told.

ANTICIPATION— Keeping readers hooked by making them guess what comes next.

CLIMAX—The turning point, which involves decisiveness or suspense.

RESOLUTION— The point in which the central conflict ends. In some cases, it follows the climax. In others, it is the climax. You cannot have resolution unless all news questions are answered.

larity contest because it fails to pinpoint the different philosophies between candidates.

DIALOGUE—Dialogue is a conversation between characters. What people say to one another is far more interesting than what they say to reporters. It is one thing to have a student tell a reporter about helping save the life of a heart attack victim. It is quite another thing to use dialogue to re-create the scene so that readers feel as though they are witnessing the event for themselves.

A way to achieve the effect of dialogue is to use contrasting opinions about controverial issues or decisions. The method is especially effective for news analysis or sports analysis. Interaction at public meetings is also appropriate.

ORGANIZATION—How to tell a story? Should you begin at the end and work your way back through? Start in the middle and then wrap back around? Or, as the White Rabbit in *Alice in Wonderland* might suggest, should you start at the beginning and go till you come to the end, and then stop?

Before beginning to write, make an outline of the plot of the story. What are you trying to say and to whom? What was the setting? Who are the characters? What event incited the conflict? What dialogue exists? What is the climax of the story? What is the resolution?

Then ask yourself, if this were a movie, how would the director tell the story? Think of all the movies you've seen over the years. In what order were the stories told? Can you pattern your story after one of them?

Does the inverted pyramid work best?

Does it work best to tell it in straight chronological order?

Maybe a combination of the two—the diamond—would work even better. In the diamond, the writer starts in the present or immediate present, introduces the drama of the story, jumps to the distant past and moves to the recent past, and finishes with an important and specific ending.

Regardless of the story shape followed, the writer must have a specific plan in mind before applying pencil to paper or fingers to keys.

ANTICIPATION—Keep readers hooked by making them guess what comes next. By writing in chronological order, you can show the unusual twists and turns in the story. One popular writing model today calls for the introduction of a situation and then takes the reader in chronological order through to the resolution and conclusion of the story.

One of my favorite leads of all time is, "She never knew she had it."

With these six small words, the reporter hooked readers and forced them to continue through the story, which dealt with a young woman with spinal bifida.

CLIMAX—The climax is the high point of interest or suspense. In one of the old Perry Mason television shows, it's where the husband admits he killed his wife for the insurance money. Everyone except Perry sits there gape-mouthed, and the judge tells the milkman he is free to go.

In the typical inverted pyramid story, the reporter begins with the climax. It's not a very effective order if you're trying to build suspense.

RESOLUTION—If you introduce a problem, readers expect you to solve it, or at least bring it as close to resolution as possible. You don't want to leave the reader hanging. If your story deals with a philosophical difference in the math department, you would want to isolate the sources of conflict, develop their characters, provide anecdotes using dialogue to make the issue real and meaningful, and finally, show how the conflict has been resolved. Perhaps the department chair has appointed a committee to propose curriculum revisions. Or perhaps the resolution is an agreement to disagree.

Note how in the story on the next two pages how the conflict is resolved.

'DON'T CRY, I'M GOING TO BE OK'

By KIM MCGUIRE
Winona (Texas) High School

AS THE PARAMEDICS loaded her stretcher into the helicopter, she caught her first glimpse inside.

In the cramped space of the helicopter, one doctor was struggling furiously to get an IV set up while the other was preparing a shot.

When the whirling blades of the propeller began to roar overhead and the helicopter lifted off, she looked down only to see the ground below her getting smaller and smaller.

It was then she thought to herself, "Please God, don't let me die."

Only an hour earlier, on Thanksgiving, Lorie Downing, senior; Bruce Wintters, her boyfriend; and his brother Blake had been deer hunting behind Eddie Haire's house on County Road 371.

"Bruce had called after my family had finished eating Thanksgiving dinner and asked if I wanted to go deer hunting with him and Blake.

"When I asked my mom, she said, 'No, you might get shot.'

"So then I decided to tell her we were just going to go over to his house, but we went hunting instead.

"If I had known then what I know now, I wouldn't have gone," Downing said.

At dusk, the trio decided to split up. Bruce and Lorie went toward the north end of the pasture while Blake stayed at the south end.

"After a while, Bruce and I decided to go back. As we were walking back through a shortcut we had found, Bruce told me he heard something moving in the woods," Downing said.

At the same time, Blake was seeing movement in the woods. Thinking it was a deer, he fired in that direction.

The bullet entered Downing's chest, went out and back into her arm, then back out again.

"I never heard the gunshot or really felt any pain. Instead, my hand jerked towards my chest as I began to scream.

"Bruce pulled my arm away from my chest, and that's when I began to bleed. I'll never forget all that blood," Downing said.

Realizing what had happened, Blake ran to their house to get help. Downing said while they were waiting for help, the only things she thought about was how cold she had suddenly gotten and the possibility she might never see her family again.

"In a few minutes, Blake and his dad, Dusty, plus Eddie and Darren Haire and Walt Miller all arrived. Throughout the whole ordeal, I was scared the most when I heard Dusty say, 'Blake, it's a lot worse than what you said.'"

Within minutes, the Red Springs and Winona Fire Departments, as well as Downing's parents and hordes of onlookers, had arrived. Because of the tremendous amount of blood Downing had lost, the paramedics called Air 1, the helicopter from Medical Center, to transport her quickly to the hospital.

"When the helicopter arrived, the paramedics cut off my jacket and shirt and started an IV going. Then, they put what they called parachute pants on me. They're plastic, and they pump them up like when you're taking your blood pressure. What they do is cut off circulation below the bleeding area and force the blood to it. Then, they loaded me into the helicopter," Downing said.

In three short minutes, the helicopter had traveled roughly 20 miles and had landed at Medical Center Hospital. Downing was immediately rushed to the trauma room of Mother Frances Hospital.

To survey what damage had actually been done, the emergency team performed an arteriogram, a process that involved inserting a tube in Downing's leg that extended to the wound around her chest area. Then, the team shot dye through the tube. Still conscious, Downing remembers the process as "stinging real bad."

The results showed that the bullet had caused some nerve damage in Downing's arm as well as completely severing an artery.

Rushed for time, since Downing's temperature had dropped far below normal, and her blood level was dropping from a normal 12.7 to 7.1, the doctors decided to remove an artery from her leg and insert it in her arm.

"As they wheeled me into the operating room, I remember seeing the faces of all my friends and family. When I saw my mom crying, I said, 'Don't cry, Mom. I'm going to be OK,' " Downing said.

Downing said the last thing she remembered before the anesthesia took effect was asking the anesthesiologist if she could have a piece of gum.

"He told me, 'No, you won't like it. It's a Weight Watchers brand,' " Downing said.

When Downing awoke, she was faced with some startling news. The bullet had missed her heart by a mere inch.

"The doctors told me it was unbelievable how lucky I was. It really made me stop and think about things I had never thought about before," she said.

During the following days of recovery, Downing said she received at least 50 bouquets of flowers, 40 balloons and hundreds of visitors, one of whom was Blake Wintters.

"The whole time we were in the pasture he kept saying, 'I can't believe I shot her.' "

Six days after the shooting, Downing was released from the hospital. However, her injuries still plague her.

"I still can't feel my thumb, index finger and half of my middle finger. It feels like there's a giant clamp on my hand," Downing said.

However, doctors have told her that the three days of physical therapy sessions she attends each week should help considerably.

Within six to eight months, Downing should have use of her radial and media nerves, which were both damaged in the accident.

Until that time, the doctors advise her to eat lots of food containing potassium in order to get her blood level back up again and basically to "take it easy."

Downing says she realizes now that the shooting was merely an accident. She did, however, say she had one regret.

"I know that a strapless prom dress," she said, "and high heels are definitely out of the question now." ★

THEME: The team didn't do as well as members expected.

Don't lead with "Given that three starters returned from a 16-8 team, the Lady Mavs did not do as well as expected."

Instead, determine why the season was not as successful as members had expected it to be, and then lead with an example that shows rather than tells. For example:

WHY?
★ Injuries
★ Bad luck
★ Attitude
★ Disorganization

DESCRIPTIVE EXAMPLE

WITH 19 SECONDS left against Parkview, Maverick girls basketball coach Jan Davis called time out to collect her young team and set up a possible game-winning shot.

"Melinda, you inbound the ball to Tammy out front," Davis barked.

"Tammy, you wait for Molly to come across in front of the basket, then throw her the ball. Molly, you roll left and take the shot here. Ramona, you set up here and put it in if she misses. Everyone know what they're supposed to do? Okay, let's do it. Let's go!"

The referee handed the ball to Melinda King and blew his whistle. Melinda tossed the ball to Tammy Ford, who dribbled the ball, waiting for Molly Perkins to break to the basket.

"Now!" coach Davis shouted, the clock now at 7 seconds left. "Get it to her now!"

But just as Ford released the ball, Molly tripped over a teammate's shoe, and the ball sailed into the hands of a shocked Parkview guard, who raced untouched down the court for a layup that sealed the win. The Mavs fell to their knees in disgust.

"That's how it was for us all year," said Ford, a 5-6 junior guard. "Bad breaks at the worst possible time. We were really snakebit."

Despite its 12-10 mark, players and coaches alike said they didn't feel as though they had a winning season.

"We had three starters returning, and we figured we'd be in the playoffs, but it wasn't meant to be," coach Davis said. "These girls worked hard, but they didn't get a single break all season. I really felt bad for them."

The streak of bad luck began two weeks before the first game when returning all-district guard Lissa McIntyre blew out her right knee in a practice. Over the course of the year, injuries forced nine players to start at least three games.

"I don't think we had the same line-up for any two games in a row," said King, who led the team with a 21.8 points per game scoring average. "It was hard to get into a rhythm, and then it seemed like we got into an emotional funk. It was like we kept expecting something to go wrong.

"And usually, it did."

Even more frustrating, King said, was the fact that one of the teams the Mavs trounced, Ysleta (76-53) advanced to the state semifinals.

"With any luck, that could have been us," King said. "With any luck at all, this could have been our year." ★

CHAPTER FOUR

FIND AN ANGLE

American high schools are more similar than different. Not surprisingly, student newspapers look and read alike, whether the school is in Connecticutt or in California. It isn't something to brag about.

Finding an interesting angle is perhaps the most difficult task of reporting any story. It begins with a promise not to repeat routine or trivial facts. Instead, the reporter vows to use an event as a springboard for an article that tells the story behind the facts, to tell the part of the story that will most interest the reader.

Attempts to define "angle" are largely unsuccessful, but I'll take a stab at it. Here goes: the angle is a point where the interests of the reporter and the reader intersect with the subject, and most stories have any number of possible angles. Some people think of angle as "point of view." It can be implied or stated. It is the selection of a central character, through whose eyes or experiences the story is related.

Some confuse the angle with the lead. It isn't.

Frankly, the purpose of the lead has been overly simplified in many journalism text-books. It's the one and only chance you have to grab the reader. It pulls the reader into the story.

True enough, but if all you wanted was to strike the reader's eye, you could begin every story with a little three-letter word, SEX. Instead, the lead represents the way the reporter chooses to tell the story, to make this subject distinct, to make the story belong to the reporter.

Certainly, the lead should seize the reader's attention, stimulate the reading of the entire story, inform and entertain. But numerous kinds of leads—summary, descriptive, narrative, anecdotal—can accomplish this.

To suggest that leads are interchangeable so long as they fulfill three or four specific purposes is insufficient. There is a difference between what is right for the subject and what is merely correct.

You find that difference by thinking not in terms of a lead but in terms of an angle. It is a multi-layered process that begins when you ask yourself, "Who is the most interesting subject in this series of events? Which stories are most compelling? Whom will the readers want to know about? And what will they want to know? How can I capture the spirit of this story, not simply the facts?"

There is a strategy inherent in the lead. That strategy is to introduce the angle. A story can have any one of a dozen or more leads. But the story has only one angle that would be best for your readership and your publication date. Furthermore, reporters take a fairly roundabout way of finding the angle. It's not a matter of theme → angle → lead → body → conclusion.

Instead, it's circuitous, with each element being determined by and determining the other parts.

Let's take the story of a teacher's retirement: Retirement stories provide rare opportunities for great features if students will take the time to do something with them. Often, reporters stack a few irrelevant facts on top of one another, toss in a predictable "I'm going to miss everyone . . ." quote and call that a feature. It isn't. It's a collection of data—cold, heartless and meaningless.

Instead, a reporter should be trying to reveal the character of the retiring teacher, to give meaning to the event, to capture the humanity of the moment. The following story, by John Bryant of the *Austin American-Statesman*, tells something more than how long the person has taught and where.

EVEN WITH 50 years of classroom experience, retiring Crockett High School home economics teacher Minta Palmer couldn't get Debra Favors to bite into a slice of mango.

"What does it taste like?" asked Favors, one of 24 second-year food students who had just prepared a glazed-ham dinner.

"It tastes like peaches," said Mrs. Palmer. "It's my gift to you."

"Well, I hate peaches," Debra complained.

Mrs. Palmer, who is being honored today with a breakfast in the school library, likes to urge students to try new foods and use good manners to eat them.

"They will be better adjusted to life," said Mrs. Palmer. "And good manners will take them places that money never will."

Mrs. Palmer, who was 71 in April, started teaching in 1938 in the North Texas German-American oilfield community of Goree in Knox County. She stayed for two years and was paid $100 a month. She taught in Shamrock and George West in Texas and 20 years in Raton, New Mexico, before she married Charles L. Palmer and moved into the Austin school district in 1964.

She was at Johnston High School for four years, then was one of Crockett's original teachers when the South Austin school opened in 1968.

That adds up to being the school district's only retiring teacher this year with 50 years of experience and lots of good memories.

Mrs. Palmer has two bulletin boards that compare what students learned in 1940 and in the 1980s. On the 1940s board, she noted that "a teacher became addicted to teaching."

In 1988, Mrs. Palmer said, "I'm still addicted."

Wednesday, her second-year students created a meal that attested to Mrs. Palmer's teaching abilities. The dinner they prepared and served to invited Crockett faculty and staff members featured an orange-pear salad, glazed ham, rice au gratin, green bean-bacon bundles, sour dough bread, cheese soufflé and chocolate cheese cake.

The semester's biggest cooking project was an unqualified success.

"I'm not hard to please, but this would be good anywhere," said satisfied eater Jim Houston, a Crockett guidance counselor for 14 years.

The third-period students took time from their meal to share plenty of the credit with Mrs. Palmer.

"She's real nice, and she helps everybody," said sophomore Deanna Ybarra. "Now I know how to set a table at home, and I can help my mom with the cooking."

Raymond Foster, a sophomore who plans to attend a cooking school and become a pastry chef, said, "She's a wonderful teacher. She's the neatest person I ever met."

Later in the morning, when the first-year food students started eating their pastry assignments, Mrs. Palmer raved about senior James Jones' lemon meringue pie.

Mrs. Palmer said having boys in her home economics classes is not new. She had male students in her classes at Shamrock High School back in 1940, she said.

Mrs. Palmer said home economics curricula in the 1980s have put an emphasis on family living and relationships instead of cooking and sewing skills.

But she still likes plenty of lab work in her classes. "Unless students are making something, they are not as happy," she said.

In her retirement, Mrs. Palmer said she and her husband will raise cattle, dogs and "lots of hell." ★

PROCESS OF ELIMINATION

Finding the right angle is sometimes a process of elimination, shuffling through the possibilities until you come up with the most compelling story.

One summer, a student at a workshop I taught at the University of Oklahoma wanted to know how such an approach would work with hard news. His school had recently changed its graduation requirements. "How do you find an interesting angle for a story like that?" he asked.

My response: Find a kid who will be affected. See if his or her situation is similar to that of others. If so, how? If not, why not?

Former NBC news commentator John Chancellor defines news as the "chronicle of conflict and change."

Find the conflict in the new graduation requirements. Explain to the reader in human terms what change means.

THINK IT THROUGH

A few years ago, I entertained the notion of writing an article about a small Texas Panhandle school that had won eight consecutive girls' state basketball championships, and 10 in 11 years. I didn't, but I spent a lot of time thinking about how I might do it. In my mind, here's how it would have gone:

I'd begin by researching the story immediately after the school, Nazareth High School, had won its 10th championship. Because seniors had dominated the team, I knew that there would be a number of new faces the next year to uphold the tradition, and I thought that would make an interesting angle. I had planned to select one of the sophomore or junior players and use her as the focal point for the story. I imagined how I could tell the story of the young woman who had attended these games since her childhood, had dreamed of playing for the Flying Swiftettes, and who now would step into the limelight.

Suddenly, the unexpected happened. The coach resigned.

My angle then switched from a player to the new coach, a young woman who had played at Nazareth years before. If you've seen the movie, *Hoosiers*, then you know the rest of the story. The team started slowly the next season, battled through a tough district schedule, qualified for the state tournament and then completely obliterated the competi-

tion to win yet another state crown.

To say the angle switched from player to coach doesn't tell the entire story. I still had to decide how to tell her story. Should I begin with the day she was named head coach? Should I begin by describing the final moments of the state championship game? Do I begin somewhere in the middle?

Once I decide where to begin, then I must find that right scene, anecdote or incident to pull the reader into the story. Is the lead descriptive or narrative? What is the verb tense? What person? What is the tone? The mood?

While journalism strives to be objective, the goal is difficult to achieve. It is the reporter's decision whom to interview, what questions to ask, which information to use, and in what order, and how to create the context—the mood, the texture, the pace—in which the action occurs.

There's nothing very objective about this process.

COMMON PROBLEMS

Whether in California, Texas, New York or Hawaii, high schools are more similar than dissimilar. They have clubs and activities. They have classes of students engaged in pretty much the same academic endeavors. They are run by adults who share a common vision, and they are supported by parents who think they pay too many taxes for what they're getting in return, unless it's a winning football season. That's the big picture.

Not surprisingly, high-school newspapers often look and read alike. High-school journalists cover the same stories and events in pretty much the same way as they did the year before and pretty much the same way other student journalists do. This isn't something to brag about. Many stories are interchangeable. Fill in the year, the name of the school, and two or three names, and the story could apply to any school, any year. Oh, to have a dollar for every time I've read

WE FROWN ON STORIES LIKE THESE

Sophomore Casey Hall is not your average student. He looks normal enough, but on the inside he is a character to behold. His off-the-wall sense of humor makes him impossible not to like.

"He's the funniest, most bizarre person I've ever met," said senior Dana Francis.

Everyone seems to think that Casey is very funny.

"He is a very clever person," said Dana Smith, junior.

Okay, so what's wrong with this? The reporter tells us Casey is funny but gives us no evidence to support the claim. Don't tell us. Show us.

Give us an example. Describe a scene. Do something. But don't simply tell us.

these leads:

- While other students slept late, swam and watched television, the (fill in name of club) attended summer camp. ✪

- The purpose of Student Council is to serve as a bridge between students and administrators. ✪

- Biff and Spike are members of a rock band, the Lost Causes, and they're working hard so they'll be big stars one day. ✪

- It's (choose one: football, basketball, baseball, etc.) season again. ✪

- (Fill in name of person) was crowned homecoming queen last Friday night before a packed stadium. "I was so excited when my name was called I could just die. This is an honor I'll cherish for as long as I can remember," she said. ✪

- College entrance tests will be administered next week. The purpose of the tests is to prepare . . . . ✪

- (Teacher's name) announced her retirement last week. She has been teaching here for 30 years. She is a graduate of Arizona State University and has a master's degree from Pepperdine University. Her first teaching job was in Somerton, where she taught for five years before moving here.
  She is married and has three children. When asked what she plans to do in retirement, she said, "Read, travel and work in the garden." She added that she will "miss the students too." ✪

- The Great American Smoke-Out is scheduled for next week. Sponsored by the American Cancer Society, the purpose of the Great American Smokeout is to convince smokers to give up cigarettes for one day, in

the hopes that they will kick the habit permanently. "We hope all smokers will participate," Principal Jim Bates said. ✪

- On Nov. 30, the Future Farmers of America traveled to Tulsa for a national convention. While they were there, several competed in various competitions. Students who won include . . . . ✪

- Blood. What does it mean to you?
  To millions in need of blood, it means the difference between life and death. Blood donations are important for those who need transfusions. Transfusions have saved hundreds of thousands of people suffering from severe bleeding, shock and blood-destroying diseases.
  The Student Council will conduct its annual blood drive next Tuesday. Students who want to donate should . . . . ✪

BEING CORRECT ISN'T ENOUGH

You get the idea. Although the stories fulfill all the requirements of textbook journalism, they aren't likely to attract many readers. In summer workshops, I tell students this is like the difference between a great kisser and a correct kisser. Who wants to be thought of as merely correct?

As a newspaper judge for high-school press associations, I've seen students take the same approaches in issue after issue. These approaches fail because they tell the big picture rather than focusing on specific people, places and times—in other words, focusing on the small picture that makes each school, each situation and each person unique.

What follows are stories that typically appear in high school publications. I've tried to show that there are no boring subjects—only lazy and careless reporters.

FANS AND FANATICS

Schools have sports teams. Teams have fans. Some of the fans go a little overboard. Hey, maybe there's a story here.

Maybe not. The first example begins with a statement of the obvious and goes downhill from there.

THE WEATHER WILL soon turn cooler, and the leaves will start to fall—and that means the arrival of football season. Fans are important to the success of the team because they cheer for the players and support them even when they lose. Coach Jimmy Duncan said the fans are an important part of the team.

"Speaking for the players and coaches, we appreciate the support of our loyal fans and hope everyone will come to the game and cheer us on to victory," he said.

Leading the fans are the cheerleaders.

"It's so important for our team that everyone come to the pep rallies and the games and scream real loud and participate in our cheers so that the players will know we're behind them win or tie," head cheerleader Penny Purcell said.

When asked, students said they enjoyed going to games and cheering for the team.

"It is fun to go to the games and watch the boys play," said freshman Becky Powell. "Even though I have no idea what is taking place on the field, I scream real loud a lot at the games."

"I feel it is my duty as a loyal athletic supporter to go to all of the games," sophomore Stuart Goldsmith said. "The best part is looking at the cheerleaders." ✪

TELL THE READER SOMETHING NEW

The following story, on the other hand, focuses on a football fan—not fans. It's interesting and fun. It develops the subject's character and personality and, most importantly, tells the reader something new.

THE FIRST GAME he attended, the players wore leather helmets and played the game in an old cow pasture. Sixty-three years and almost a thousand games later, Wallace Simpson is planning for another football season.

"I ain't missed but one game since 1928, and that's hard for some people to imagine, but I've been healthy and in town so I never saw a reason not to go," said Simpson, a retired engineer whose three sons played for the Bulldogs back in the 1950s. His youngest son, Heath, quarterbacked the 1958 Bulldogs to their only state football championship in the school's history.

"I saw my first game—a 35-0 win over Cleardale—in 1928 when I was 14 years old, and from that moment on, Bulldog football was my passion," Simpson said. "I played for four years here—four of the worst teams in the school's history, I might add—and then went to school over at Commerce so that I'd be close enough to home to go to all the games."

Every game except one, that is.

"My senior year in college, I was married, and my wife was expecting our first child," he said. "She was getting real close to delivering so I decided it would be best if I stayed home rather than going to the game. Good thing too. My son was born at 2:30 that morning, and we lost the game anyway. I'm just glad that the one game I missed was a loss rather than a win. I'd hate to think that I missed a game that we won."

Simpson served 16 years on the school board and was president of the Football Booster Club for eight years. "I don't miss all of that a bit," he said. "But when I get tired of going to games is when they'll need to plant me six feet under. I may be just another old fool, but I love them Bulldogs." ★

FOREIGN EXCHANGE STUDENTS

All too often, stories about foreign exchange students rehash clichés by focusing on food, hobbies, how schools differ and similar silliness. Do we really need another story that says, "I like being in (fill in the name of your school and community) because the people are so friendly, but I miss my family and friends"? I don't think so. Here's one of my all-time favorite losers:

IN CASE YOU HAVEN'T noticed, Huckleberry High School has two new special additions, and they are Michelle and Claudia Shafi. Michelle is 16 and a senior while Claudia, who is 13, is a freshman.

When asked how she likes HHS, Michelle replied, "Very much." Some of her hobbies are needlepoint, playing basketball, belly dancing, swimming and sewing. She also likes Kevin Costner and saw *The Bodyguard* four times in

ONE CAN FIND A BETTER WAY TO WRITE IF ONE TRIES

Yucky headline, huh? Makes you wonder, "one what?"

Rather than the stodgy "one may find . . . ." lead, it is better to refer directly to the subjects.

For example, rather than "On Friday night, one might find members of the Film Appreciation Club at the local theatre . . . .," here's a better approach:

If it's the opening night of a much-anticipated film, they're there, sometimes dressed in tuxes and long gowns, sometimes in cheap T-shirts they found at a thrift shop downtown.

"They" are the members of Oscars Anonymous, a hearty bunch of cinema lovers who look forward to the night of the Academy Awards as eagerly as others anticipate Christmas morning or prom night.

Beirut.

Claudia's hobbies include sewing, belly dancing and creating art. Singing is also a favorite hobby of hers, having sung in the Greek Orthodox Church Choir in Beirut.

When asked what Claudia and Michelle did in Beirut, they described the beaches and said they had picnics, went to movies and went to school, which they started when they were only 3 years old. Michelle also likes to do homework, which is a change from what you will find here (Ha, ha).

Now that these two girls have been introduced to HHS and the student body, you might want to talk to them and ask them about their country. It will help if you know French, for their English is not yet up to standards although it appears to be better than some students at HHS (Ha Ha). ✪

LACK OF EMPATHY

What a sad article. Here, you have two girls from war-torn Lebanon, and all the reporter can find to ask them about is their favorite food.

I came across another story a few years ago about a young girl who, with her family, had escaped the Killing Fields of Southeast Asia. Rather than capturing what certainly was a harrowing tale, the reporter asked every dumb question imaginable.

What is your favorite color?

What is your favorite food?

Are schools harder in this country?

What is your favorite extracurricular activity?

Such lack of empathy was appalling. Who cares what her favorite food is? Who doesn't know that foreign schools are harder? Doesn't it seem reasonable that her favorite extracurricular activity may be staying alive? With minimal effort and imagination, the reporter might have captured the heart of the situation.

CLAUDIA SHAFTI remembers the first time the jets flew over Beirut, her hometown.

"We thought it was some kind of demonstration," she said.

Suddenly, an explosion threw her to the floor, and she lay there, listening to the screaming American-made F-17s as they pounded the city with 2,000-pound bombs. The invasion of Lebanon had begun.

"People here now think of Beirut as a war-torn city," Claudia said. "But it wasn't always so. Just a few years ago, it was considered the Paris of the Middle East, and it was a wonderful place to grow up."

That was until the civil war began.

"The Christians were fighting the Moslems, the Syrians were everywhere, the PLO had come into the city, and it was just a mess, a horrible, dangerous mess," Claudia said. "We heard gunfire every day, every night. We saw dead bodies on the streets. Our beautiful city was reduced to ruins."

That's when her father decided to take his family to the United States. In September, Claudia's father, mother and younger sister, Michelle, arrived here. Michelle is a freshman.

"It is so different. I'm trying to get used to the language, the food, the culture," Claudia said. "One thing I have grown used to is the silence. No jets. No bombs. No death." ★

CONSIDER CURRENT EVENTS

In writing these stories about foreign exchange students, consider the current events of their country. How can you use those events as an angle? For example, in the days prior to the fall of the Berlin Wall, I came across a story about a West German youth. What did he think about the collapse of the Soviet empire? Had he been to Berlin, and what were his thoughts about the divided Germany? Can he explain the growing popularity of neo-Nazis?

A similar story involved a student from Japan. In the 50th anniversary of the surprise attack on Pearl Harbor, it would have been interesting to get her perspective on the event. She could have talked about Japan-bashing by Americans. Equally interesting angles can be found for students from any country. What we don't need are more stories about how America differs from their countries, how students are getting accustomed to hamburgers, shopping malls and driving on the right side of the road.

These stories about exchange students need not be boring. Case in point:

FOR 18-YEAR-OLD Kari Hati of Finland, North Mesquite High School is not as academically challenging as the small school he attended in his native country last year. That's why he doesn't spend much time on homework here.

Jose Antonio Perez of Barcelona, Spain, a high school student at Greenhill School in Dallas, finds that American schools place more emphasis on factual knowledge than on creativity.

Maria Kim Helena Lidbeck of Sweden doesn't understand why American schools have so many rules. Such practices as going to detention hall, wearing identification badges and not being allowed to walk through the halls during lunch hour are unheard of in her native land. But at Skyline High School in Dallas, where she is a junior, they are a vital part of everyday life.

For these exchange students and many others, attending school in Dallas is dramatically different from attending school abroad.

In interviews with six exchange students from Finland, Sweden, Denmark, Ecuador and Spain— each of whom attends a different public or private school in the area—no real consensus emerged as to how American schools stack up against foreign school systems.

But they all agreed that the language barrier makes learning harder—regardless of the subject matter.

"The language—it's horrible," says Christian Pederson, a Danish student and currently a 10th grader at St. Mark's School of Texas. "Some days, when I come home from school, I have to look up 20 different words to see what they mean. I learned English, not American English, before I came here. There's a difference."

Saane Norgard, another exchange student from Denmark who is a junior at the Episcopal School of Dallas, faces a similar challenge. "I spend more time studying here, partly due to the language and curriculum," she says. "School is harder because I have to take it in English. I don't know if it would be harder if it was in Danish."

Most exchange students already speak English when they arrive here, according to Nancy Bryant, area coordinator for the International Education Forum, a California-based, non-profit organization that matches American host families with foreign students. Still, the most difficult task facing exchange students, she says, is learning to think in English.

"All our students speak fluent English and are screened vigorously for their English language skills, academic skills, health records and their ability to get along with other people," she says. "Initially, they have a hard time because they're thinking in their native languages. The breakthrough comes when they think in English."

Ms. Bryant believes that the quality of American education depends on how much each student is willing to put into it. "All my students are eager to come here, and I'm sure it's not because they think it will be easy. Yet, in spite of the language problems, they tend to do well." ★

Now, let's look at the cliché articles and try to determine how they could have been approached.

CLICHÉ—SUMMER CAMP

• While other students slept late, swam and watched television, the (fill in name of club) attended summer camp at Florida State University. Attending the camp were (fill in names of students).

"It was a lot of fun, and it broke up the monotony of the summer," club member (fill in name of club member) said. "It gave us a head start on the year." ✪

CREATIVE ANGLE—SUMMER CAMP

SUNBURNED AND EXHAUSTED, her throat parched and her feet swollen, junior cheerleader Linda Moretti rolled out of her dormitory bed—a flimsy hard-rock mattress, resting on a set of springs that screeched at every motion—at a quarter past six in the morning.

"Get rolling girls," a dorm resident boomed. "We don't have all day. Breakfast served in 10 minutes"

Twenty-five minutes later, Linda and the other members of the varsity cheerleader squad marched out onto the Florida State University football field to begin another day of drills under the blistering sun.

"Anyone who thinks cheerleading is just hopping around and squealing needs to come here for a few days," Moretti said. "This is the Marine boot camp of workshops. There's nothing very

WELL, THAT'S A DUMB QUESTION

"It is not the answer that enlightens but the question," said dramatist Eugene Ionesco. His insight about words on stage is also applicable to words in newspaper and yearbook copy. Given the banality of the answers below, imagine what the questions must have been like.

• *I took art because I like to draw.*

• *I took Algebra II and Geometry because I want to take Trig, and you have to take Algebra II and Geometry in order to take Trig.*

• *Being in a club is important because it makes you feel like you're a member of an organization.*

• *(On using the library): It's the best place I know to find a book.*

• *(On homecoming): I was so very surprised when my name was announced. This honor means a lot to me because it is something that was voted on by the whole school, and it's something I'll cherish for as long as I live.*

PERSPECTIVE • 41

glamorous about it."

The purpose of the workshop is to forge a tight-knit unit than can fire up even the most jaded of fans. It isn't for the meek or the weak.

"Cheerleading has gotten a really bad rap," senior Christi Zulani said. "Too many students think it's just a popularity contest. If any of us are popular, then surviving this camp has meant that we earned that popularity." ★

Cliché—Club news

• The student council is hard at work planning for another successful school year. Among the projects planned include raising money for the Ronald McDonald House, planning the Christmas food drive, and helping with prom preparations. ✪

Creative angle—Club news

IT WAS 20 DEGREES outside, but with the wind chill, it felt more like 20 below. Four students were huddled around the electric heater in the small trailer. Suddenly, there came the dreaded sound of a car engine. A short argument ensued, resulting in one of the four people being pushed outside—to sell another Christmas tree.

Why would students subject themselves to such punishment?

"Service is what this organization is all about," said Student Council President Ben Wilson. "We don't want to get a rap of being in this just to pad our college entrance forms. We really want to help."

Student Council members helped the Evening Optimists sell $10,000 worth of trees, with the funds going to the Ronald McDonald House. Other Council projects included working concession stands and collecting clothes and toys for the city's youth shelter.

Next week, the Council will begin its preparations for the April 10 prom.

"We realize that the prom is several months away, but an event as large as this requires months

of preparation," vice president Rita Beller said. "Last year, we were late in reserving a site, and were almost forced to have the prom at the school cafeteria. Can you imagine how furious juniors and students would have been had we been forced to have prom in the cafeteria?"

Despite the demands of the job, Council members say the extra work is worthwhile.

"Even though it is hard to keep up with studies at times, being on the Council is a great honor and I hope it helps when it comes to scholarships," junior representative Stephanie Watts said. "And it's very satisfying to be able to do something nice for people and good for the school and community." ★

Cliché—Sports season starts

• It's (choose one: football, basketball, wrestling, track, baseball, etc.) season again. Members of the team include . . . . ✪

Creative Angle—Sports season starts

COACH BILL JACKSON pushed his cap back on his head and rubbed his hands across his face, obviously tired and frustrated by his junior quarterback.

"I told you, when the end comes across the line of scrimmage, you flip the ball to the tailback," he told Brad Simmons while jabbing his finger in his chest. "Now, try it again."

For Jackson's Lions, the season has been a series of "try it agains." The loss of 16 starters off last year's 9-2 team, plus the decision to go with a new one-back offense has the team scrambling to prepare for the opening game.

"We found out last year that we were getting most of our big plays out of the one-back set," Jackson said. "So we've switched from the Houston Veer because I think the one-back set will be the offense of the '90s."

The offense features more formations and puts more pressure on the quarterback and ends to read defensive alignments.

"We hope we can spread out the defense, which has to respect the possibility of the pass,"

> Finding the right angle is sometimes a process of elimination, shuffling through the possibilities until you come up with the most compelling story.

● ● ● ● ● ●

Jackson said. "We're a little ways from having it all down, but we're getting there."

The success of the offense will rest largely on the shoulders of Simmons, who played sparingly as a sophomore.

"Brad has tremendous ability," Jackson said. "He's a smart kid, a good runner and a very strong passer. Once he becomes comfortable with the system, he could be unstoppable."

Simmons will be joined in the backfield by senior Randy Voss, a second-year starter who ran for 852 yards last year while gaining second-team all-district honors. However, the offensive line was decimated by graduation—only guard Alan Moore returns. Both wide receivers —key elements in a one-back offense—have only junior varsity experience.

Defensively, the Lions return four starters: tackle Jeff McNair, end John Maher and outside linebackers Jim Sparks and Lavon Gannon.

"We're going to be green for a few games, but I think we'll put it together quickly," Simmons said. "Everyone is excited about this team. We think we can make up in hustle what we lack in experience."

The Lions open the season Sept. 6 at home against Port Pampano. ★

Cliché—Homecoming queen

• (Fill in name of person) was crowned homecoming queen last Friday night before a packed stadium. "I was so excited when my name was called I could just die. This is an honor I'll cherish for as long as I can remember . . . ." ✪

Creative angle—Club news

FOR KAREN MAYS, the joy of being named homecoming queen last week was tempered by the concern she felt for Larry Buckner, a 6-year-old at Matthews Elementary School who was undergoing surgery in Memphis for a tumor in his leg.

"It was truly thrilling to win, but I spent all day thinking about Larry," Karen said. "I couldn't take my mind off the fear that he and his family must have had. I wore a ribbon with his name on it."

Larry was taken to St. Jude's Children's Hospital in Memphis for the surgery. Karen met Larry at the Ronald McDonald House, where she is a volunteer.

"When Larry was five, doctors found a tumor in his leg," Karen said. "The tumor was removed, and he went through chemotherapy to remove any final traces of the cancer. This second surgery was to determine whether the chemotherapy worked."

Doctors found no new signs of the tumor.

"Winning homecoming queen was great," Karen said, "but nothing like the feelings of joy that I had when Larry's parents told me the good news." ★

Cliché—Teacher retirement

• (Fill in name of teacher) announced her retirement last week. She has been teaching here for 30 years. She is a graduate of the University of Kansas and has a master's degree from the University of Missouri. Her first teaching job was in Plainville, where she taught for five years before moving here.

She is married and has three children. When asked what she plans to do in retirement, she said, "Read, travel and work in the garden." She added that she will "miss the students too." ✪

Creative angle—Teacher Retirement

LUCY SWANSON ran her hand across the desk and inhaled deeply. In three weeks, her 30-year tenure as a mathematics teacher will end, and she is feeling the mixture of nostalgia and exuberation that comes with retirement.

"My husband and I own a little place in New Mexico, and we want to spend as much time there as possible," she said. "There's nothing quite like sitting on your patio, looking out across the desert toward Santa Fe as the sun sets behind the mountains."

But Ms. Swanson admits that many of her thoughts on those Indian summer days to come will probably take her back to her long career as a math teacher.

"I never wanted to be anything other than a teacher," she said. "I've had an opportunity to touch so many lives, to really be a part of the world as it changes and not just be a spectator. "

When Ms. Swanson arrived here in 1962, she was one of the thousands of college students, imbued with the enthusiasm of the new Kennedy Administration.

"We were out to change the world, and I

WELL, THAT'S A DUMB QUESTION!

Athletic coaches are notorious for their propensity to engage in coachspeak—the art of answering a question without saying anything. In fact, when it comes to high-school newspapers, it isn't really a fair accusation. Often, they are responding as best they can to meaningless questions.

For example, what kinds of questions could have prompted these responses?

• *We are looking forward to the season. If everything falls our way, we could win a few games.*

• *The ground game was successful because of our offensive line.*

• *I think they ran to the best of their ability but not potential.*

• *They got their heads bashed in, but they're better people for it.*

• *If you don't look at the losses, we had a pretty successful season.*

suppose to a degree, we did," she said. "I think it is interesting that I came to to the classroom just after the Berlin Wall was built and am retiring in the year that it was torn down."

Teaching all those years had its challenges.

"Once, a boy put a snake in my desk drawer. I almost had a heart attack. The boy is now a school teacher himself," Ms. Swanson said. "Back in the 60s, some boys put my Volkswagen Bug on the guard rail. But I was lucky. I was never the object of meanness but rather playful pranks."

Looking back, she's seen a lot of changes in students.

"Kids today are so much more worldly than they were 10 or 20 years ago," she said. "The kids in the 60s weren't nearly as radical as people think. The schools have changed as society has changed, but it's odd that the kids pretty much remain kids, and that's what I'm going to miss most of all." ★

Cliché—College boards

• College entrance examinations will be administered next week at Hillside Community College. The purpose of the college entrance exams is . . . . ✪

Creative angle—College Boards

EVERY SATURDAY morning, junior Quan Nguyen rolls out of bed at 6:30, drives 45 minutes across town to Hillside Community College, and then spends the next three hours studying math.

She hopes this time invested will make the difference in her dream to attend Yale University.

"I know the competition for entrance is incredible, and I need to score as high on my entrance exams as possible so I'm hoping these classes will give me that extra advantage," she said. "I think I'll do fine in the verbal section, but I've always had a rough time with math."

Altom is one of a number of students who are attending Saturday morning classes at local colleges to help them prepare for college entrance exams.

"I want to go to the University of Virginia, and I don't want to have to worry about whether I'll be accepted or not," junior Vu Pham said. "So I'm taking a class that's helping me with the verbal section of the SAT. It's also helping with my regular classes."

School counselors say the college prep classes are a good investment for some students.

"I'm not sure they're right for everyone," said Mrs. Evelyn Richmond. "But the classes have been shown to help students raise their scores by as much as 15 percent, and for some students, that extra 15 percent is the difference between being accepted by Harvard or Stanford, or going to a local college." ★

Cliché—Great american smoke out

• The Great American Smoke-Out is scheduled for next week. Sponsored by the American Cancer Society, the purpose of the Great American Smokeout is to convince smokers to give up cigarettes for one day, in the hopes that they will kick the habit permanently.

"We hope all smokers will participate," Principal Judith Heihn said. ✪

Creative angle—Smoke out

AS A YOUNG COACH, Bill Smith would puff down three or four packs of Winstons a day. "It's how I dealt with stress," he said. "Some days, the pressure of the job was so much that I'd have two cigarettes going at the same time."

But all that ended three days after his 45th birthday. He had a heart attack and underwent open-heart surgery to repair arteries, constricted after years of smoking.

"I laid in the hospital bed and thought about my family, that I'd never watch my daughter graduate from high school or kiss my grandchildren, and I cried and vowed never to touch another cigarette," Smith said. "And I haven't."

That was five years ago. Not only has he kicked the habit, Smith is encouraging others to do the same. He is one of the catalysts behind the school's annual observance of the Great American Smokeout and a supporter of a proposal before the School Board to implement a campus-wide anti-smoking policy.

"I started smoking when I was 15," Smith said. "I thought it was cool. Pretty soon, I realized how disgusting a habit smoking is, but I was hooked. I was a young coach, under a lot of stress, and I couldn't quit."

Smith underwent triple bypass surgery in early October. Doctors took five lengths of artery from his legs to replace the clogged blood vessels near his heart.

"I remember thinking as they wheeled me

into surgery, 'I'm too young to be doing this.' " Smith said. He added that doctors told him the vessels were constricted because of all his years of smoking.

In the wake of Smith's smoking-related medical illness, teachers have hopped on the bandwagon to promote a policy for designated smoking and non-smoking areas.

Principal Judith Heihn said a committee had already been working on such a policy for almost a year.

"Our smoking committee included non-smokers and smokers, and we had been proceeding slowly, which you have to do to make sure everyone accepts the new policy," she said.

The school is also observing the American Cancer Society's Great American Smokeout Day by placing banners, posters, balloons and informational literature around the school this week to increase awareness of the dangers of smoking.

Smith said he hopes it won't take surgery to convince others to quit.

He added, "If anyone needs a little additional incentive to quit, I can show them a pretty nasty scar on my chest." ★

CLICHÉ—THE CLUB TRIP

• On Nov. 30, the Future Farmers of America traveled to Tulsa for a national convention. While they were there, several competed in various competitions. Students who won include . . . . ✪

ORIGINAL ANGLE—THE CLUB TRIP

EACH MORNING, Saturdays and Sundays included, Susan Clark rises at 5:30 a.m., tosses some cold water on her face and walks 400 yards to the barn on her father's dairy farm. There she spends the next two hours petting, grooming and cleaning her prize steer, Rusty, and occasionally sneaking him junk food.

"He really likes barbeque potato chips," Susan said. "Don't ask me why."

This ritual—rain or shine, temperature be damned—has been going on for 18 months, and Susan hopes the big pay-off is near.

"The State Fair is in two weeks, and I think I've got a good shot at winning Best of Show," she said. "That's what all this work has been for. I want that blue ribbon."

For students in Future Farmers of America, such is the stuff of great dreams. FFA students know they're stereotyped as ropers and hicks but figure the occasional razzles are small prices to pay for what could be big payoffs later.

To wit: the Best of Show steer at the State Fair is often sold for as much as $20,000.

"If I win, my college education is paid for," Susan said.

And if not?

"Well, I've loved taking care of Rusty, and I've made a lot of friends in FFA," she said. "No matter what happens, I think I've come out ahead." ★

CLICHÉ—BLOOD DRIVE

• Blood. What does it mean to you? To millions in need of blood, it means the difference between life and death. Blood donations are important for those who need transfusions. Transfusions have saved hundreds of thousands of people suffering from severe bleeding, shock and blood-destroying diseases. The Student Council will conduct its annual blood drive next Tuesday. Students who want to donate should . . . . ✪

ORIGINAL ANGLE—BLOOD DRIVE

JOHN SPIVEY KNEW it was bad, but he wasn't prepared for this. His 17-year-old daughter, Hillary, bruised and swollen, connected to half a dozen monitors, lay in critical condition at County Memorial Hospital.

Thirty minutes earlier, doctors were frantically working to save her life after a drunk driver had slammed, head-on, into her Volkswagen bug. Although she was wearing a seatbelt, she suffered serious head injuries, a fractured leg and numerous cuts and bruises. The driver of the other car was killed immediately.

"She lost a lot of blood," Spivey said of his daughter, who is now a junior at Temple University. "If there had been a shortage, she might have died. You never think about how important it is to have a good supply of blood available until something like this happens to you or someone you love."

This is why Spivey, a senior history teacher, is again chairing the annual blood drive next Tuesday. ★

WE FROWN ON STORIES LIKE THESE

What does the word "recession" mean? If you said, "a temporary slowdown in economic activities," you are absolutely right. We're having a recession here. And it has some students worried.

"I want to find a job when I graduate, but right now it's not looking too good," said Tom Jones, senior.

"People need to work, and right now, there just aren't many jobs around," added Mary Brown. "But I'm confident it will turn around soon."

Don't tell us what a recession is. Tell the reader how the recession is affecting individuals in your community. Focus on individuals and their situations rather than droning on with definitions and bland quotations.

CLICHÉ—TEACHER OF THE MONTH

• **JANUARY'S TEACHER** of the month is English department chair Cheryl Hankins, who teaches English literature, AP English and speech. She is sponsor of the Debate Team and has coached the team to the finals of the state debate tournament, which occur next week in Philadelphia.

A graduate of Penn State University, she began teaching here in 1974. Hankins, who earned her masters degree in English from Temple University in 1980, was named English department chair in 1985.

"I enjoy teaching the students here."

Describing her teaching philosophy, she said, "I think every child can learn and that it is my job to find that place in each student so he or she will want to learn." ✪

CREATIVE ANGLE—TEACHER OF THE MONTH

• **THE STUDENTS AT** Harlandale High School are turning out for a different kind of adventure.

It has nothing to do with football or basketball or any other ball. Harlandale students want entry into the world of test tubes, laboratories and experiments.

Dan Martinez, it seems, has gotten his point across.

"Kids are now putting their marbles where it counts," said Martinez, Harlandale's science department chairman. "They want to be challenged to higher concepts of thinking."

Those ideals may sound a bit lofty, but the proof is in the numbers. More than half of Harlandale's 2,200 students are enrolled in science classes. New physics classes have been added to meet the demand, and 100 students recently were turned away from chemistry classes because every seat was filled.

There are various reasons for this surge in the sciences, but at Harlandale, administrators say all indications lead to Martinez, the school's popular, do-everything science teacher. Martinez is The *Light's* "Teacher of the Month" for November, an award given in conjunction with the Hispanic Association of Colleges and Universities.

Martinez believes the sciences are a way to raise the expectations of Hispanic students. His classes are explanations of new concepts, which Martinez hopes will push his students toward fields in medicine, engineering and high technology.

Martinez has a personal stake in how his students do because he is deeply embedded in the community around the predominantly Hispanic high school, where he has taught for 15 years. He is a Harlandale product. He grew up in a neighborhood near the school and today lives only a mile from Harlandale.

He believes a large part of his teaching responsibilities are tied to his involvement in the community. A teacher who is not a part of his community loses a key ingredient in identifying with his students.

"How can you solve the problems of a community by isolating yourself in another part of town?" he asked. "You won't solve any problems by being aloof.

"People have to see you in action. You have to go to the football games, extracurricular activities, the *quinceañeras*, and just show the kids that you care."

Martinez is an unabashed booster of his students. He believes they are as capable and talented as students anywhere else in the city. They only need a boost to believe any subject is within their reach.

"Knowledge gives you confidence," Martinez said. "It's that will, that desire, that takes you as far as you want to go.

"I try to get them started." ★

CLICHÉ—THE CLASS ACTIVITY

• **THE SPEECH CLASS** is currently participating in mock trials. The purpose of the mock trials is to duplicate the action in a courtroom and to teach students about the judicial process.

"Being in mock trials is very interesting," junior Sam Smith said. "I want to be a lawyer some day, and this is good training." ✪

CREATIVE ANGLE—THE CLASS ACTIVITY

• **TERRY JAMESON'S** lawyers did everything they could to convince jurors that a plastic bag of "crank," a methamphetamine, was confiscated from his school locker without his consent, violating his right of privacy.

They argued that Jameson should be found not guilty of possessing the drug.

Six teenage jurors disagreed.

Jameson, a fictional character, had the best mock trial team in the state. The "attorneys" were students from Westlake High School. Although their defense did not succeed in a practice classroom trial Thursday, they have fared better in competition.

The Westlake team, which has won competitions at the district, regional and state levels, will be matching courtroom wits with 23 teams from other states in a national mock trial meet Friday and Saturday at the Dallas County Courthouse, said Alice Oppenheim, a lawyer who has helped prepare the students.

"These students are an exceptional combination of talent and energy," Oppenheim said. "Austin and the state of Texas should be proud of them. I've enjoyed working with them. If anybody is cynical about young people today, these students would change their minds."

Westlake's mock trial program has come a long way, said Jack Woods, a teacher for 35 years, who started the program four years ago when he began working at Westlake.

"The first year it was too new, and we did not have a successful program," Woods said. "The team fell apart when we got to division competition." Students were involved in other activities and were not committed to the program, he said.

"The commitment has gotten stronger each year," he said. "I think that is the reason we won the regional and state competitions."

The team of seven senior students went to district competition after placing first among 16 Westlake teams, Woods said. Members of the top team are Kristen Silverberg, Bryan Taylor, Jennifer Bradley, Karen Kocks, Trudi Donaldson, Tiffany Gurkin and Alexander Renwick.

Silverberg, who plans to go to law school and then go into politics, said the mock trial experience has given her skills to use in everyday life.

"I guess I really enjoy the practices," Silverberg said. "It has taught us all so much. One thing that is extremely important in mock trials is the ability to be flexible.

"You have to be able to respond to any charges by the other team," she said. "That means you have to be clear on the facts. It helps you in real life to understand your own position and to be able to defend it to others."

At a practice trial last week, the student argued first for the prosecution and then for the defense in the case of the fictional State of Arida vs. Terry Jameson. In competition, students have to argue both sides of the case. Team members came to the classroom court in professional attire. Other students acted as the jury, bailiff, witnesses and courtroom observers. When the judge, played by Woods, arrived, the courtroom suddenly became quiet.

The Jameson case, which will be argued at the national competition, involves two issues being considered by the U.S. Supreme Court. They are a student's right to privacy regarding a school locker and the authority of a school official to take that right away, Woods said.

The national competition is being sponsored by the Dallas Bar Foundation, which created the first high school mock trial program, Oppenheim said.

The foundation, along with the Dallas Bar Association, sponsored the state competition. District and regional competitions were sponsored by Austin's Young Lawyers Association. ★

CLICHÉ—STUDENTS IN A BAND

ROCK 'N' ROLL is here to stay, as witnessed by juniors Biff Willows and Spike LeMond, who are members of a rock band, the Lost Causes.

"We started playing a few years ago over at Spike's house," Biff said. "Pretty soon, we picked up a few gigs at parties and stuff. We really want to make it big, to play in the huge arenas and have a lot of groupies and stuff. I mean, my personal goal is to be on Beavis and Butthead some day. That would be cool."

Spike said the band has a wide range of influences. "We like the harder stuff: Metallica and Scorpions, for example. The whole point is to make a lot of money and meet girls." ✪

CREATIVE ANGLE—STUDENTS IN A BAND

SHOWCASE

By CHRIS BARTON
Sulphur Springs (Texas) High School

"**THIS IS A FARCE** of an interview, I have to tell you," concedes Jim Smith.

And it's true. It's often impossible to get Smith or his younger brother Rick to

The "Teacher of the Month" story (page 44) was written by Daniel Cavazos of the *San Antonio Light*, San Antonio, Texas. The Mock Trial story on Terry Jameson was written by Brenda J. Breaux of the *Austin American Statesman*, Austin, Texas.

comment on their family's Dixieland jazz band with anything but offbeat asides or twisted one-liners.

Relating his early musical career, Jim recalls an eclectic folk trio he formed with his parents. "That was pretty irrelevant to what we're doing now, but it was my start in showbiz. We usually played the community center circuit."

"All the way from Sulphur Bluff to Hagansport," Rick helps out.

Later, when Jim describes their two performance ventures to New Orleans as "war," Rick offers a cheerier view:

"It was like springtime flowers tossed to and fro."

If Jim and Rick, a senior and a junior, seem to play well off each other, it's because they've had lots of practice. Along with their brother Jeff, a 1987 graduate, each has played a musical instrument since third grade and for the past eight years has been a member of the Sulphur River Jazz Band.

"Our dad had bought the instruments each of us would play before we could even talk," says Jim, the band's trumpet player.

After Rick had learned the trombone, the band began to form. Along with Jeff on clarinet and their father Hank on banjo and vocals, Jim and Rick were joined by Loren Seely on bass.

In 1984, Mark Chapman became the permanent drummer. Once the band jelled, their performances included spots at church socials, service clubs and the Fall Festival—the gig Jim calls "that great nurturer of the arts."

"And who could forget Tots on Parade?" Rick asks.

"Our first really big gig," admits Jim.

Of all the concerts the Sulphur River Jazz Band has given in its eight years, at least two are particularly memorable to the Smith brothers. The first, a performance at the Country Club, was "the one where everybody got drunk and left," Rick recalls.

"Not the band," clarifies Jim. "The audience. We got paid $300 for playing pool in the back."

Another memorable gig sticks out, not because of the audience of the band itself but because of the exotic behavior of the other performers on stage.

"We were playing for a bunch of Catholic luminaries, and we shared the stage with some people from the South Sea islands," Jim says. "They weren't wearing shirts, and they were carrying spears. They kept playing with Mark's

drums, and when one kid climbed on top of the drums, his father knocked him off with a spear."

As unstructured as their performances often are, the Sulphur River Jazz Band's rehearsals are even more so.

If the bassist is late or no one is available to replace Jeff, the band simply does without. Rick sits slumped back in a couch and shifts his eyes from ceiling to floor while Jim plays, and during Rick's solos Jim wanders around the room, empties his spit valve, grabs a mute off a shelf and returns to his straight-backed chair in time to pick up on his cue.

"Our rehearsals are not very structured at all," Rick says. "We just learn the music and play it."

"Not necessarily in that order," Jim adds. "The freedom of Dixieland is what appeals to me. You can just play what you want to, within limits."

That freedom includes improvisation—one of the integral features of Dixieland jazz. On "St. Louis Blues," a band favorite, "a lot of times we'll just keep taking solos indefinitely," Rick says.

"We once stretched it into 15 minutes at a gig," says Jim, who also gravels the song's vocals in an impression of jazz great Louis Armstrong. "It just depends. Jazz is such a flexible form. But since you're making stuff up, you have to listen to what everyone else is doing or you'll clash."

Rick and Jim agree that part of their band's tightness and improvisational skills arise from the family element, particularly when Jeff is home to join in.

"Rick and I and Jeff can tell what each other will play," Jim says. "It's like we're on the same wavelength. We can predict each other's musical response."

"Sometimes we'll even pick up our horns and play the exact same note," adds Rick.

Being without Jeff, both as a brother and as a clarinetist, has altered how the Sulphur River Jazz Band sounds as well as how Jim and Rick fit into the band's musical scheme. Sometimes, they have to go as far as to play the clarinet parts on trumpet or trombone.

"I have to adapt my style a little bit and play a few more runs and licks," Rick says. "It doesn't sound as good with no clarinet. That takes away from the music."

Jim, however, finds a few advantages to Jeff's absence. "There's less going on, and it's not as cluttered," he says. "We have more freedom because the instrumentation is not as full."

Besides, Jim adds, "We get a larger cut of the

paycheck." ★

THE STUDENT WITH A DISEASE

Rarely do student journalists capture the trauma and the heartbreak facing teenagers who must deal with catastrophic disease or serious injuries. Many stories reflect the same amount of distance that reporters want to put between themselves and the diseases.

CLICHÉ—THE STUDENT WITH A DISEASE

• **JUNIOR BENNY LUPINO** is in Boston, where he is undergoing chemotherapy for leukemia. The cancer was discovered over the summer. Because of the disease, Benny has been forced to quit the high school football team. However, his mom said he is working hard to keep up his studies. "He wants to graduate with his class," Mrs. Etta Lupino said.

Benny is also a member of the National Honor Society, the Latin Club, the Jazz Band and the yearbook staff.

"We are all praying for a speedy recovery," NHS sponsor Beverly Richmond said. "He's a wonderful young man, and if anyone can beat this, Benny can." ✪

CREATIVE ANGLE—THE STUDENT WITH A DISEASE

It's not much of a story. The reporters either fear infringing on the privacy of the person or fear that any discussion of the gravity of the situation is unwarranted or sensational for its own sake so they gather quotes from safe sources—his mother, the NHS sponsor. Benny is all but ignored.

It need not be this way. Consider the following story, sent to me years ago by a colleague. I assume it was written by a professional, but I'm not certain where this article appeared. Granted, this is the work of a professional who writes beautifully. Still, we should strive to imitate the best. And this is.

JOHN FILBECK WAS more afraid of never playing football again than he was of

cancer. A 13-year-old has his own priorities. In the fall of 1978, increasing pain in his legs forced him out of the Pop Warner league in West Pittsburg, California. The doctors found a rare and fast spreading tumor—neurofibrosarcoma—near his spine. As John lay in the hospital after surgery, his teammates paraded his jersey around the field.

In early 1979, John's father took him to Dr. Jordan Wilbur at the Children's Cancer Research Institute in San Francisco. The boy's first question was, "Will I die?" and the second, on hearing that he could but might not, was "Can I play football again?"

"Not this year," said Wilbur. "Maybe next."

John chose to hear, "Next year for sure," and that prospect sustained him through the next 18 months of treatment.

Wilbur prescribed a nasty brew of four drugs and radiation therapy. Each time John entered the hospital for another round, he tried to psyche himself like an athlete. He shaved his head to preempt the effects of the chemotherapy. He led the cheers for other sick kids on the floor. He reminded himself, as his stomach heaved again and again, what a coach always said: "Pain is mental, John." And: "If you're not hurting, you're not helping."

The strain aged his face, put lines of character on an already expressive brow. But the round-eyed fear showing in the picture above is still that of a little boy. The doctor is telling him that although his tumor has shrunk dramatically, he still might not be fit to play.

In August, John finished his treatment. He was in the clear—for now, perhaps forever. Eight times in three days, he telephoned Wilbur with the same question. When the doctor at last consented, John returned to the hospital to have the permission slip signed.

Tan and cocky, he strutted down the hall. He was wearing shoulder pads. When he got down on the shiny floor to demonstrate his four-point stance—a 96-pound defensive tackle—the wan children around him gaped in delight, and the nurses rubbed his head as if it were a magic lamp. ★

SURVIVING THE SCARS OF INCEST

By BRENT STINSKI
City High School, Iowa City, Iowa

*Names have been changed to protect the identity of the sources.

HER HAZEL EYES have given up crying about it. Now they just gaze back with cool acceptance, like they were looking at a scar, a bitter memory. She remembers that destroying thing that stole a piece of her life years ago. Incest.

It's taken her five years to look at it like this. Today she doesn't cry. Today she doesn't hate, use drugs, or live in depression like she did for so long. No, now Dede* '89, realistically sees what happened between her and her brother and has moved on. She's a lucky one.

At City High there's a lot like her—teens who have dealt, or are dealing, with incest. Some are recovering. Others have been abused and keep it a secret. Maybe some will be abused tonight.

Chances are, you either unknowingly know an incest victim—he or she could be one of your friends—or you are one. Considered to be the best recent report on incest, *The Secret Trauma: Incest and the Lives of Girls and Women*, by Diana E. H. Russell, states that incest is of an alarming frequency. One in every six girls and one in every ten boys is an incest victim before the age of 18. If that holds true, then there are about 160 incest victims at City.

"Incest basically is sexual behavior with a family member," says Ronnye Wieland, a therapist at Iowa City's Mental Health Center. She says incest can be any type of sexual contact, even just fondling, and that only about one-third of all incest actually involves intercourse.

"It can be touching in inappropriate places by any family member," Wieland says. Any relative can cause the scarring effects of incest. Lifelong effects like depression, intense stress, difficulty in establishing relationships, and flashbacks (the same kind experienced by Vietnam Veterans).

WHEN SUSAN* '89, talks about her uncle, you can hear the anger and fear in her voice. When Susan was 5 years old, her uncle started sexually abusing her. He was stopped nine years later.

"I sleep with a red stick," she says. "It's like a baseball bat, but only smaller. I'm scared he'll come and try to hurt me."

"You see, he carries a knife with him. And every time he sees me he puts a hand on that knife, and he just stares me down. I get cold chills; I start shaking and just run.

"That's why I sleep with that red stick."

That kind of fear has been with Susan for five years—ever since her uncle was reported to the police and forced to stop the abuse. But Susan, like many incest victims, finds she still loves him. Many incest victims find that even though they want to hate the abuse, they can't.

"My family's very important to me," Susan says. "I hate my uncle, but I love him because he's my uncle. I hate what kind of person he is, but I cannot hate him. He's my uncle."

Dede says she might have once loved her brother. Once, that is, when incest wasn't a part of their lives. But Dede remembers how she used to look up to him: the way any 11-year-old would to their older brother of 4 years.

"He was in high school, and I was in junior high," she recalls. "I was a little kid; I had a little mind. It was kind of neat at first because my older brother was finally paying attention to me."

He betrayed her admiration and trust. "He was the only male in my life that I looked up to," she says. "He was my older brother. He was supposed to protect me and take care of me. And then he does this.

"When you are a little kid, you trust everybody. When I was still a little kid, my trust in the world was totally shattered."

The betrayal of trust, therapists believe, is one of the most damaging aspects of incest. "If a child cannot trust a relative, then they lose the ability to trust anyone," says Mary Ellen Lester, who is Susan's therapist. "The child is confused about what to believe. She is often told, 'This won't hurt; you'll like it,' and yet she knows inside she doesn't like it at all. Soon, she thinks that she can't trust her own feelings."

The victim can't even trust that her own emotions are valid. She's too insecure to be mad, too scared to be happy. All because the one she trusted lied to her, and she believed it.

In order to escape this insecurity and pain, "victims often self-medicate with illegal drugs," says Lester. "They don't want to face the pain of the recovery process."

Not wanting to exist with the aftertaste of being

abused, Dede turned to drug abuse at the age of 15. Now, she says, she's sure she did it to escape the effects of her brother's incest.

"If I couldn't leave or make it stop, then I'd check out of my head and go to a safe place until whatever was happening was over. That's how I dealt with it." She pauses. "Or not dealt with it. Whichever."

Her self-abuse evolved into self-hate and self-blame. "It was easier to hate myself than to hate my older brother," she says. "I felt like: Why didn't I stop this sooner? Why did I let this happen in the first place? I felt like it was my fault. I hated myself; I hated him; I hated everybody."

Lester says that kind of self-blame is "something characteristic of almost every incest victim."

"Children don't understand that feeling bad doesn't make them bad," she says. "They think it's their fault, and they carry this assumption into adulthood. Recovery means realizing they are good people who had something bad happen to them."

THE CRUELEST THING about incest is that it cripples. Victims are too insecure or too scared to run for help. So they just keep it a secret, actually living with it. But only when victims shatter their secrecy can they begin changing from victim to survivor.

After three years of abuse from her stepfather, Missy* '92, broke her secret. Her anger, translated into action, inspired her to turn him in to the police. He was found guilty for sexual abuse and spent three weeks in jail. Missy was punished by her stepfather for three years. He got three weeks.

"It seemed like I was getting the punishment and not him," she says. "I was court-ordered to do all these things, like go to a counseling group. He was court-ordered to go to the groups too, but he never went."

But the counseling group Missy was forced to go to turned out to be a godsend, showing her the way to recuperation. "(Recovery) is hard, but it's worth it," she says. "There are times when you go into depression and you don't want to work at it, but there are also times you feel really good about yourself. When you make it through a group session, you just feel really good."

Wieland leads an incest group at the Mental Health Center. "It's really mostly educational," she says. "We talk about taking care of one's self, learning how to be assertive and learning that their feelings are okay."

IF YOU HAVE EVER been abused, consider the advice every victim will give you: find help.

According to Susan, abuse is a desperation you don't have to deal with. "Get help," she pleads. "It's the only way you can get on with your life and put your past in your past. You have no future if you can't deal with your past."

Susan has decided to put that past away. "I'm not going to let my uncle take the rest of my life," she says. "I will not let him have that. He's taken too much from me already. That bastard's not going to get any more." Susan began therapy one year ago. But, she says, she feels she is only one-fourth of the way to full recovery.

Incest's memories don't plague Dede today. "I've buried him," she says.

She's known that for a while now. It came to her last summer after she checked herself into a drug treatment center in the wake of her most intense period of drug use. She remembers: "They brought my brother there to the treatment center, and we talked about it. He sincerely told me that he wasn't trying to hurt me, that he wasn't really thinking about what he was doing. The reason, he told me, was because I was somebody he trusted, that he couldn't do that to somebody he didn't trust.

"That doesn't make it all okay, but in that meeting I kind of let it go. It wasn't any big flash of lightning or revelation. It just kind of happened. I realized: Okay, this happened. Okay, it sucked. And I'm holding this big resentment against him, and I have for five years. Where is it getting me? Nowhere. I have to let it go now. I don't need to hurt about this anymore.

"I've hurt enough."

Dede has given up drug abuse and says, with confidence, that her life is back in order. She has made her recovery.

"Recovering from incest means ending the self-blame," Lester says. "It means dealing with the depression, feeling the pain and letting go of the past."

Dede knows she will never forget her past—the scars will always be too painful for her to do that. But at least now she accepts her life, herself. And those hazel eyes that used to cry are now looking to the future. ★

THE BATTLE OF LITTLE BIG HORN

AS REPORTED BY THE UNTRAINED HIGH-SCHOOL STUDENT

History consists of one amazing event after another. Good writing makes it come alive forever. Lazy writing, though, drains it of all its life. For example: Here's how a poorly trained reporter might have handled an article on the fate of General George Custer.

MISTAKES TO AVOID

Second person, question lead

Have you ever been shot by an arrow and scalped? Well, General George Custer was. Custer and a lot of his men got together and went on a field trip to Little Big Horn. While they were there, they were attacked by Sioux Indians and killed in a massacre.

Definition from Webster

Webster defines massacre as "the act or an instance of killing a number of usually helpless or unresisting human beings under circumstances of atrocity and cruelty."

Editorial comment

Well, you can bet General Custer wasn't helpless, but that didn't seem to matter because he's dead just the same. And the whole thing has really upset some people.

Quote that provides no meaningful information

"This is very upsetting," commented President U.S. Grant. "Custer was a good soldier and was loved by all. We are going to miss him."

Anonymous quote for no good reason

An unnamed soldier remarked, "I hate to hear about soldiers getting killed because I know it could happen to me."

List of names

Members of the Seventh Cavalry who were killed included . . . .

Quote cliché

When asked if he was pleased with the tribe's performance, Chief Sitting Bull was quoted as having expressed, "And how. Heap big victory."

Obvious information asked

Asked if he would comment on future battles, Chief Bull proclaimed, "We are not looking ahead. We fight them 'um, one battle at a time."

Editorial comment

The Seventh Cavalry didn't look so good this time out, but you can bet they'll get their act together and come on strong in battles to come. ★

GRAMMATICAL LEADS

Because they often emphasize the news questions "why, how and so what," grammatical leads are excellent ways to open interpretive or analytical stories.

Also, grammatical leads provide a welcome relief from typical leads emphasizing who, what, when or where.

Here are a few we highly recommend:

• PARTICIPIAL PHRASE—A participial phrase begins with a present tense verb or past participle (a verb working as an adjective) and features action. Often, it answers the news questions "why" or "how."

As a present participle:
Cashing in on his dreamy pout, droopy blue eyes and cute tush, Billy Cacophony pursued his dream of rock 'n' roll stardom, despite his inability to sing or play a musical instrument. "Just look how far good looks and nothing more took Bon Jovi and The New Kids on the Block," he reasoned.

As a past participle:
Stunned by the desecration of his beloved 1968 Mustang convertible, Principal Melvin Adams formed vigilante groups to track down seniors responsible for the outrage.

• GERUND PHRASE—Begins with a gerund (the "ing" form of a verb working as a noun) and features action or an interesting detail. For example: Jogging is boring.

Typing 30 words a minute with a minimum of three mistakes and without breaking a finger nail is the requirement for passing Mrs. Joyce Bigby's business class.

• INFINITIVE PHRASE—Begins with to plus the simplist form of the verb and features purpose or dramatic action. Also, can create a minor note of suspense.

As an adverb:
To maintain his last thread of sanity, Latin teacher John Vector dismissed class.
"The kids think they speak Latin in Latin America and that 'pro-bono' is a U2 groupie," he muttered in disgust.

As a noun:
To cash in on her brother's fame, looks and dance steps is Janet Jackson's recipe for success in the rough and tumble world of entertaining a crowd of ditzy girls.

• PREPOSITIONAL PHRASE—Begins with a preposition and features one aspect of the story which the reporter feels deserves special attention.

After reading the staff editorial denouncing the administration's dress code, the principal tossed the student newspaper to the floor, stamped his feet and screamed, "Heads will roll."

• NOUN CLAUSE—Features the substance of announcements, decisions or beliefs, and begins with that, how, why, whether, what or when.

That vocational education and all electives except foreign language be eliminated from the secondary curriculum was the proposal of a group led by Mortimer Huxley.

How the state plans to finance public secondary education in the 1990s was the focus of a weeklong confrontation between the Governor and the Legislature.

• TEMPORAL CLAUSE—Features the time element and begins with when, while, before, since or as soon as.

When students return to school next fall, they will encounter new discipline, parking and attendance codes.

While Principal Melvin Adams talked to freshmen about the evils of vandalism, six seniors were painting pink and green happy faces as well as creative graffiti on his prized 1968 Mustang convertible.

WE'D LIKE TO SEE MORE LEADS LIKE THESE

• CONCESSIVE CLAUSE— Begins with though or although and expresses difficulties overcome or unusual circumstances.

Although he had failed to turn in a single assignment or pass a test, super jock Biff Stanley was genuinely shocked that he failed to pass World History. "But I'm the quarterback," he argued

Although Rhonda Rah Rah misplaced her pom pons, hairbrush and mirror, she was still able to lead cheers and meet her friends at the football game.

• CONDITIONAL CLAUSE—Begins with if or unless and expresses speculative interest or condition.

Unless the Jeffersonville Bobcats come up with a plan to replace their porous defense, stagnant offense and uninspired coaching, they stand a good chance of remaining the district's doormat for decades to come.

If the prom were held tonight, students would have nothing to eat and would dance to whatever music could be generated from a boom box.

COMPARE & contrast

FOCUS ON A SUBJECT

In a teenager's life, one thing is always true: the need for money is the same. Some teens can get money by working in stores, or by doing odd jobs, but perhaps the most popular way to earn fast money is through baby-sitting.

Baby-sitting at first glance seems to be the ideal job. You can sit and watch television and eat other people's food. At the same time, just keep an eye on their kids, and soon you've got a small fortune in your pocket. However, baby-sitting does have its share of problems.

For one thing, children don't always do what you tell them to do.

"Once, I had a boy lock himself in his room and begin tearing his shelves down," sophomore Clyde Zeigler said. "Another time, an 8-year-old let the family's dogs out of the back yard. It took me an hour to round them up."

Most students who baby-sit say they are paid at least $3 per hour and work from 7 p.m. until midnight. In addition, the kids usually go to bed at 9 p.m., leaving them three hours to talk on the phone or watch TV.

"Baby-sitting is boring, but it's easy," said Christy Dayton. "I usually talk to my boyfriend on the phone, or sometimes he comes over and we watch movies together."

Most students said that they baby-sit once a week.

"Generally, I go out one night on the weekend and baby-sit the other," Christy said. The money she earns will be used to pay for gas and food, she added. ★

FOCUS ON AN INCIDENT

It only took a second.

Sophomore Clyde Zeigler turned his back on Josh long enough for the mischievous 8-year-old to open the backyard gates, allowing the three black Labradors to escape into the neighborhood.

"I really panicked," Clyde said. "The last thing Mr. Nelson, Josh's father, told me was to make certain the dogs didn't get out of the yard, and just like that, they were gone. I chased them down for an hour."

Welcome to the wonderful world of baby-sitting, where anything goes.

"On good nights, it's the best job in the world," junior Katie Dayton said. "But when things go bad, they go really bad."

For example, one night, a 5-year-old Katie was baby-sitting locked herself in a closet.

"I didn't have a key, and the light in the closet was off. She was screaming bloody murder, and I thought the neighbors were thinking that I was torturing her," Katie said. "Eventually, I had to get a screwdriver and remove the door knob. Boy, was that ever a nightmare."

The problem with baby-sitting, students say, is that little children rarely appreciate the gravity of their deeds.

"Once, when I was baby-sitting, this little boy put his cat and her four kittens in the dryer and turned it on," Lisa Gray said.

"By the time I found them, three of the kittens had died, and the mother was totally freaked out. I had a hard time explaining what happened. Even now, I can hear that poor cat screaming." ★

CHAPTER FIVE

DESCRIBE IT

By appealing both to the senses and to the emotions,
journalists can encourage readers to judge
the action in terms of their own experiences.

I like leads that take me somewhere, that transport me to another place and time. I want to be there, and I want stories to take me. I don't want to read a lead that says: The city's homeless rate reached record high levels, a spokesman for the mayor's office announced.

Instead, an effective lead shows the problem:

RAY TUGGED the plastic garbage bag that served as a raincoat in a mostly unsuccessful attempt to stay dry, drew a few last puffs from a cigarette stub he found on the floor of a 7-11 store and joined the back of a line of down-and-out men, waiting for a warm bunk in the warehouse that serves as a shelter for the homeless on nights like this one.

"It must be 15 degrees out here," said Ray, who refused to give his last name. "It seems like every time the weather turns bad, this damn line gets longer and longer."

Ray is right.

A city official announced yesterday that the homeless rate has reached record high levels. ★

Journalism purists may not appreciate this more colorful approach. But high school students would most likely appreciate a descriptive lead that takes them out of the classroom or library and on a tour of the city's homeless shelters. And I think teachers would rather see students reading the school newspaper than wasting their time playing video games.

The strength of any descriptive piece lies in its use of details in an attempt to appeal both to human emotions and to physical senses: sight, smell, hearing, taste and touch.

In an article about a man who suffered near-fatal brain damage in a bicycle accident, the reporter said the brain "resembles nothing more than a large, soft, very wrinkled walnut. It weighs almost three pounds. Of that, about 2 1/4 pounds is water and the rest tissue. The combination explains why the brain is often described as looking like Jell-O, but the better comparison would be mayonnaise. Push your finger into this gray blob of protoplasm, and it will adhere."

Now that's descriptive. And it only appealed to two of the five senses. Each of the next three leads use selective details to create an image that carries with it an emotional response. Not only do readers see something, but they also feel something as well, even if that something is a queasy feeling in the pit of their stomachs.

■ DESCRIPTION OF A PLACE

NINE RED LEATHER chairs rest behind the mohogany table in the properly paneled and softly carpeted auditorium in the central administrative building on West Cabell Street.

All of the chairs are equal—but one is more equal than the others. It is the fifth chair, the one in the middle of the table. The back of the chair is slightly taller than the rest. This one is reserved for Dr. Marvin Layne, who for the past 11 years has served as school board president. From this post, Dr. Layne has guided the district through several of its most turbulent years.

Flanked to the left by blue-tinted photographs of school board presidents dating back to 1911 and to the right by U. S. and Illinois flags, the 64-year-old college marine science professor has used this seat to cajole, intimidate and hammer through policies and procedures that he says have saved the district from disaster. ★

■ DESCRIPTION OF A MOMENT

IN THE BACK of ambulance 703, paramedic Hank Harky battles to keep a 17-year-old breathing, but the young man's airways are rapidly contracting. The teenager is suffering a heart attack from a drug overdose.

With sirens blaring and emergency lights flashing, the ambulance races along R. L. Thornton Freeway at 72 mph shortly before 10 p.m. Thursday, bearing down toward the Veterans Administration Medical Center.

"How far, Ben?" paramedic Harky shouts through a small window to his partner, driver Ben Bryan, who is working hard just to keep the shaking ambulance in one lane.

"Twelve minutes. We can still make the cut over to Parkland," the driver yells above the din.

The pain and excitement are exacting a toll on the patient, and his heart starts to beat erratically. Despite the intravenous medication he is receiving in his left arm, he starts grabbing at his chest and screams painfully between each laborious breath.

"Do it," paramedic Harky shouts to his partner, who revises the ambulance's destination to Parkland Memorial Hospital because it is closer.

This is a typical run on "box" 703, Dallas' busiest ambulance and the 11th busiest in the country, according to a national survey. ★

■ DESCRIPTION OF A PERSON

WALKING INTO A SMALL coffee and pizza shop, South grad Lisa Spindler cannot help but steal the attention of those inside. One by one, everyone in the room takes quick glances at the woman who searches for a vacant table. Dressed in a long trench coat, overlaying a white shirt, with a peach sweater wrapped around her dark jeans and a black hat that surrounds her porcelain-like face untouched by make-up, Spindler could be one of the models who have helped create her growing fame.

Spindler, who graduated from South 14 years ago, has made a career out of her love of photography that began in high school. Her career began primarily with fashion photography, but her current project tells the story of a homeless man through nude photographs.

"When I was younger, I used to look at many magazines, especially European publications," she said. "I always wanted to be a photographer after looking at these very powerful images."

After thanking the waitress who brings her tea, Spindler resumes her train of thought.

"I decided to borrow a camera and take Jack Summers' class. I took photography for two years at South, and it wasn't until the second year that the pictures started clicking, and I started to get a feel for the camera. That was the first year that I won awards for my work. I cannot remember how many. I think eight, but I won more awards than anyone else in southeast Michigan."

As Spindler speaks, she absent-mindedly drags the tea bag around the bottom of the cup by the string. She pauses only for a short moment to take a sip of tea.—*Julie Davis, Grosse Pointe South High School, Grosse Pointe, Michigan.* ★

APPEAL TO THE SENSES
Successful description does more than describe. It appeals to the senses and emotions. It generates empathy between the reader and the subject by forcing readers to judge the action in terms of their own experiences.

Identifying the theme and determining the angle will assist you greatly in collecting detail. For example, the reporter in the story on page 58 has decided to tell the story of PALS, a peer drug counseling program by examining its positive influences on a specific student, Joey Eberhart. So, the theme of the story is "For Joey Eberhart and students like him, PALS has not only saved his life but allowed him to save others."

Now, the reporter has to decide on an angle, how to approach the story. She attends several sessions in which Joey counsels younger students. She interviews Joey,

'THIS ISN'T FUN ANY MORE'

By STEPHANIE MCCOLLUM
Central High School, San Angelo (TX)

SHOWCASE

AS THE TEACHER wrote notes on the blackboard for the class to copy, a student readjusted the bundle she was cradling in her arms.

"She's burping," explained Michele Acevedo, junior and proud mother of April Marie, a bouncing five-pound flour baby. Mrs. Darlene Hoggett, home and family living teacher, continued to scribble notes on the board.

Mrs. Hoggett reminded the class that their baby books were due the following Monday.

"If you've been carrying 'it' all week," she said, "go ahead and give 'it' a name."

"What if you don't know how to spell the name you gave the kid?" asked an unidentified "father."

The home and family living teachers, including Mrs. Hoggett and Mrs. Gay Young, designed the unit on parenting to answer questions students may or may not have about parenting, according to Mrs. Young. She stressed that she wanted the students to realize the responsibilities involved in parenthood.

For one week, the students carried sons or daughters made out of 5-pound sacks of flour and stuffed pantyhose. The flour babies replaced the traditional hard-boiled egg last year after Mrs. Young heard about the flour babies from a friend. Mrs. Young said that the idea of using eggs had become outdated after seven years. She decided that the flour babies are more life-sized and therefore got the point across to her students. She added that cases of "egg-napping" had caused some students' failing grades.

"I love it when they make comments like, 'This isn't any fun,' " Mrs. Young said. She explained that she did not object to students having fun at school, but "I have a very serious motive behind it."

As part of her effort to stress the responsibility of childhood, her home and family living classes take up units "in sequence"; teenage pregnancy is taught first, followed by marriage and parenting.

Mrs. Young stressed that the unit was not all ruffles and pink lace—the unit includes some serious topics. One speaker planned for the classes is a mother of a handicapped child who talks about her experiences. Topics covered in the unit are abortion, child abuse and how to handle incest.

Along with getting a preview of parenthood, Mrs. Young said that the students seemed to enjoy the project. She said that a group of students who were eating lunch off-campus received some strange looks from curious adults. Junior Tracy Ballard even received a warning from a Department of Human Resources worker not to mistreat her child. Not to worry—the doting mother had made a trip to Angelo Community Hospital, along with junior Gigi Kassay, to seek bottles and birth certificates for her child.

The class project also created financial opportunities for senior Sheila Hopkins, who began work on her flour baby at the beginning of the semester. Ms. Hopkins sold disposable Cabbage Patch diapers to her classmates at 25 cents each. Mrs. Young reported that most of the "children" in her fifth period class are bedecked in the latest in babywear.

Mrs. Hoggett's class geared up for the "prettiest baby" contest. The proud parents introduced their children. The babies' attire ranged from footy-pajamas to sunshades and drew many snickers from the class, despite Mrs. Hoggett's warnings to the contrary. "Don't ever tell a mother, 'Your baby looks just like a little monkey,' " the teacher admonished.

"He's gonna be a basketball player cause he's got long legs," junior Vanalyn Ocker boasted. Such displays of pride were evident among the "fathers" when they dressed their sons in clothing they wore as infants.

The votes were in. The class voted "Spanky," the son of junior Gene Hernandez, as winner. The "father" admitted feeling "good" about his son's accomplishment. Hernandez added that his child was very quiet, and "he didn't wet his pants either." ★

WE FROWN ON LEADS LIKE THESE

• THE "HAS ANYONE TRIED THIS BEFORE" QUESTION LEAD— Question leads, especially the second person "Have you ever . . . ." or "Do you know . . . ." leads should be rejected immediately.

What's wrong with them? They create an artificial connection between the subject and the reader. If the story is about someone or something, the reporter should focus on that person or thing rather than asking rhetorical questions.

Besides, the question lead provides the reader nothing. It's the reporter's job to answer questions rather than pose them. For example, a lead like, "Have you ever been bungee jumping?" is artificial and rhetorical if the assumption by the reporter is that few readers have been.

Have you ever jumped off a bridge without a parachute? Well, Leslie did. Leslie is a bungee-diver, and she said it is real fun.

"You might want to try it some time," she said.

his counselors and the students he counsels. But she decides to angle the story on the relationship between Joey and a younger student, Brian Kennedy.

Finally, she opts to begin the story by describing one specific, though typical, counseling session. Notice how the theme, the angle and the description work together to pull the reader into the story by evoking images and emotions.

IT IS HARD TO TELL whether he is more tired or bored or ashamed as Brian Kennedy rubs his hands through his greasy, coal-black hair and then down across his chin that has yet to grow anything more than peach fuzz. He stares down at the table or darts his eyes across the room. He refuses to look forward.

For sitting across from him is Joey Eberhart. And Joey is mad.

"Damn it man, I can't believe you did this to me," Joey says. "I can't believe you did it to yourself."

Brian, a freshman, knows he has let Joey down. He closes his eyes and speaks slowly.

"You don't know what it's like out there. I just couldn't turn it down. I really didn't want to get drunk. Getting drunk isn't that much fun anymore. But I got stuck with the wrong people."

Joey understands. Three years ago, he was a ninth-grade drunk himself. Today, the senior is a member of PALS—teenagers who licked their own abusive habits and now help younger kids beat their own. Still rail-thin, like he was when he was popping pills and boozing, Joey's skin is a translucent orange-yellow, the result, he says, of a vegetarian diet. ★

DESCRIPTION MAKES A POINT

We learn a lot about Brian and Joey in these five paragraphs, and what we learn is relevant. The description isn't a random collection of details. It makes a point. Some writers overwhelm the reader with details that fail to add anything substantial to the story. (For example: Joey's favorite band is Smashing Pumpkins. His favorite food is meatless spaghetti. The person he'd most like to meet is Robin Williams.)

Unless you're being paid by the word,

there's no excuse for verbosity. Compare the story above to this flat, one-tone story that takes a more typical approach:

A GROWING NATIONAL concern about the prevention of alcohol and substance abuse has led to the development of the Peer Advisory program in Pine Valley schools.

PALS began three years ago in the Brookland district by an initial grant from the federal government. Students who are part of the PALS program voluntarily take part in an initial 16- to 20-hour training program and monthly two-hour training sessions throughout the school year.

Senior class president Cindy Greene, member of PALS, said, "Peer Advisory is a worthwhile organization because students have fellow students who can understand the problems they may be facing in their day-to-day lives."

PALS volunteers visit ninth and tenth grade homerooms every Tuesday and also offer Lunch Bunch every Thursday. Lunch Bunch is held during all lunches and openly discusses a different topic each week. ★

The following leads contain information that fails to advance the action.

■ **EXAMPLE A**
Sitting in a room filled with broken radiators and jumbled desks, valedictorian hopeful Joanna Brown looks across the brim of her wire-rim glasses and expresses her feelings about life, how she divides her time between social and academic activities and how she still maintains the highest GPA in a class of 271.

■ **EXAMPLE B**
In England, soccer fans are just as likely to get bashed in the head by someone and then crushed into a steel fence. Last year, six people were killed at a soccer match in Liverpool. Pine Valley High School also has a soccer team, but it's more laid back.

■ **EXAMPLE C**
The Spanish Club started off this year with the breaking of a piñata. Club members

EDIT FOR STYLE AND SUBSTANCE

On June 11, 1993, Texas newspapers reported that 83 percent of teachers responding to a survey by the Texas Federation of Teachers say they see a significant problem with student discipline and misbehavior. Summarized the *Dallas Morning News*: "More than 1,400 teachers from 200 school districts across the state painted a picture of schools rife with profanity, threats and disrespect of school rules."

Now, you want to update and localize this story for your school paper. A non-thinking student reporter would rehash the story from the daily newspaper, going so far as to attribute information to the newspaper itself. The lead to this story would have been, "Violence, particularly against teachers, is a growing problem in schools, according to a survey conducted by the Texas Federation of Teachers."

A more ambitious reporter might talk to school officials, but the story would still focus on the results of the survey. This lead might be "Students are relying on their fists and, in some cases, knives and, frighteningly enough, even guns to solve their disagreements with teachers, said school officials, who added that campus violence is reaching epidemic stages."

However, the reporter who thinks both verbally and visually would look for a descriptive anecdote to hammer home the point that violence happens to individuals and has little to do with statistics and surveys. The lead to this story (see complete story, page 164) might be:

JAMES MILLER WAS CALLING roll in his first-period history class last month when one of his 14-year-old students started shouting, throwing paper and walking around the

room. The Stockard Middle School teacher's cue to send him to the office came when the boy pulled a marijuana cigarette out of his pocket.

But before Mr. Miller could fill out the principal's referral form, witnesses said, the youth punched him repeatedly in the face, slammed him against a chalkboard and knocked him out.

A classroom full of stunned eighth-graders looked on as the boy kicked the unconscious teacher in the chest and fled.

Mr. Miller was left with a broken nose, loose teeth, eye damage and bruises. He has been on medical leave since the attack Jan. 7 at the Oak Cliff school.

In Dallas and other urban school districts across the nation, the safety of teachers and principals is a growing concern.

In the 1991 fall semester alone, there were 47 assaults against Dallas Independent School District staff members, district security reports show. In each of the two previous school years, the total for both semesters was about 60 assaults. ★

— Anna Macias, *Dallas Morning News*

GET A REAL QUOTE

Editing weak content is an exercise in futility. Every story must have a theme that is thoughtfully conceived and an angle that is developed through observation and interviewing.

Take, for example, the following story about Jell-O wrestling, in which the principal participated and, as expected, was pretty much ganged up on. Everyone, it seemed, wanted to bury him. But here's the quote:

"I felt like the event promoted school spirit. I wanted to see a positive image from everyone and for students to have fun with the other schools."

I doubt this quote reflects his thoughts as he was wiping Jell-O out of his eyes, hair and ears. I'd like to know what was really going through his mind.

WE FROWN ON LEADS LIKE THESE

• THE "WHAT EVERYONE ELSE IS REPORTING" LEAD These stories summarize information from other publications rather than providing original reporting.

Last month, Time magazine reported bungee jumping is growing in popularity throughout the United States. Bungee jumping, Time stated, is the act of leaping off bridges and having an elastic cord spring you back up, right before you smack the ground.

According to Bungee Illustrated, more people are into bungee jumping these days than sumo wrestling.

"It's the nation's fasting growing sport, involving 150-feet rubber bands," David Marks, a bungee jumper from West Virginia, stated in the magazine.

TRAIN REPORTERS TO SEE THE ACTION

This exercise, created by H. L. Hall of Kirkwood High School (Kirkwood, Missouri) asks students to rewrite each paragraph, making it as descriptive as possible. Students are free to use their imaginations to create scenes as they think they may have existed. The purpose of the exercise is to spur students into thinking descriptively.

❐ Jeff Wagner, senior, ran more than 500 miles during the summer to practice for the cross country season. The temperature was more than 100 for nine consecutive days. The high temperatures caused other runners who were also practicing to vomit.

■ *Up and down country lanes, heat waves rose from the sweltering pavement, the result of nine consecutive 100-plus days. In the distance, a pack of young men—sunburned and drenched in sweat—slogged forth, battling the record temperatures in preparation for the fall cross country season. Leading the pack, Jeff Wagner pushed on, rolling up more than 500 miles this summer, hanging tough at times when others dropped to the sides of the road, sick at their stomachs and gasping for breath.*

❐ Four students spent the summer lifeguarding at city pool. Whistling down children for running and breaking other pool rules occupied much of their time. They also operated the concession stand and battled throbbing headaches and sunburn. The best part, they said, was watching other teen-agers.

■ *The lifeguards' life isn't as glamorous as it's made out to be. Sure, they get a killer tan and a plenty of time to check out members of the other sex. But they also must sell hot dogs, Cokes and candy while keeping tabs on hordes of elementary and junior high kids whose primary interests almost always include running on wet pavement. A typical day is likely to conclude with a hammering headache and a sunburn.*

❐ Students stood in line for hours to buy tickets to a Grateful Dead concert. One student got in line 84 hours before tickets went on sale. Traffic jams the night of the concert delayed the start of the concert by one hour. There was standing room only, and the crowd went wild.

■ *The line started to form days before tickets went on sale. One student waited in line for 84 hours to snatch front row seats. For what? The Grateful Dead, one of rock 'n' roll's most celebrated bands, a group that survived the 60s intact and whose appeal stretches from 50-year-old former hippies turned investment brokers to 15-year-old skateboarders.*
As usual, the band didn't disappoint. The standing room only crowd went wild when Jerry Garcia and group stormed onto the stage, despite an hour delay due to a traffic snarl created by the throngs of "Deadheads" coming to see the show.

❐ Four students participated in the Moonlight Ramble, a 20-mile bike ride at night. Jon Byrd, sophomore, attempted to ride under a rope barrier at the start of the course. The rope caught on the seat of his bike and threw him to the ground. He still won first place.

■ *Sophomore Jon Byrd overcame a rough tumble at the beginning of the Moonlight Ramble—his bike seat snagged on a rope barrier, tossing him to the ground—to win the 20-mile night rally over three other students.*

also learn, little by little, the culture of Spanish speaking countries and how to learn Spanish, too. The Spanish Club will hold its next meeting next Tuesday.

IS IT SIGNIFICANT?

In example A, what is the significance of the broken radiators and jumbled desks? Why mention her wire-rim glasses?

In example B, the story concerns the high school's soccer team. Focus on it. That soccer is popular in England is irrelevant.

In example C, who cares how the Spanish Club began the year? Provide the specific incidents and details that show the process by which students come to appreciate a different culture. Breaking a piñata isn't one of them.

Consider these next two stories. The first involves romantic obsession, a provocative topic rarely covered by high-school newspapers but certainly a reality among American teen-agers. Rather than taking a wide-angle view of it, the reporter chooses to focus on a specific girl and her experience with an obsessive young man.

SHE THOUGHT HE WAS going to kill her. He had been angry before, even punched his hand through a window once, but he had never threatened her, never scared her like this.

Now he was out of control. He pushed her into a corner and then shoved her back down when she tried to escape. "All I could think was 'I have to get out of here. I just started crying.' "

That was a month ago. Today, Julie (not her real name) has ended her relationship with Jim (not his real name), but he didn't give up without a fight.

"He'd circle my house, leave me little notes, stare at me in class," Julie said. "He kind of lost it."

Other high school students have similar stories. Obsessive love is all too real for many teenagers . . . . ★

CREATE THE DESIRED IMAGE

This is far more effective than a "Webster defines obsession as. . . . Many students are

involved in obsessive relationships." Even though we haven't described Jim or Julie, we have described the situation sufficiently to create the desired image.

The next example involves long distance relationships, and again, note that it focuses on a specific couple and uses their experience as the universal experience.

NANCY AND BILL WERE the darlings of last year's senior class. They dated all through high school and even into the first year of college. But there was a problem. Nancy attended the University of Maryland, Bill the University of Virginia.

"We'd see each other on weekends and talk to each other on the phone a lot," Nancy said. "But I began to feel that I was missing out on my college life, and so I started thinking about breaking up."

Bill had gone one step farther.

"I was still technically going with Nancy, but I started dating a few women at UV," he said. "And I started seeing my relationship with Nancy as a drag."

During the Thanksgiving weekend, Nancy and Bill agreed to break up.

"I still loved Nancy, but the long distance relationship wasn't working out," Bill said.

Too often, it doesn't.

Counselor Mike Barry said . . . . ★

Now, pick up with whatever statistics and other general information needed to fully develop the story. Make certain to return to the narrative about Nancy and Bill.

STRIP STORIES TO A SINGLE THEME

I picked up this trick from Rob Thomas, formerly of John Reagan High School in Austin. What he's done is attempt to strip subjects to a single sentence and then rebuild them around stories—not data.

For example, he finds a review of a book about teen-agers and their jobs, and suggests it to his staff as a story idea. Most staffs would rewrite the article or, maybe, find the book and rehash it.

But Thomas' staff will look for the local

WE FROWN ON LEADS LIKE THESE

• THE WACKY COMPARISON LEAD—Also known as the "most people think but not me" lead.

Most people think that jumping off a bridge is crazy, but not Judy. Judy loves it! She doesn't use a parachute either. Is this wacky or what?

• THE "I'M TOO DUMB OR LAZY TO COME UP WITH A FEATURE LEAD SO I'LL JUST LAY OUT THE FACTS AS I SEE THEM" LEAD—Also known as a "Dragnet, Just the Facts Ma'am" lead. It doesn't attempt to interest the reader. It just dishes out facts in no particular order. For example:

Senior Judy Smith is a bungee-jumper. Bungee jumping is a sport in which persons are attached to a long, elastic cord, much like a huge rubber band, and then jump off bridges or other high suspension structures.

Asked why she does it, Judy said, "Because it's fun."

and timely angle, and will place at the heart of the story a teenager—a Reagan student—rather than the book or the author. As a result, the article will have personal impact. The following example shows the kind of shoddy efforts we see often in the student press.

EDUCATORS ARE concerned that part-time jobs are robbing teenagers from receiving a full high-school education, according to Cameron Barton, education professor at the University of South Carolina and author of *Teenagers and Their Work*. ★

■ **PREDICTABLE LEAD.** While this isn't plagiarism, it makes no attempt to localize the information.

FOR MANY STUDENTS, putting in a full day's work means more than sitting in class from 8 to 2. More and more, students are working four-, five-, even eight-hour shifts daily at minimum-wage jobs.

However, part-time jobs are an increasing concern to educators, who worry that students lose more than they receive in their pursuit of a weekly paycheck.

According to *Teenagers and Their Work* by Cameron Barton, education professor at the University of South Carolina, "We are challenging the myth that part-time work is good for teenagers. In fact, our findings suggest the opposite," he stated in the book. ★

■ **UNIQUE ANGLE.** This lead localizes the situation to the school in a descriptive, appealing manner.

AT TWO each afternoon, while most of the students at Reagan High School are bent over their books, struggling against afternoon torpor, trying to hang in there for two more hours, senior Ricky Moreno is headed out to the parking lot.

He has an hour to dash home, change clothes, grab a bite, then drive to Tom Thumb where, for the next eight hours, he'll handle customers' questions and complaints, issue refunds, send cashiers on their breaks and in general keep things running smoothly at the front of the store.

YOU SAID IT, FRIEND!

Use the verb "said." Avoid synonyms, such as:
- believes
- feels
- says
- states
- expressed
- commented
- according to
- remarked

"Explained" may be used occasionally but only if the quote presents an obvious interpretation or clarification. You may believe an idea or feel an emotion, but you cannot believe or feel a direct quote. You may use synonyms for "said" if the synonym implies an emotional tone or action, such as whimpered, screamed, complained, whispered, charged or argued. Synonyms are usually reserved for dialogue—not quoted material.

For example:

"I told you to quit hitting golf balls in the journalism room," Miss Offset snapped.
"Oh golly gee, I'm just trying to have a little fun," senior Billy Ingrate whined.

See pages 83 and 85 for more help.

Ricky is the customer service manager. It's a very responsible job for a teen-ager, and Rick is proud of it.

"It's teaching me responsibility," he says, "how to deal with my own money and how companies work inside and outside."

But many educators, sociologists, labor leaders and parents would disagree. Increasingly, they're critical of such after-school work.

In Florida, Hawaii, Nebraska, New York, North Carolina and Ohio, state legislators are debating laws that would limit the number of hours teen-agers can work. Tennessee already has passed such a law. ★

■ PREDICTABLE LEAD

THE MARCHING MATADOR Band was named top band in each of the nine contests it entered this year, and the choir and orchestras also had successful years. ★

■ UNIQUE LEAD

AS USUAL, THE MUSIC HALL was one of the loudest places on campus, although the noise wasn't made by trumpets or saxophones but by hammers and circular saws. For four days, carpenters worked frantically to build a new trophy case that would hold the more than 50 trophies won by music groups this year.

Standing off to the side, Ron Nail, music department director, placed his hand on drum major Ben Garcia's shoulder and said, "Who would have thought that we'd be doing this today?"

Not many.

In its second year under Nail's direction, the band has surpassed all previous accomplishments. And Nail said he wants to make certain the school's musicians understand how much he appreciates their efforts.

"The music banquet is next Tuesday, and I wanted to show off our awards in the new trophy case," Nail said. "It is extraordinary what these kids have achieved this year." ★

Now, try a few of your own with these sentences:

1. The Student Council had a busy year.
2. She was a popular and excellent teacher.
3. The National Honor Society participated in many charitable activities this year.
4. Computers made a big difference in the school this year.
5. Soap operas remained popular with students.
6. The death of a popular sophomore after a long bout with cancer had a tremendous impact on students.
7. A spirit of volunteerism swept through the school.

THE RIGHT WORD

• You'll read this in every book about writing, but it needs to be repeated: Concentrate on action verbs and specific nouns. If you have a choice among words, select the one with the narrowest meaning.

Choose specifics rather than generalities:

STRONG	WEAK
Air Jordans	shoes
Toyota Camry	car
Trudged	walked
Jabbered	talked
Stetson	hat
Stroked	touched

You get the idea.

WRITE THE WAY YOU THINK

• Go to the thesaurus when you know there is a better word but can't think of it. Never use it in the futile attempt to prove to everyone what a great vocabulary you have. Readers won't be impressed.

So if you're writing about video games, say, "Red-eyed and washed-out for hours and slouched over Mortal Kombat, his latest video addiction, Zippo continued slamming buttons and blurting, 'Die, Mother.' "

Don't write: "Imbued with a veritable plethora of vexation augmented by his physical dissipation, Zippo engaged the computerized entertainment facility, thus terminating his video adversaries."

MAKE IT COUNT

• Make certain the description contributes to the development of the story's theme. Don't describe for the sake of describing. For example:

PRINCIPAL MADGE O'BRIEN said it is an honor to be nominated as Administrator of the Year but added she really doesn't expect to win.

"I'm pleased that the faculty thinks enough of me to nominate me for this award," O'Brien said wistfully, her pretty blue eyes looking up over her half-moon glasses. "It's like an Academy Award. I'm thrilled to be nominated, but I don't expect to win."

Wearing a white silk blouse and blue skirt that looked more like a first-grade teacher than a principal of a tough high school, O'Brien said softly that she appreciates the support she has received from students and teachers alike. ★

WE FROWN ON LEADS LIKE THESE

• THE "I'M NO JOURNAL-IST BUT MY CREATIVE WRITING TEACHER LOVES ME" LEAD—While description is a goal, you want to avoid overkill and pretentiousness.

Ominously, anxious eyes visible and invisible gazed up from the Cypress-filled banks of the Guadalupe River, its bone-chilling waters running gently over oval, white stones, to the visage of a young woman as she inched to the rim of the bridge. Would she do it? Would she take the plunge? The spectators sat transfixed, frozen both by the frigid waters and the anticipation of the next jump.

In a flash, Sue Bob answered their questions by diving like an eagle into the voluminous gulch, the hot, stinging air rushing through her helmet and goggles. As the elastic rope snapped her back from the jaws of death, she realized she should have brought with her another pair of underwear.

The description here has little impact on her nomination, and the story really goes nowhere. What she wears, the color of her eyes and how she speaks are not shown to be relevant to the theme of the story. With another angle—an anecdote that shows why she was nominated—they could be. For example:

MADGE O'BRIEN stared over the top of her rimless, half-moon glasses, straight into the junior's eyes and said, "One more mistake, Mister, and you're out of here."

The junior nodded, not daring to meet her cool-blue glare. He didn't confuse the soft voice for a lack of authority. He knew she'd do it.

And the rest of the school has learned that O'Brien is all-business even though she looks more petite than potent. In fact, faculty members are so impressed that they nominated her for state administrator of the year.

"Women administrators are a relatively new phenomenon," O'Brien said. "The stereotypical administrator is a male and often a former coach. So women have had to fight to enter the higher echelons of administration and then fight even more for respect once they arrived."

Respect is not a commodity in short supply when it comes to O'Brien.

"I've taught here for 25 years and have seen six or seven principals here in that time, and Mrs. O'Brien is as good as any of them, and better than most," science teacher Edwin Holt said. "She comes from the classroom and is sensitive to the needs of classroom teachers. She's tough, but she's fair. That's what has impressed me the most about her."

Even students say O'Brien is a cut above.

"She's open and honest, and she treats us like equals," Student Council President Liz Collier said. "She doesn't patronize us, and she's made the Council a partner in some decisions affecting students. Working with her has been a real pleasure." ★

The purpose of description is not merely to show but to help the reader understand why the visual details are important. Specific details allow the readers to see not only what you've seen but also to appreciate why the subject is interesting and important.

DESCRIPTION OF NEWS

Nor is description confined to features and other non-timely content. The lead of a next-day news article can be as descriptive as the reporter wishes to make it.

As the city editor of a weekly newspaper in California, I was forced to cover school board meetings. I don't wish this on my worst enemy. School board meetings are deadly tedious unless the subject of sex education comes up. And then everyone turns into Jihad warriors.

Unfortunately, sex isn't discussed much at school board meetings. Budgets are. So are outcome-based education and higher order thinking skills and performance assessment models and all kinds of educationspeak, which explains why most people would rather watch six hours of "Full House" than attend a school board meeting.

Still, school boards make decisions that have a direct impact on students. When this happens, you'll be expected to report them. If your school board is accommodating, it will meet a day or two before deadline so that your stories will be fresh and timely. Sadly, school boards are not renown for their obliging tendencies. To wit: Meetings often end late on Monday nights, forcing parents to choose among their childrens' education, Monday night football and a good night's rest.

Consequently, you are responsible for reporting news about an event that students wouldn't attend, even if it opened with Pearl Jam. Furthermore, it's your job to make students want to read about it, to know what happened and why, to understand what the decision means to the average Sally and Joe in the halls.

It can be done.

Let's assume that the school board votes 4-3 to shut down a school. Citing declining enrollment in the district, the board votes to close Kennedy High School and divide its students among the three other schools in the district. It's not a popular decision.

How do you cover this?

Above all else, you must remember that your job is to answer not only all news questions—who, what, when, where, why and how—but also all reader questions. "How much?" and "so what?" come to mind.

Answering all the applicable questions does not enslave you to the summary lead. In fact, you may even use the inverted pyramid form so long as you begin the story with the most important idea or angle. In developing this idea or angle, you may use a straight news lead (and there's nothing that says a straight news lead cannot be descriptive) or a free-form approach.

You will choose the approach based on your determination that one approach more effectively communicates the content of the story. So, you'll use an anecdotal lead because you believe it best tells the story. Or you'll use a news lead that emphasizes "why" because you believe it best tells the story.

The point is this: you will have options available to you, and you will choose the option that best fits the tone, style, readership expectations and content of the story. You will not use the inverted pyramid merely because "that's what we've always done."

Let's return to the matter at hand. The School Board has voted to close Kennedy High School. To adequately report this story, you must begin by collecting the fundamental data: Who voted in favor of the plan? Why? Who voted against? Why? How many students will be affected? Where will they go? When will this go into effect? How much will it cost? How much will it save? What will happen to the faculty, staff and administration at Kennedy? What was the percentage of enrollment decline that prompted the board's decision?

These details are part of the "tight" descriptions that allow space for the more colorful and emotional descriptions. Finding answers to the questions will mean that you'll have to interview a wide range of people. Editors/reporters always have to do second, third and fourth visits to establish these specifics. But it must be done.

Let's assume now that you've collected this information. Are you through? No. Reporting this information alone is likely to result in a dry article that is equally unlikely to be read. Rather than writing the predictable news lead, you should look for the descriptive human interest angle. Students are far more likely to read a story about the impact of a school board decision than they are a story about the decision itself.

A decision is abstract. The effect is concrete.

First, you need to interview students. You could wander up and down the halls, asking the people you bump into, "What do you think about the board's decision?"

I can predict their answers: It stinks. Let's go for a more unusual, provocative lead. If the school has been around for any length of time, it's probable that two or three generations of family members are graduates of the school. That being the case, interview Grandpa, Pa and Junior.

Perhaps you have a young woman who was to be the last of nine children to graduate from the school. What are her thoughts? Perhaps a teacher would have retired next year after having taught her entire career at the school. What are her plans?

Sit down with three or four members of your staff and brainstorm. How many other angles could you find for this story? It's almost unlimited. Your major restraints will be time and space. You don't have an infinite amount of time to devote to the article. And the publication does not have an infinite amount of space. So you must pursue the story from what you think will be the most lucrative direction, select and organize your data, determine the key news element to the story and then choose an angle that best presents that news element.

WE FROWN ON LEADS LIKE THESE

● THE "FALSE ALARM" LEAD—This is a lead that provides fraudulent anticipation of nothing. For example:

On a hot Saturday afternoon, a blood-curdling scream echoed through the Snake River canyon. Was someone falling to his death? Was it a heinous murder?

No, Todd jumped off the 150-foot bridge on purpose. He is a bungee jumper! And he said it is a lot of fun.

THE PORTRAITS OF sophomore Laura Hall's eight brothers and sisters are scattered around the school. Her oldest brother, Rick, was an all-state basketball player in 1984. His photo hangs in the boys' gym. Her sisters, Teresa and Rebecca, were both chosen "Most Likely to Succeed" several years ago. Their photos are in the oak trophy case in the senior hall.

Laura had hoped that her senior picture might one day join them, collecting dust next to the plaques and trophies that the school has accumulated over the past 40 years. It won't happen. Not because Laura isn't an honor student. She is.

But next year—Laura's senior year—the school won't exist. By a 4-3 vote Tuesday, the school board voted to close the school and divide its students, faculty and administrators among the district's three other high schools.

For Laura and hundreds of others, the decision was devastating.

"Every day I walk these halls, I am conscious that my days here are numbered," she said. "Since my freshman year, I've looked forward to being a senior, going to the football games, homecoming, the prom. I remember watching my sisters and brothers and knowing that one day, my time would come. And now, it's all gone."

School Board President Donald Sweatt was among the four members voting in favor of the plan to close the school. He was joined by Richard Moreland, Kathy Mayeux and Mary Richter. Voting "no" were Doug Abel, Alvin Miller and Wilma McCormick.

"It has been an unpopular move, but sometimes you have to do what you know is right, whether it's popular or not," said Sweatt, a retired Army officer. "I graduated from Kennedy. I know what these kids are going through, and I feel for them. Believe me, I do. But we could not endanger the entire district to save this high school."

The board cited declining enrollment as the primary reason for its decision. Since 1986, enrollment at the school has dropped 25 percent—from 1300 to just over 950 this year. District officials say they expect another decrease next year.

"The economy here is flat," Superintendent Lois Sexton said. "We have no new businesses moving in, and we're losing population each year. Until the economy picks up, I don't see how we can expect enrollment to stabilize."

Dr. Sexton said the district will save $2.1 million by closing Kennedy. She added that at this point, school officials are more concerned with reassuring Kennedy students that they are committed to as easy a transition as possible.

"Under the best of circumstances, moving to a new school is difficult," counselor Bob Murphy said. "We will be working especially hard to see that this move is as painless as we can make it."

For Laura Hall, that isn't good enough.

"No matter how hard they try, we're still going to be the new kids at school," she said. "We won't hold the offices. We won't edit the yearbook or be homecoming queen. We'll be at school, but we won't be at our school." ★

SPORTS DESCRIPTION

Look for the theme of the story, and then find a way to illustrate the theme. Describe a scene. Capture a moment. Tell a story. For example, the volleyball team is in the midst of its best season in history. The typical story will say something like this:

THE VOLLEYBALL team has compiled a 27-3-2 record, its best in school history. Leading the state's fourth-ranked team are Tara Fumerton, Sara Kurth and Rachel Hurley.

Head coach Greg Vraspier said, "The team has been playing real well so far, and we think we can go a long way once we get in the playoffs. If we maintain our focus and intensity, we could challenge for the state crown."

Members of the team include . . . . ★

Unless readers already have an interest in volleyball, they are not likely to read this story. If they're interested, they probably go to games or follow the team in some other way. Thus, this story tells them nothing they don't already know. How can sports provide meaningful and compelling information for both the fan and the non-fan? By concentrating on the psychological or emotional elements of the game: fears, disappointments, frustrations and aspirations.

Note how the following lead puts readers in the middle of a quiet locker room seconds before the start of a big game so that they can be a part of the dynamic tension of the moment. Also notice how the reporter uses interpretation to place the season into a historical context. It's the winningest season in history. The team won its first victory over West in five years. Success is the result of an intensive off-season regiment.

By STEVE DOOLITTLE
City High School, Iowa City, Iowa

SHOWCASE

INSIDE THE GIRLS' locker room, the volleyball team waits. The players are nervous with anticipation. Clustered together, the players display emotions in different ways. Some yell, scream or laugh. Others are quiet, searching for inward motivation. Silently to themselves, they all wonder: will we win the match?

But winning is not the only thing on their minds. They hear the crowd assembling in the gymnasium outside, producing a noise sounding like the slow, steady beat of a drummer. To the players, the fans are a distant rumbling but a reality they will soon face. They know that tonight the bleachers will be filled. Their ability, skill, team unity and emotion will be displayed to all their fans.

And the fans come for all types of reasons. They come because they know a player on the team, because they expect to cheer on the team that represents their school and because they want to have fun. But most of all they come because this year, the Central High School volleyball team is a team that can make things happen. A team that has been opening the eyes of people throughout the state.

A HISTORY LESSON

"We're number one," senior Tara Fumerton yelled while running across the court after beating Cedar Rapids Washington in four games 17-15, 10-15, 15-12 and 15-7. Even if, according to Division 4A ranking, they were number five, after the emotional victory, CHS felt as though they were number one.

This year with a 27-3-2 record, the volleyball team is having its best season in school history. They've already set the CHS record for most wins in a season and have a chance to win more at district and state. The impressive season began earlier this year when they beat West High for the first time in four years.

The secret to the team's success seems to be its stamina.

"We've been outlasting most of our opponents," head volleyball coach Greg Vraspier said. "In the final games of our matches, our opponents have been slowing down and reacting poorly. But we've been ready on our feet and jumping to play until the very end."

For the moment, the volleyball players are basking in the glory of their success. Their satisfaction is well deserved after the intensive training they have been through over the summer.

"We were determined to improve during the off-season," Fumerton said. "So we went to the weight room three times a week and conditioned by running stairs at Hawkeye Arena. Our strength is what makes us better than other teams."

Vraspier agrees that the players' increased strength has been key to their success.

"They hit the ball so much harder and with so much more force," he said. "They never fade at the end of games."

THE FUTURE

With the MVC tournament and a match against Linn-Mar coming up before districts, the volleyball team just has to work on the tiny details. Although careless errors are hard to eliminate, CHS wants to keep them to a minimum.

"The careless errors are the only things that slow us down," Vraspier said.

CHS is being recognized as a contender throughout the state.

"We're in that situation where all the other teams are gunning for us. We're a team to beat, and we'll continue to be a team to beat," he added.

Vraspier said he is optimistic about the team's chances at districts.

"When we enter districts, we'll be going for revenge against Davenport North. They've beaten us twice. Now we're going to beat them. After we win, we should be on our way to state. I hope we win state, but this is the first year in a long time where CHS actually has a fair chance.

"Whenever I'm asked, 'just how good is your team?' I remember an experience I had earlier this season," Vraspier said. "I was sitting in the stands when some players from a varsity team that I had previously coached came up to me and asked if it would be possible for them to play on our varsity team. I said 'no' and thought to myself, 'maybe the freshman team.' " ★

WE FROWN ON LEADS LIKE THESE

- THE 'BUT WAIT!' MAYBE NOT LEAD—This lead creates an artificial situation rather than accurately describing a real one.

Armed with a sword and shield, the man charges into battle. His opponent blocks every swing of his mighty blade. Exhausted from fighting, the man lets his defense down, giving his enemy the perfect opportunity to attack.

With one slice of a sword to the leg, the man is on the ground, clutching his mutilated leg and screaming in pain. Before long, the opponent has killed the disabled man—a mighty slash that splits the man's head open—and the battle is over.

But wait! There is no blood. The corpse hops up from the grass and is shaking his enemy's hand. No longer enemies, these two are now friends! The two gallant warriors are participants in the annual Round Top Shakespearean Festival.

Tis better to fall on your own pen than write such a silly lead.

Here's another exceptional sports lead. Note how the combination of the third person narrative and the description captures the anticipation of the coming season. Note also the interesting and informative direct quotes.

By DUGGAN PHILLIPS
Stillwater (Oklahoma) High School

SHOWCASE

DROPLETS OF COLD autumn drizzle fall, land and slide down the reporter's slick winter jacket as he walks in through the gym doors. His momentary icy chills and shivers from the outside are suddenly swept away and replaced with the humid, sultry sweat of a drenched, rain-forest-like atmosphere.

Screams and bouncing vibrations surround him as he starts to walk down the steps to the gym floor. Through the yells of the hustling players and the vibrations of the pounding balls, he does see one thing very clearly. The Pioneers' basketball season is once again alive.

As the season nears, expectations and longings for a fresh start are strikingly clear.

"I've been excited since the end of last year about this new season," head coach John Phillips said. "I think everyone was disappointed by the outcome of last season so I've been looking forward to a fresh start and a clean record for a long time."

The Pioneers' last season came to a halt after an early-round loss to Sand Springs in the state regionals, closing the season with an 8-15 record.

After last season's record, most players' views center on the characteristics that set this year's team apart from others in the past.

"I think as a team we are a lot closer than the teams of the past," Brady Despain said. "We've worked hard during the summer and have come a long way."

Coach Phillips agreed.

"We have the makings of an excellent team," he said. "The players right now are unselfish and put their individual desires aside for the success of our team. I think Casey Stengal, manager of the New York Yankees, said it best when he said, 'It's easy to get the players. Getting them to play together is the hard part.'

"Our players on the court right now can play together as a team, and, as far as I'm concerned,

that's the best thing a coach can ask for." ★

Finally, note how this descriptive lead is used to capture the feelings of a group of young women, whose season ended weeks earlier than they had hoped. This lead serves as a smooth and effective transition into the body of the story, which is not a compilation of statistics but a discussion by the players of when and where the wheels flew off.

By LAURA MATTHEWS
Westlake HS, Austin, Texas

SHOWCASE

ALL WAS SILENT except for the sounds of the gravel grinding beneath the bus tires, and the air was suffocatingly heavy with disappointment. Faces started blankly out of the half-opened windows, lost in their own thoughts, as an artificially bright voice cut through the gloom.

"Hey guys, remember that spike in the Georgetown game? We really took 'em by surprise with that one . . . ."

There was lack of success stories for the varsity volleyball team to recall after its playoff loss to Taylor. But even with a season record of 21-8 and a three-way tie for first place in the South Zone, the volleyball team members, who expected their season to end weeks later than it did, were less than satisfied.

"It's really hard to read about the state playoffs now because I keep thinking we could have been there," coach Jane Patterson said.

"It's real tough to be on top and have people gunning for you. It's a really mental game at that point," she added. "The other teams have everything to gain and nothing to lose, and you're just the opposite. It was like we were the only game of the season for a lot of the other teams."

Leander, Georgetown and Taylor psyched themselves up enough to beat Westlake in the last three games of the season, putting Westlake in a three-way tie for first place with Leander and Taylor.

"After Leander, it was like 'what happened, what went wrong?' so we all worked on our mental preparation and all the other things we thought we had done wrong," Patterson said. "We really got ourselves primed for the Georgetown game, and then we lost that too." ★

ACADEMIC DESCRIPTIONS

A much overlooked source of powerful content is the typical classroom speaker. These persons spend their time and effort to talk to high school students because they believe they have something to say. And the messages they bring can and should be made into educational experiences for the entire school. This certainly is the case in the story below:

By LORI LESSNER
Eastlake (Ohio) North High School

JOE MUHARSKY knows what it's like to hear the agonizing screams of an American soldier tied to a tree while being skinned alive and to have gasoline and salt water poured all over his raw body.

Muharsky knows what it's like to hold a friend and watch him bleed to death in the jungles of Cambodia while President Nixon makes his 1 1/2 hour speech denying allegations that American troops were in Cambodia in 1969.

As a member of the U.S. Navy Black Berets, Muharsky has been to hell and back. He spent 22 months of his life in combat along the Mekong Delta during the Vietnam War.

Muharsky, a graduate of North in 1965, is an annual speaker for Mr. Ray Smith's senior democracy classes as well as for Mr. Bob Beutel's senior government classes. He returned to North once again on Nov. 12 and 13.

Muharsky told students simple yet incredible facts about the horrors of the war which he witnessed first-hand. He also discussed his opinions based upon his knowledge and experience in the Vietnam War.

"I'm not saying you have to agree with me. They are my opinions, but I want to leave you with questions to make you think. I certainly don't have all the answers."

"I think the Vietnam War is the most tragic mistake this country ever made. World War II, Korea, Vietnam—all wars are the most horrible things. If you think they are glamorous, think again," Muharsky said.

In patrol boats that lacked armor, Muharsky would go on raids in canals located in Vietnam and Cambodia. He used guerilla warfare in the jungles against the Viet Cong (whom the Ameri-

cans referred to as "Charlie") as well as against the second enemy, the North Vietnamese Army.

"You have one-tenth of a second to feel sorry for the buddy of yours who was blown away with an M-16. The .223 caliber bullet travels 4,000 feet per second to kill a human being. You know you are next unless you keep fighting. I became something over there that really bothers me," Muharsky said.

Muharsky contrasted World War II with the Vietnam War. In Nam, there was no such thing as a front line. Instead, people fought as individuals. Success was determined by which side had the lowest body count after a battle.

Muharsky recited facts that are etched in his memory forever. He said that out of 3 million Americans who served in Nam, 175,000 became disabled. Thirty percent of the men in his platoon died by friendly fire. They never even saw the enemy. Fifty-five thousand veterans committed suicide upon their return home because the American public badly rejected them. There were also few jobs available for them because of their limited education.

"Why did so many veterans kill themselves?" Muharsky said. "Well, psychiatrists believe that who you are going to be and your development occurs between the ages of 18-25. The boys coming home fell into that category and only knew how to kill. The war determined that. They had nowhere to turn."

Muharsky also stated that he thinks there are Prisoners of War (POWs) still in Nam.

"I believe there is good evidence towards the allegation that many captured servicemen were left behind in Southeast Asia. I would not go back to rescue them unless I knew for sure they were alive and in a specific location we could find by helicopter."

"I think Muharsky is very dedicated to the veterans. I see him as a strong-willed person," Smith said. "He has an interesting story to tell."

Muharsky can tell of the flashbacks he experiences daily. The smell of cat food makes him smell the rotten flesh in a jungle once again.

Muharsky can tell why all the American troops carried not one, but two dog tags around their necks for identification.

"If you are about to be blown up, you put one tag under your tongue. This way, because rigor mortis sets in, you can still be identified and sent home for a proper burial," said Muharsky.

Vietnam veteran Muharsky remembers what

WE FROWN ON LEADS LIKE THESE

• THE "I NEVER MET-A-PHOR I DIDN'T LIKE OR A CLICHÉ EITHER, FOR THAT MATTER" LEAD.

• *The divers were fueled with the excitement of the jump . . . .*

• *Spectators on the ground were full of anticipation . . . .*

• *The air was thick with suspense . . . .*

• THE "IF TED TURNER CAN COLORIZE CASABLANCA, I CAN BUTCHER SHAKESPEARE" LITERARY ALLUSIONS LEAD . . . .

• *To be or not to be. A bungee diver that is. Bungee diving is. . . .*

• *Four score and seven years ago, our fathers brought forth on this continent, a new nation, conceived in liberty and dedicated to the proposition that all men should go bungee diving!*

• *King Richard II may have traded his kingdom for a horse, but we'd give just about anything for a victory in next week's game against Jefferson.*

those 22 months on the Mekong Delta felt like every single day that passes.

Muharsky knows. He was there. ★

This story is so much more effective than the typical "Joe Muharsky spoke to Mr. Ray Smith's senior Democracy classes about his experiences in Vietnam. Muharsky said the war was 'the most tragic mistake this country ever made.' "

What makes this such a special story is the empathy the writer feels for the speaker and the extremes to which she goes to capture the power of his message without sensationalizing or sermonizing. Instead, she provides an unflinching and unglamorous look at what it must have been like in the midst of a firefight and what it has meant to the men who were there.

RECREATE THE SCENE

Perhaps you're saying: "We don't have time to attend all of these activities that you want us to write about. We are high-school students, and we're expected to attend class and satisfy all the hoop-jumping which that entails. A few of us also participate in other programs, and band directors aren't always so understanding when we tell them we need to skip rehearsals to watch the homeless stand in the rain.

"So how are we going to describe events we haven't witnessed?"

First, failure to witness an event is often an error of staff management and planning. Know what's happening and when, and be there. Or assign someone else to cover the story.

Second, learn to take your senses with you to class, to work, to school activities and to social events. You must learn to see, hear, taste and feel your world, to be aware of your environment so that you can recreate it when the situation demands.

While it should never be the primary mode of operations, scene recreation is a viable substitute when you absolutely, positively cannot be there yourself. This technique is used repeatedly in the professional press when the reporter cannot be on the scene of a story. For example, a story in a Miami newspaper dealt with police raids on alleged crack houses. The reporter described how police kicked in the door, chased a suspect into a bedroom, threw him onto a bed, stuck a gun in his ear and said, "You blink, and your brains will be splattered all over this mattress."

The reporter wasn't sitting on the officer's shoulder during all of this. In fact, he wasn't there at all. But he interviewed the officers in such depth that he was able to re-create the scene. He had them describe the apartment. Were there dirty dishes in the sink? Were the beds made up? Were the ashtrays bulging with cigarette butts? He had police officers tell him what the apartment smelled like. He asked them if they could remember what was playing on the radio when they kicked the door in.

This technique is difficult and time consuming, but the pay-off is substantial. For example, the lead of the story on page 71 is one of the most powerful I've ever read in a student publication. The image of the young mother, who is rocking her baby and crying, is unforgettable.

GIVING UP CHILD MEANS 'TRUE PAIN'

By CLARE BUNDY
Duncanville High School

A GROUP OF candystripers stand around the nursery, holding incubator babies. It's "loving time." Another young girl steps in with her mother and picks up a baby, too. She is not in a uniform, but in a hospital gown, for the baby she holds is her own—and it's her "loving time."

It's also time to say goodbye.

"I sat in a rocker and held him and rocked him, and I cried and cried and cried," Amber, a senior, said. "I wanted that moment to last forever so I could always hold him and always be there for him.

"But I knew I couldn't. That's what hurt."

Amber was 16 years old when she gave up her child for adoption. The factors: "a meaningful relationship turned sour, failure of contraception, and little-to-no parental support," she said. "I was also only a sophomore in high school, and I had a desire—a need, really—for higher education."

Whatever the reasons or reasoning involved, they didn't lessen the hurt of losing her child. She remembers the day: June 19, 1985, and she vividly recalls the rest of the memory.

"When the time came to let him go, to set him down in the crib, I was still crying and I walked away," Amber said.

"But as soon as I reached the door, he started to cry. And I knew that if I turned back to get him, I'd never be able to leave the room.

"So I just walked out."

This traumatic situation was also an ironic one for Amber, who at 8 years of age decided she wasn't going to have any children.

"Coming from a big family, I knew how much time and energy it took to raise children," she said, "and I thought as an adult I'd be too selfish to devote all of that time and energy to one person."

Yet when she found out about her pregnancy, she said, she changed her mind. She didn't want to give up her child.

"But my parents forced the decision of adoption on me," Amber said. "I didn't have any choice in the matter; no alternatives were given."

The adoption was closed through Catholic charities, and though she said she felt "99.7% good" about her child's new parents, she reserved the other .3% for herself.

"I think I would have made a good mother," Amber said. "I have a good sense of judgment and three little sisters as experience.

"I know what it takes to make a family," she said, "but I also know it wouldn't have been complete without a father. That helped with their decision."

For it was all "their" decision in the end. Amber said that by the time her son was born, she "just wanted to hold him, just feel his presence," she said. "I wanted to feel his tiny body resting on my chest."

And she did get to hold him—for five days Amber mothered her child before leaving the hospital. The time she had with him was helpful as well as painful.

"It helped in that the experience was good. I felt good about it," Amber said. "Everything from breast feeding to changing diapers was a new, yet old, experience.

"It hurt because I knew that what I was holding and experiencing would never be mine."

When her son turns 21, however, he will be free to contact his mother. But Amber said she is not sure if she'll ever be emotionally prepared for their meeting.

"But I would still die to see him," she said.

And what would she say?

"I'd tell him that I love him and always will, no matter who or what he becomes," Amber said. "And I'll tell him the truth about what happened between his father and me. And what's happened to me because of it. There's no reason to lie to your children."

Yes, there is still a "strong maternal bond," and Amber said there always will be; this experience has left its mark on her now more than ever.

"During the pregnancy, I was loving the child, but I was apathetic to the situation," she said. "Now I either speak cynically about it, or I cry. I never used to cry."

This was evident as she stated the one word that described the whole ordeal:

"Pain," she said, tears streaming down her cheeks and falling onto her sweater.

"True pain." ★

WE FROWN ON LEADS LIKE THESE

It has been a year of ups and downs for Mr. Pinchon. He taught at York and was recently married. Those are definitely ups.

More recently, however, he was diagnosed with leukemia, a form of cancer.

That's a definite down!

No commentary required.

'AMERICA IS LIKE RUSSIA'

By MARK KNOBELSDORF
Tarpon Springs Senior High School
Tarpon Springs, Florida

SHOWCASE

HE SMOKES Camel Lights. He wears Harley Davidson boots. He worships Jim Morrison.

Greg Descours is a 16-year-old James Dean who doesn't dig America. He is ready to go home.

"You may call it homesick, but I had my doubts about living here as soon as I arrived." Greg looks in the air and smiles. "My first house mother was 72 years old, and we couldn't relate. We'd watch movies on the HBO that I paid for, and she always talked and tried to explain things. I finally threw the TV remote against the wall and broke it."

Dismayed with his elderly house mother and disillusioned with Dixie Hollins, his first American high school, Greg was happy to find refuge with a family in Palm Harbor.

"I was very glad to leave Dixie Hollins. It was dirty there, and there were fights every day." He shakes his head and places a crinkled cigarette in his mouth.

"Tarpon is a lot better; the people are friendlier, but on my second day at a football game, they (the administrators) busted me for smoking in the stands and told me I have to go to a smoker's clinic. I tell them that I quit smoking myself, but five months later they're still on my back for it."

Pulling out a shiny silver Zippo lighter from the pocket of his Levi's, Greg ignites his cigarette. He takes a drag and explains the difference between high school in America and France.

"In France you're allowed to smoke on school grounds. School doesn't start earlier than eight in the morning, and the classes have longer breaks between them. A lot of the schools are older and more traditional looking, if you know what I mean."

Greg brushes his fingers through his curly brown hair, then cracks his knuckles.

"No offense, dude, but students in France are more concerned about their future than American teenagers. I'm not saying American kids aren't smart, but in France, nobody puts their head on the desk and sleeps during class."

Wrapping his fingers around the can of warm Coca-Cola on the table, Greg lifts the container to his mouth and hastily swallows the liquid as if it were a burden.

"I'm getting sick of drinking this so often," he says, wiping a dribble of cola off his chin with the sleeve of his denim shirt.

"In France you can drink beer when you're 16 and liquor when you're 18. When I was 14, I bought 20 liters of liquor and two cases of beer at the supermarket to celebrate my birthday. People that want to drink around here have to hide in the bushes to enjoy a can of freedom. I mean, it's kind of fun hiding from the pigs, but who waits until they are 21 to drink beer?"

Revealing a tattered billfold, Greg proudly pulls out a creased photograph of a pretty girl standing in a grassy field. Her hair is long and brown, and she's smiling like the Cheshire Cat.

"This girl is waiting for me in France," he claims, lifting the photo close to his face. "I think the girls in France are a lot better looking. Not that there aren't real good looking ones in Florida, but in France they don't eat all the hamburgers and greasy foods, and overall they have better bodies."

Sometimes Greg likes to head out to the beach to check out the scene, but he misses the atmosphere of his native shorelines.

"It seems like in America, everyone is afraid of being natural. At a lot of beaches in Europe, the women walk around without worrying about covering their breasts. I mean, it's no big deal to be naked. Over here, it's like a crime to sunbathe in your own backyard."

While Greg says he has adjusted well to the American lifestyle, he is looking forward to returning to his family in Le Puy between Lyon and Monaco on May 10. He contends that Americans have every right to be proud of their country in the same way he favors his homeland.

"When I said America is like Russia, I meant you have to be 21 to enjoy everything the country has to.offer. It seems like you have to be real small or an adult to enjoy life here, and it's hard if you're a teenager. There are just so many cops around here, but I guess you can still have fun." ★

CHAPTER SIX

TALK TO PEOPLE

Face it, the sources aren't going to come to you. Those who do probably aren't worth using. To be a reporter, you have to overcome your shyness—then get out there and talk to real people.

Ask a group of publications students why they enrolled in journalism, and chances are, most of them will respond, "Because I like to write."

I've always hoped a few would answer, "Because I like to talk to people." That's because powerful writing begins with keen, insightful reporting, and the heart of reporting is interviewing. Good reporting is about 80 percent interviewing, and good interviewing is more than the hit-and-run encounter where the reporter asks a quick "What do you think about . . . ." to the first person he or she bumps into.

Shortly after the Persian Gulf War, I talked at a state press association convention about "How Student Journalists Covered the War." Consistently, the stories were outdated, vague and bland, primarily because reporters asked dumb questions such as "What do you think about American involvement in the Middle East?" to anyone they encountered on campus. Consequently, the stories consisted of large quantities of jingoistic, ill-informed and sometimes downright dopey comments.

"I think we ought to nuke them back into the Stone Ages," many students said. Other comments were neither so perceptive nor informed.

Fortunately, a precious few reporters knew how to cover such a story. They knew that the theme of the story was fear and a sense of loss. And so they interviewed the people most likely to possess these emotions—the families of soldiers who were sent to fight in the deserts of Kuwait.

These stories packed a wallop. An Oklahoma paper wrote of one family's first Christmas without Dad, who was a staff sergeant. The story was accompanied by a photograph of the family decorating the Christmas tree—the first tree, by the way, that Dad had not been home to pick out himself. It was a moving and powerful story because it touched on the emotions that each of us would feel had we been in that situation.

The key to successful reporting is the first lesson: Find the right person to interview. Build your story around the person who is closest to the subject of the story. If you're writing a story about teen runaways, talk to teen runways or members of their families. Don't build the story around adult counselors and social workers. Quote them, yes. But focus the story on runaways. Again, it is best to select one or two persons to stand as universal examples. You want to show how this person or these two persons represent a larger truth about all runaways.

This is no small endeavor. You will spend a good part of your time finding the right person to interview. Look hard. Ask around. Be willing to follow unlikely leads. The perfect source exists, but you can't expect to find that person at your doorstep prepared to hand you written comments.

"Hi, my name's Jack. I heard you are doing a story on teen runaways. Well, I'm your man. Ran away two years ago. Live in a trash dumpster. I've taken the liberty to type out a few comments. Feel free to use them as either direct or indirect quotes. If you need more information, you can reach me through my answering service. Thanks—and have a good day."

If this is what you're expecting, reconsider journalism.

You must find the perfect sources, get to know them, listen to them, watch them and, most importantly, earn their trust.

A good interview entails getting as much out of a source as possible. This means that the interviewer must listen, react to the response and then follow with perceptive questions.

Imagine for a moment that Arnold Schwarzenegger is coming to town and you're granted an exclusive interview. What kind of impression do you think you'll make if you begin by asking, "Mr. Schwarzenegger, what is your latest picture?"

The two most important elements of an interview are preparation and poise. Preparation should come first, of course. It should consist of thorough research of the subject and a careful list of preliminary questions. Poise comes during the interview—it covers every aspect of the interview from greeting the subject to terminating the discussion. Poise also includes putting the subject at ease, following-up on leads, building up to tough questions and "keeping cool" if and when the subject gets nasty.

But we're getting ahead of ourselves.

To prepare for the interview, the reporter should figure out who are the primary sources, who are the secondary sources and how these people can be reached. Don't be embarrassed to contact people. Most of us like to be interviewed. It's ego-inflating. No one wants

to walk into the office at 8 A.M. Monday and find Mike Wallace and the "60 Minutes" crew waiting with microphones drawn, cameras buzzing and some strange person who points a finger at you and says, "That's him. He's the one who did it!"

But short of that, most folks find being interviewed a pleasant experience and will gladly grant you a few moments of their time. Realize that they are doing you a favor so conduct yourself professionally.

Make an appointment if possible. Clearly define the purpose of the interview.

Give sources an idea of what you plan to discuss so that they can prepare as well. Use your common sense about this. Don't tell the source, "I need to interview you for an exposé we're producing." Administrators don't particularly want to hear this. Besides, what you think may be an exposé or investigation may turn out to be something much less inflammatory once you speak to all of your sources. Now, a few more tips:

• Arrange for privacy. Don't be interrupted by telephone calls, secretaries, gofers or others who are likely to stroll in and out of the person's office.

• Never attempt to see someone under false pretenses.

• Be there on time.

• Dress appropriately—not too far above or below the subject. Neutral.

• Show up prepared. Bring pencils, pens, pad, tape recorder if possible.

• Do your homework. Look at news, magazine or reference articles about the topic.

Talk to friends or to colleagues of the source. Find out as much about the person and the topic as possible before you begin the interview.

• Like a lawyer, you should anticipate the answers to most of the questions you plan to ask. Unlike the lawyer, expect to be surprised now and then. You want the source to state ideas in interesting ways and to present examples with vivid details. Welcome conviction.

• Prepare a list of questions, but be ready to deviate from it.

What do you ask? David Knight of South Carolina suggests to students that they consider the kinds of information that people tend to want to know about: Family, sex, politics, music, work, aging, religion and recreation.

He then suggests that they apply these to the news questions (who, what, when, where, why and how) as well as to the elements of news: timeliness, currency, prominence, oddity, impact, human interest, proximity and conflict.

It's a good idea to frame these questions so that they will elicit anecdotes. Try to get your source to tell you stories.

Anticipate your interviewee's mood. For example, what tone might you have to take if your job is to interview the coach whose team lost by one run for the third consecutive year and to the same team in the state championship baseball finals?

Be polite. Make people you're interviewing feel special, as though they are a part of an important moment which, if you are doing your job professionally, they will be. You won't get anywhere if you take on an attitude that suggests, "Let's get this over with because I gotta go to my girlfriend's house."

TYPES OF QUESTIONS

It is also good to consider the different types of questions that you can ask. The reporter who wishes to make the source feel at ease might begin with questions that the source can answer quickly, giving him or her a sense of control. Who? What? When? Where? Get them saying "yes and no," and they figure, "This is easy. I can handle this."

Then, hit them with other questions that may not be "yes or no" but that they can easily answer. For example:

What is the last good book you read? Who are your heroes? What are your hobbies? How do you spend your leisure time? What was your childhood like? What were your childhood ambitions? Who were your childhood heroes? What annoys you? What do you say are your worst weaknesses?

The answers to these easy questions might provide keen insight as you attempt to frame more difficult questions. While you may begin the interview with simple questions, use them only as long as it takes you to develop a rapport with the source. If you walk into the person's office and happen to notice that she has a photograph of her children on her desk, it is better to ask, "Tell me about your children" than "How old are they?"

The first question gives the subject a broad base of possibilities. Similarly, avoid "yes/no" questions. Questions that begin with "do, are, can, will . . ." tend to be "yes/no" questions.

Note how the following questions call for a one-word answer:

• Do you plan to run for re-election?
• Are you happy with the team's play?
• Can the team overcome this loss?
• Will the board approve the bond proposal?

Ask timely and relevant questions—questions that will elicit as much information as possible. The best question is the one that brings the highest return with the smallest investment in words.

Rather than, "Are you satisfied with the team's play?" ask, "What do you think about the team's play?"

But make certain your question is prop-

NO, YOU CAN'T JUST INTERVIEW YOUR FRIENDS!

Every story needs a minimum of two quotes. Quotes give stories credibility, timeliness and interest.

• Quotes must be firsthand. Don't lift them from other publications. If readers want to read quotes from *Newsweek*, they will read *Newsweek*.

• Quotes must be real. Don't interview your friends or friends of your friends. Many students are turned off by their school newspapers and yearbooks because they consist of the same quotes from the same people, page after page.

• Quotes must be valid. The sources must have knowledge about or experience with the subject. Compared to freshmen, upperclass students are experts. So are adults in charge of groups or decisions.

The insight conveyed in the quote should be precise, relevant, timely and packed with a newsworthy viewpoint.

erly worded. I remember an interview with John McKay, former head coach of the Tampa Bay Buccaneers in the National Football League—a team that set an NFL record for consecutive losses. Asked "What do you think of your team's execution," McKay responded, "Sounds like a good idea to me."

So be sure you ask for precisely what you seek.

Another type of question asks the source to analyze something. "How" and "why" questions force the source to think, to mentally connect different facts and situations.

Still another type of question asks the source to respond to hypothetical situations, a kind of "what if" inquiry. These questions are especially good for personality profiles. However, make certain the hypothetical situation is relevant. Avoid the "if you were on a desert island, what kind of Cheese Whiz would you most want to take along?"

Finally, most of us enjoy being asked our opinion. These questions allow us an opportunity to create a favorable image of ourselves. So it is with sources. To be interviewed is an indication that someone thinks we're experts. Then, to be asked our opinion about an issue or event is doubly gratifying.

CONDUCTING THE INTERVIEW

Talk casually. Ask brief, concise questions. Good interviewers do about 20 percent of the talking. You won't learn much if you're doing all the talking. While the interview should assume a conversational tone, the opinions should be dominated by the source, not the interviewer.

Empathize with the subject. Try to understand that person's point of view. Listen in a non-judgmental way. Don't agree or disagree with the subject. Gasping, rolling your eyes or frequently responding "Duh" are highly discouraged.

At the same time, convey acceptance.

You'll elicit more spontaneity by responding "yes" or "I understand" or "That's interesting" or by providing non-verbal clues, such as nodding, smiling, etc. But they must be genuine.

Don't personalize the interview. If you reveal your feelings about a subject, it may prompt the source to tone down his or her answers or tailor them to be in line with yours. Students sometimes ask questions that all but scream how they feel about a particular issue. Avoid these so-called "frame up" questions. For example, avoid asking a question in the following manner: The Supreme Court's decision in the Hazelwood case was a disaster. What is your opinion?

BETTER: The Supreme Court's decision in the Hazelwood case elicited strong opinions on both sides. What is your opinion about the decision?

Record sights and sounds as well as quotes during the interview. Pay particularly close attention to gestures, inflections, voice tone and regional accents if they are meaningful for the story. Observe body language. Does the source twitch uncontrollably? Sweat profusely? Does the source try to stare you down? Does he or she avoid looking you in the eye?

I once worked with a man who attempted to intimidate reporters by getting literally in their faces. Like former President Lyndon Johnson, he tried to press the flesh, and his technique more often than not worked.

Pay close attention to the person's environment: What art is hanging on the walls? What would it say about the new principal if he had a large photograph of Josef Stalin hanging on his wall?

What does his or her desk look like?

What kind of clothes does the source wear? How does he or she wear them? In some cases, you can judge a book by its cover.

Still, while body language and environment are important, your primary goal will be to glean from the source the best information possible. Always look for the dynamic comment, the dazzling quote that establishes the theme of the story. Polished politicians know that reporters are searching for "sound-bite" quotes, and they are quite adept at giving them more than a few. Find those quotes that are a window to the soul, that may say more about the subject than the words themselves individually may denote.

Of course, make certain you record specific data such as dates, names, spellings, ages, etc. Your memory can be relied upon for concepts and anecdotes, but specific figures are elusive. Write them down. If you have any questions about a fact, double-check. A 25-inch personality profile can be sunk due to a simple factual error in the lead.

Don't be afraid to ask the source to repeat or clarify a statement. It is your job to control the interview. Sometimes the interview might wander off in directions you did not anticipate. If this new direction offers great possibilities, go with it. If not, bring the interview back on track.

CONCLUDING THE INTERVIEW

Don't expect the source to read your mind. Don't ask, "Is there anything I haven't asked?" or "Did I forget anything?" Ask instead, "Is there anything you'd like to add?"

Conclude the interview on time. If you promised the source that the interview would take 15 minutes, be prepared to leave in 15 minutes. Of course, if the source agrees to extend the interview, so be it. But never keep the source guessing when you'll be finished. And never, ever force the source to call an end to the interview. The perceptive reporter will know when the interview should conclude.

Close on a positive note. Tell all sources how much you appreciate their time, their hospitality and their honesty.

Request permission to contact the source at a later time and date should additional information or clarification be required.

Chances are, you won't be able to read all of your notes. So get a number and best time to call, just in case.

WORDS OF WISDOM

You may think you've just made the best friend you ever had. Good sources have a way of making you feel special. Perhaps you are. But never sacrifice your own integrity or the integrity of your publication by suggesting to the source that he or she can dictate when the story will run, on what page it will run or how much of the interview will be used.

Never promise the source that he or she can read and edit the story prior to publication. In writing certain stories about highly technical matters, I have allowed sources to read portions of stories to check accuracy, but I have never allowed a source to change a quote or determine the angle or tone of the story.

Never accept "off-the-record" comments. I once knew a man who would make outrageous comments in public meetings and then blurt out, "That's off the record." It took only a few times before he learned his lesson: If you tell it to a reporter, it isn't off the record.

Some sources will attempt to bully you by providing ghastly, even slanderous quotes, and then quip, "of course, that's off the record." If you ever accept off-the-record information, then you have compromised all the information you receive from the source.

Time after time, reporters have been burned by sources who claimed certain information was "off the record" merely because a portion of an entire interview, they thought, was closed. Your philosophy should be, "If you don't want to see it in print, don't say it."

SUMMON YOUR COURAGE

Many young reporters are too shy—or think they are—to properly conduct an interview. They think, "I'm just a reporter

WHY WOULD A SOURCE WANT TO TALK TO YOU ANYWAY?

Most importantly, people like to talk about themselves. People are flattered to be approached by a reporter and even more gratified to be asked to talk about themselves.

Beyond that:

• It's an opportunity to obtain recognition and publicity for their work.
• It's a chance to tell their side of the story.
• It's a chance to be an "educator" of the public as well as a figure of authority.
• It's a chance to clarify positions or eliminate misunderstanding.
• It's a chance to influence or impress others.
• It's a novel experience.
• It's ego-inflating.
• It provides the source with a touch of immortality because their words may be frozen in print.
• The source believes in freedom of the press and wants to support a viable, relevant publication.

WHY DID YOUR INTERVIEW FAIL?

✓ You had no idea why you interviewed this person.

✓ You didn't prepare for the interview. Instead, you walked in, interrupted the source and asked, "So what can you tell me?"

✓ You didn't bring a pencil, pen or pad. You brought a tape recorder but forgot to bring a tape, which wouldn't have helped anyway because the batteries in the tape recorder were dead.

✓ You had no idea when the story would appear in print. "I just write 'em and hand 'em in," you told the source.

✓ When they weren't stupid ("What is your favorite food?"), your questions were vague, soliciting comments that restate the obvious ("What is the purpose of the Future Teachers of America?")

✓ Even when the source provided interesting information, you didn't follow up or probe questions that needed to be clarified. "Yeah sure, you know who killed JFK. Now, just once more, tell me the purpose of the Future Teachers of America?"

✓ You wore blue jeans that are too sizes too small and one of those T-shirts that doesn't cover your belly-button to interview the school board president, who is also a Methodist preacher.

✓ You went into the interview with a preconceived notion rather than listening to what the source said and meant. In fact, you told the source, "I know you're a crook, and I'm here to prove it."

✓ You didn't listen to the answers. Instead, you drummed your fingers on the table as though you couldn't wait to end the interview. You yawned every two or three minutes.

✓ You talked too much. Rather than asking the question and waiting for the source to respond, you answered for him or her.

✓ You allowed the interview to wander off track or to interrogate you about your opinions.

✓ You were insensitive to the source. You referred to the source's children as "rug rats." You asked if he buys his ties at Discount World.

✓ You overstayed your welcome. To make matters worse, you barged back in 10 minutes after the interview ended and said, "I forgot to ask, 'What did you say your name was?' "

✓ On the way out of the office, you take the last peppermint from the candy tray and say, "See you in the papers!"

for the student newspaper. Why should the superintendent want to talk to me?"

They fail to appreciate their importance to the staff, the students and the community. You are entrusted with an opportunity to meet with persons who may be unavailable to the average student. You carry the responsibility to act as the eyes and ears of all potential readers.

This is no small obligation, and you must rise to the occasion. Despite the stereotype of reporters as loud, insensitive louts, the great majority of reporters I have known are essentially quiet, introspective and serious. However, they do not allow their placid natures to interfere with their jobs of getting their stories. Nor do they confuse a reclining nature with passivity. They are relentless in their pursuit of a story even though they don't make a lot of noise during the chase.

So, you must rise to the occasion. Many photojournalists admit to a certain shyness but claim that they overcome it when they raise the camera to the eye. Looking through the lens creates an invisible barrier behind which they can hide. In other words, students personally are not taking the pictures. Instead, students are an extension of the camera.

You may need similar tricks to overcome your shyness as well. If so, then visualize yourself as an extension of the readers. I do not mean to suggest that you wrap yourself in artificial pomposity. But pursue the story as you think a daily newspaper reporter would. If you see yourself in this role long enough, it will become apparent to you what others have long since realized: that you are in fact a reporter for a worthwhile publication. You become a journalist as well as a student.

CHAPTER SEVEN

PUT IT IN ORDER

Now that you've collected all of this information,
you must do something with it. Begin by asking, "What part
of this story will most interest my readers?"

I came across an article in a Houston newspaper which said that some of the nation's top students are poor, disorganized writers. One reason, educators theorized, is that students spend so little time writing in schools.

Experienced writers always use order, transition and attribution to develop fluent copy. It's second nature. I once interviewed a basketball coach who toured Africa with a group of students. The coach literally wrote the story for me. All I had to do was string his quotes together, never giving a thought to order, transition or attribution.

For a beginning writer, it may not have been so easy. As an instructor of workshops and seminars, I've found that order and transition are the most difficult concepts to teach, with attribution (who said each quote) following closely in third. Why? Because they require the higher order thinking skills of analysis, interpretation and synthesis that students need to develop.

Part of the problem with organizing a story is a failure to collect enough information to compile a story. A random collection of unrelated facts isn't fodder for good storytelling, no matter in what order it's placed.

But even with students who have gathered sufficient information, marshalling that information and putting it in order remains a formidable obstacle. Many opt to tell the story in chronological order, whether it holds any news value or not.

For example:

HOMECOMING WAS held last week.

The day began with a parade during which the homecoming princesses rode down the middle of town on a fire engine. Then, a pep rally was held during which students voted for homecoming queen.

That night, the Lions played the Clearview Panthers to a 21-21 halftime tie. At halftime of the game, Linda Elkins was named homecoming queen. In the second half of the game, Ron Stone scored from two-yards out with six seconds left to lift the Lions to a stunning 28-21 win over the top-ranked, undefeated Panthers.

Head coach Roland Grewe was so shocked by the win—the team's first this year—he had a heart attack on the sidelines. The search for a new coach continues next week after the funeral when the school board interviews Bobby Bowden, who stunned everyone by quitting the Florida State Seminoles and applying for the position, saying, "It's the only job I ever really wanted." ★

This isn't exactly getting to the point. Fortunately, getting to the point isn't always the best route for high school reporters to take unless they're writing those three-inch club or class briefs. But for the major news and news/feature articles, narrative styles are more compelling.

The inverted pyramid, with its emphasis on shoehorning the 5 W's and How into a single sentence paragraph, is rarely an adequate writing and reporting tool for a non-

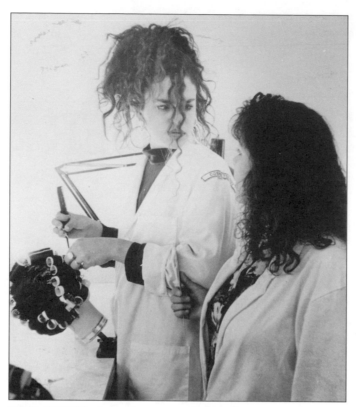

HAIR IRONY. A good reporter sees past the clichés and statements of the obvious and then allows the subjects to relate the narrative in their own words. *Photo by Hilda Cavazos, Milby HS (Houston, TX).*

daily student publication even though integral parts of the inverted pyramid—particularly the use of the quote/transition/quote structure—are viable for many reporting styles. Regardless of how the reader is drawn into the story, the body of the article should be built upon direct quotes and transitions.

Unfortunately, too many stories contain no quotes, dumb or silly quotes, or stacks of quotes. The reporters fail to work with the quotes, opting instead to pile one on top of the other—a tactic certain to befuddle even the most patient readers.

Consider the following scenario: Three students from your school, located in an upper middle-income suburb, join 16 other students who volunteer to repair homes in an inner-city neighborhood. The inner-city neighborhood—with its rows of run-down homes—is a bit of a shock to the students,

who are more accustomed to well-manicured lawns and clean, tidy streets. Let's examine each approach.

✓ THE NO-QUOTE APPROACH

THREE STUDENTS helped repair homes in an inner city neighborhood this summer. The students—Ralph Smith, Jim Jones and Joanie Johnson—were part of a project sponsored by the First United Methodist Church. The project combines two existing programs—the United Service Project, in which kids from suburban areas repair homes in the city, and Servants at Work, in which members of the church repair homes of people physically unable to do so themselves.

The three students worked on the home of Tony Lema of 2120 Lennox Avenue. The house needed a new roof. Students said they enjoyed the work and were happy to be part of the project. ★

✓ THE DUMB QUOTES APPROACH

THREE STUDENTS helped repair homes in an inner-city neighborhood this summer. The students—Ralph Smith, Jim Jones and Joanie Johnson—were part of a project sponsored by the First United Methodist Church. The project combines two existing programs, the United Service Project, in which kids from suburban areas repair homes in the city, and Servants at Work, in which members of the church repair homes of people physically unable to do so themselves.

"We worked on the home of Tony Lema of 2120 Lennox Avenue," Smith said. "The house needed a new roof ."

Jones said they enjoyed the work.

"We were happy to be part of the project," he added. ★

✓ THE STACKS OF QUOTES APPROACH

THREE STUDENTS helped repair homes in an inner-city neighborhood this summer. The students—Ralph Smith, Jim Jones and Joanie Johnson—were part of a project sponsored by the First United Methodist Church. The project combines two existing programs—the United Service Project, in which kids from suburban areas repair homes in the city, and Servants at Work, in which members of the church repair homes of people physically unable to do so themselves.

"We worked on the home of Tony Lema of 2120 Lennox Avenue," Smith said. "The house needed a new roof. Lema is unable to do the repairs because he has heart trouble."

"We were told the neighborhood was pretty violent, but the people I met were friendly and really nice," Johnson said. "Every day, Tony cooked us a different Mexican dish. One day, he cooked us some corn tortillas with beef and beans. The homemade tortillas were a lot better than the fast-food kind that we get in our neighborhood."

"We saw a lot of homeless people," Smith said. "That was really sad. If you live in our neighborhood, you don't even know that homeless people exist. You hear about it on TV, but you never see them."

"We really enjoyed the work," Jones said. "We were happy to be part of the project." ★

MAKE IT MEANINGFUL

The last story provides enough information to help an editor/reporter team turn the copy into an entertaining and meaningful story. They could begin by looking for a more compelling lead.

WHEN RALPH SMITH volunteered to come to the inner city for one week this summer, he was warned what to expect.

"We were told the neighborhood was pretty violent," the 13-year-old said, "but the people I met were friendly and really nice."

Smith and two friends, Jim Jones and Joanie Johnson, were among 18 students from suburban communities who took part in the City Service Project, in which they spend part of the summer fixing up homes in the mostly Hispanic neighborhood. The project combines two existing programs—the United Service Project, in which kids from suburban areas repair homes in the city, and Servants at Work, in which members of the church repair homes of people physically unable to do so themselves.

The students were part of a crew that repaired the roof of Tony Lema's home at 2120 Lennox Avenue. Lema is unable to do the repairs because he has heart trouble.

The student volunteers, though, experienced culture shock. For one thing, the rows of run-down homes with small yards were a strange sight for teens used to wide-open spaces and well-manicured lawns.

But the change in scenery led to an unexpected bonus.

"Every day Tony cooked us a different Mexican dish," Johnson said. "One day he cooked us some corn tortillas with beef and beans. The homemade tortillas were a lot better than the fast-food kind that we get in our neighborhood."

But food wasn't the only difference the students found.

"We saw a lot of homeless people," Smith said. "That was really sad. If you live in our neighborhood, you don't even know that homeless people exist. You hear about it on TV, but you never see them."

That aside, students said they learned much from the project.

"It wakes you up to reality," Jones said. "A lot of my friends spend all of their time in their cozy little homes and have no idea what is going on in the rest of the world. A lot of people out there need help, and it was very gratifying to be there for them. As much as anything, they need to know that people care." ★

You'll notice that the last quote is new and required additional reporting. I hate those "It was fun" and "I was proud to take part" quotes. If you are patient and persistent, you can get people to communicate this message in a fresh, compelling way. However, you must ask better questions than, "Are you glad you participated?"

Instead, try something like, "How did the week change your view of social problems?"

News isn't the only area of the student publication to suffer from the organizational pitfall of the chronological order. Quite a number of sports stories and entertainment reviews do so as well.

SPORTS EMPHASIS

The "report 'em as they play 'em" strategy for sports writing is a recipe for disaster. No one waits two or three weeks for the paper to arrive to learn whether the team won or lost. And it serves no purpose to rehash the play-

DON'T START FROM THE BEGINNING

Chronological order may work for some stories, but it rarely works for sports game summaries, concert reviews or record reviews. For example:

SPORTS

The game began when we kicked off to the Buzzards, and then they scored on a 23-yard pass. Then we scored but missed the extra point, and then it was halftime. The bands then marched. Then, they kicked off, but we didn't score again. But they did in the fourth quarter, and the game ended. They won.

CONCERTS

The Hangnails' concert was awesome. The dudes stormed on stage and ripped into their number one hit, "Lizard Gizzard." They played "Snake Bake," and then they played "Frog in my Egg Nog." Also, they played some other songs, and then we all went home half-deaf.

RECORD REVIEWS

The Hangnails' third album, "Lizard Gizzard," is totally awesome. The first song, "Snake Bake," is about this reptile who's in love with this girl, but she thinks he's gross. It's awesome. The second song, "Frog in my Egg Nog," is about this guy who has a really awesome girlfriend. It's awesome. The third song is—you guessed it—awesome.

by-play of each game. Instead, build the story around the common elements – threads of continuity—in each game. For example, in each game, the weather played a role. Or in successive games, the team lost key players to injuries. Or in game after game, the team staged a late rally to win.

Or, as in the case below, the team—depending on three returning starters from a 16-8 squad the year before—in game after game snatched victory from the jaws of defeat.

Compare the following story to the sidebar example on page 34.

THE LADY MAVS lost two out of their last three basketball games to finish the season with a 12-10 record and in fourth place in district.

The Mavs beat Ysleta, 76-53 on Jan. 7. Melinda King led all scorers with 31 points, followed by Tammy Ford, who scored 17. The Mavs led at the end of the first quarter, 24-10, and at the half, 51-30. Leading 66-39 going into the fourth quarter, the starters were pulled out of the game.

Three days later, the Mavs fell to Parkview, 59-56, even though they held the ball trailing 57-56 with 19 seconds left. King again led all scorers with 22.

In the last game of the year, the Mavs fell to Aurora, 63-49. Molly Perkins led all scorers with 18 points.

"These girls worked hard, but they didn't get a break all season," said coach Jan Davis. "I really felt bad for them."

King was chosen first-team all-district, and Ford and Perkins were selected honorable mention all-district. King led all scorers with a 21.8 points per game average. Other leading scorers were Ford (11.1), Perkins (10.2) and Ramona Griffin (7.6). ★

This story fails because it attempts only to rehash the events. The common elements that made the season so disappointing for the players are ignored. The heart and soul of the story—that these girls who fully expected to compete for a state championship didn't qualify for the playoffs—isn't addressed. Instead, the story bogs down in a quagmire of statistics and play-by-play rehash.

By finding these common elements and then using direct quotes to explain them, you can write informative and entertaining stories. But no one—not even the players themselves—will read a story that recaps the season, game by game, play by play. They may scan it for their names. But they won't read it.

ENTERTAINMENT REVIEWS

Nor are students likely to read movie or concert reviews that rehash, in chronological order, "what happened" or record reviews that examine the album song by song.

Entertainment reviews will be among the most popular content in your publication only if the writer knows the subject matter and approaches it from a fresh and insightful perspective.

In the case of a movie review, it is not enough to rehash the plot. Readers want to know whether the movie is worth the $8 ticket. You can't tell them this merely by listing the characters and giving a synopsis of the story. If you liked the movie, tell the reader why. If you didn't like it, explain why. Compare and contrast it to other movies. Most importantly, consider the intent of the film. Was it funny? Was it supposed to be funny? Was the dialogue realistic? Was the action believable? Were the characters convincing?

What were the performers trying to do, and how well did they do it?

If you use this question to approach restaurant, book, television, theatrical, film, record and concert reviews, it will force you to abandon a food-by-food, chapter-by-chapter, character-by-character and song-by-song approach.

PACK A WALLOP

The following story is one of the finest examples of story-telling that I've read. The article deals with the struggle of a mother to overcome her daughter's suicide.

The story packs a wallop. Its use of descriptive scene re-creation and narrative, coupled with its clear, logical organization and superb use of transitions makes it one of the most powerful stories ever published in a student publication. Pay attention to the use of direct quotes and transition sentences.

By STEVE DOBBINS
Duncanville High School, Texas

SHOWCASE

"DON'T BE MAD. I took some pills," Karen Keaton cried as she stooped over the toilet.

A few hours later, the 14-year-old freshman died after a series of coronary arrests.

Only that morning Karen had sat among her friends in the crowded church pew listening intently to the pastor's sermon.

And that very same day, she had eaten a big Sunday lunch with her parents and her two little sisters.

And that afternoon, she had applied at Burger King for her very first job.

And only hours earlier, she had giggled and gossiped with her best friends while experimenting with a new hairstyle.

And that spring day had been happy, relaxing and pleasant for the Keaton household.

But sometime about 10 that night, after the rest of the family had gone to bed, Karen went into the bathroom, closed the door and opened the medicine cabinet. One by one she swallowed each of the 250 heart pills taken from her mother's recently refilled bottle.

For Karen, the pain was short-lived. For those she left behind, the pain will never completely cease.

Though it has been almost six months since her daughter's death, Mrs. Linda Keaton still feels Karen's presence in their home daily. "We often find ourselves waiting for the front door to open and Karen to pop in just like she always did," she said.

Even after realizing how many pills Karen had swallowed, Mrs. Keaton believed her daughter would survive the ordeal. "She walked herself into the emergency room," she said. "I thought she'd just get her stomach pumped, and then we'd go home and everything would be OK."

Four hours and six coronary arrests after Karen had been admitted into the hospital, the doctors told Mrs. Keaton that Karen's brain was dead, and if she lived, she would be a vegetable.

Two hours later Karen died.

"Those few hours seemed like an eternity," Mrs. Keaton said.

She describes the first few weeks after Karen's suicide as a period of shock. "I just felt numb," she said. "I couldn't feel anything. It didn't really start hurting for a couple of weeks."

The initial shock eventually began to wear off. "After the shock, you start to feel angry," she said. "You want revenge for your child's death. You want someone to blame it on.

"Then you start to feel guilty. You begin to think 'If only I had done this or that differently.'

"Even now I find myself constantly tracing back to see if there was something I could have done or something I could have noticed," she said.

Karen did not show the usual signs of depression before she committed suicide. "She didn't seem depressed at all," Mrs. Keaton said. "But it was always so hard to tell with Karen when she was unhappy. She was so energetic. She could hide her feelings from everyone."

Mrs. Keaton said she believes Karen's suicide was not premeditated. "I don't think she realized the finality of suicide," she said. "On television, people are always attempting suicide. But they really don't die; they just get attention and sympathy.

"We'll never know why she did it," she said. "We can speculate, but we'll never really know for sure."

Mrs. Keaton attributes Karen's suicide to peer pressure. "A few months earlier she and her friends started experimenting with alcohol," she said. "It worried me, but I really couldn't stop it. All of the kids were drinking.

"Maybe Karen just couldn't cope with the pressures of keeping up with everyone else," she said. "What she wanted to do and what everyone else wanted her to do went against each other. She couldn't deal with that."

Still, suicide was against the image Karen put forth. "Several of her friends had talked to her about suicide, and it had been she who had talked them out of it," her mother said.

If she had ever thought about suicide before, she never made her thoughts verbal. "She never told anyone," Mrs. Keaton said. "Not even her closest friends.

"She had lots of friends, but she only had a

"AVOID SYNONYMS FOR SAID," HE REMARKED

■ *Use said unless the person definitely yelled, whispered, blurted, etc. Be careful with loaded words such as "admitted, explained, charged, accused, demanded" or any other verb that comes close to editorializing. Note how the word admitted implies some sort of wrongdoing.*

❑ *WEAK: Principal Bertha Newhouse admitted she needed help to lead the school.*

❑ *BETTER: Principal Bertha Newhouse said she needed help to lead the school.*

■ *Avoid synonyms such as declared, remarked, commented or expressed.*

■ *Avoid qualifiers such as "when asked....."*

few close friends. And even those were kept at a distance."

Karen's suicide had a devastating effect on many of her friends. "Some of them took it harder than the family did," Mrs. Keaton said. "For a month we had them here every night. They were trying to cling to her. They wouldn't let her go."

The friends reacted in many different ways. "Some of her friends who were drinking sobered up; others turned to drugs," Mrs. Keaton said. "One of the girls was a camp counselor this summer. Another one still dreams of Karen every night. It's had a diverse effect on everyone."

Karen's suicide was a traumatic experience for her two younger sisters, Michelle and April.

Michelle, an eighth-grader, still finds it difficult to talk about Karen. "For a long time, Michelle wouldn't go down the hall where Karen's room was unless someone was with her," Mrs. Keaton said. "She kept telling us Karen was just playing one of her jokes, and she would pop out of the bedroom door and laugh.

"It's easier now that we've made the room into the baby's room."

Michelle still doesn't talk much about her sister's suicide. "It took her a while to learn to deal with it. I'm sure she thinks about all of it a lot, but she is getting better," Mrs. Keaton said.

Two-year-old April was sent to stay with friends during the days after Karen's death. No one ever told April that Karen was gone, "but somehow she knew," Mrs. Keaton said.

Before Karen's death, April would knock on her oldest sister's door and call out her name. Karen would let her in and play with her. "April worshipped Karen," Mrs. Keaton said. "But since Karen's death, April has not once said Karen's name. For a while she kissed Karen's picture every night before she went to bed, but to this day she has not spoken Karen's name."

A few weeks after the funeral, the family took April to the cemetery. "We explained to April that this was where Karen was," Mrs. Keaton said. "We tried to get her to say Karen's name, but she wouldn't. As we were walking off, April suddenly stopped and looked back. Softly she said, 'Bye bye.' Somehow she understood Karen was gone."

Mrs. Keaton has adjusted slowly to her daughter's death. "At first I didn't want to see any teenagers," she said. "Her birthday and my first trip back to the high school were especially painful. The next really tough time is going to be Christmas. It's going to be hard."

Some days it is really difficult for the family to cope with their loss. "But we have rules," Mrs. Keaton said. "One is we never not mention her name. Karen is a part of all of us. We don't want to forget her, but we have accepted her death.

"Also, we haven't been afraid to say suicide. It isn't a disease."

Mrs. Keaton has found that she must go on with her life. Much of her time has been devoted to the High on Life program here at the high school. Also, she has been researching the causes and effects of teenage suicide as well as helping to organize a local chapter of Students Against Drunk Driving (SADD).

"At first I kept saying, 'Why Karen?' Now I'm starting to think maybe her death can help save 3,000 other lives," she said. "That's what I'm working for. I want suicide to stop.

"Kids who commit suicide don't realize the finality of the act," she said. "Life has its peaks and valleys. When you're in the valleys, you have to look forward to the mountains. They're there, but so many kids can't see them."

Mrs. Keaton is quick to point out that suicide can happen in any family, regardless of their economic background or culture. "Parents need to take seriously anything their kids say," she said. "Take the time to listen to them. Take an interest in their lives."

Since the death of her oldest daughter, the Keatons have found themselves becoming more protective. "I find myself watching for things," Mrs. Keaton said. "I'm not sure for what. I'm just watching." ★

ORGANIZATION STRATEGY

Several points to be made about the story:
• The lead uses a scene re-creation to pull the reader directly into the story and then uses repetition in the next four graphs to take readers from the time before Karen's suicide to the days just after the funeral, an approach that sets the scene for Mrs. Keaton to enter the picture.
• The writer allows Mrs. Keaton to tell her own story—and it is a story so forceful that it requires little intervention by the reporter.
• The story displays genuine common sense. The writer understands that the best narrative is usually told in chronological order.

WHO SAID THAT?

Journalists use attribution to identify the person who is quoted. Unless you attribute information to a source, readers will assume that the newspaper stands behind the information printed. If the information is wrong, the reader will blame you—not your source. So it's a good idea to attribute information to a source. Here are a few tips to help:

What is said is more important than who said it so place the attribution after the quote and start a new paragraph immediately after the attribution. For example:

❑ WEAK: Principal Bo Simmons said, "I am going to run over you in my truck if you don't get out of my way."

❑ BETTER: "I am going to run over you in my truck if you don't get out of my way," Principal Bo Simmons said.

But sometimes, "who" is more important than what if the "who" is an important person. For example:

❑ WEAK: "I quit. I've had it up to here. My bags are packed, and I'm rolling out in the morning," Superintendent Anita Change said.

❑ BETTER: Superintendent Anita Change said, "I quit. I've had it up to here. My bags are packed, and I'm rolling out in the morning."

Place "said" after the name because the name is more important and because the person-said order is easier to read.

❑ WEAK: "You can't leave me with this mess," said Principal Bo Simmons.

❑ BETTER: "You can't leave me with this mess," Principal Bo Simmons said.

Don't bury the attribution. Identify the source after the first sentence of a multi-sentence quote. This method focuses on the story itself without using extra words. It also promotes easier reading and allows for a shift of emphasis.

❑ WEAK: Superintendent Anita Change said, "I am going to run over you in my truck if you don't get out of my way. I told you once, and I ain't going to tell you again. This here's your last warning. Move it or lose it!"

❑ WEAK: "I am going to run over you in my truck if you don't get out of my way. I told you once, and I ain't going to tell you again. This here's your last warning. Move it or lose it!" Superintendent Anita Change said.

❑ BETTER: "I am going to run over you in my truck if you don't get out of my way," Superintendent Anita Change said. "I told you once, and I ain't going to tell you again. This here's your last warning. Move it or lose it!"

Use indirect quotations for factual information when the source's exact words are not necessary or when the direct quote is unclear.

❑ WEAK: "Approximately 200 persons showed up for the dance," chairman Ron Dukes said.

❑ BETTER: Approximately 200 persons showed up for the dance, according to chairman Ron Dukes.

Use explain only when someone is indeed explaining something.

❑ WEAK: "We are pleased that the SAT scores have improved," assistant superintendent Bob Francis explained.

❑ BETTER: "Our new strategies that focused on math, reading and writing skills were responsible for the improved SAT scores," assistant superintendent Bob Francis explained.

Every time you introduce a new direct quote, begin a new paragraph.

THE STATE OF USING 'STATE,' ACCORDING TO THE . . . .

■ *Use state only when a source reads from a prepared text. For example, if the principal reads a statement at a press conference, then use stated.*

■ *Use according to when the source is a written report or letter that announces conclusions.*

❑ *WEAK: The number of poor school-age children became increasingly concentrated in the West and Southwest during the 1980s, the U. S. General Accounting Office stated.*

❑ *BETTER: The number of poor school-age children became increasingly concentrated in the West and Southwest during the 1980s, according to a report by the U. S. General Accounting Office.*

■ *Avoid according to as a synonym for said in a direct quote.*

❑ *WEAK: "I've never seen a dumber group of seniors in my life," according to Principal Shirley Borden.*

❑ *BETTER: "I've never seen a dumber group of seniors in my life," Principal Shirley Borden said.*

HAVE YOU EVER USED SECOND PERSON CORRECTLY? HERE'S HOW!

Have you ever been hit by a truck? Well, Irene. She was on the way to school, stepped off the curb and was smacked right between the eyes by a Ford pickup. When asked how she felt about it, she said, "Not so great."

Boy, do I hate those question leads so I urge students to avoid second person. However, second person works quite well when the reporter is writing about the reader. The story above is Irene getting hit by the truck. It's not about the reader. Does the reporter actually expect the reader to answer, "Why yes, I do know what it's like to be hit by a truck!"

Of course not. But reporters often write about subjects or events that are real to the readers. Use second person when the reader is personally involved in the action.

EXAMPLE 1

Your car engine is knocking, your wool sweaters are dirty, and you need a haircut. Taking care of all of these chores may cost a tiny fortune, you lament as you thumb through the Yellow Pages.

Not necessarily.

All this can be done, at a fraction of the regular cost, by students. In public schools, colleges and private trade schools, students are studying every sort of trade and profession—horticulture, dentistry, small-engine repair, cosmetology, dry cleaning. And they need something—or someone—to practice on.

Because they are still learning, these students charge much less than professionals. But, of course, there are strings attached.

First, your needs must mesh with those of the students. For instance, the auto repair students at the high school won't fix your car's transmission if they are studying brakes when you call . . . .

EXAMPLE 2

Your coffee maker doesn't keep coffee hot anymore, and your electric blanket doesn't keep you warm. And both appliances broke after the warranty expired.

If you're like many people, you toss out the broken appliance or donate it to Goodwill, the Salvation Army or another charity, and hope it will find new life in someone else's hands. You figure the appliance isn't worth the cost of returning it to the factory and paying for repairs.

Well, you may be mistaken. A number of fix-it shops and factory-authorized or factory-owned service centers are located in the western suburbs. You may be able to get your appliance repaired with a minimum of inconvenience.

EXAMPLE 3

Ripped apart. Torn at the seams. After dating him for a year, you realize it's over. You still like him. It's not something he did. It's just that, well, your time has run out. The time on that little meter in your heart has expired, and you're out of pocket change.

"I'll tell him tomorrow, after school," you tell yourself. But you know it won't be any easier tomorrow. Besides, if you tell him now, he'll have time to find someone else to take out Saturday night.

So you draw a deep breath, stand back a foot or so and tell him it's time that he hit the road.

Jack.

Mrs. Keaton describes the scene at the hospital, her reaction following Karen's death and funeral, her attempts to understand Karen's motivation, the impact on Michelle and April, and finally her resolve to give meaning to Karen's death.

• So often, long stories bog down into a series of dull, data-driven paragraphs. Not so here. The writer uses the anecdote about April at the cemetery in the middle of the story to propel the reader through to the end.

• The story closes with a powerful quote that gives it a sense of resolution and even momentum. We are left with a powerful image of Mrs. Keaton, watching. Just watching.

The writer, Steve Dobbins, said he interviewed Mrs. Keaton four or five times, each time thinking that he had enough information to finish the story only to find that he needed more. Fortunately, she was willing to accommodate him.

She probably recognized as we do that this young man was on something of a mission himself.

WHERE DO I START?

No one said this is easy, okay? The reporting alone requires a substantial commitment of time and effort. Then, after interviewing, observing and listening, the reporter must make sense of all this information. Not surprisingly, many reporters develop an acute case of writer's block.

Getting started is the most difficult part of writing any story. It is difficult because the reporter hasn't decided how to tell the story. If you can decide in what order to tell the story, then finding a lead becomes much easier. So how do you decide the order in which to tell the story?

Unfortunately, there are no formulas. Veteran reporters write their stories as they go. As they collect information, they unconsciously catalogue it. "This quote will work well here. I'll use this information to develop the lead. I can end with that quote."

The more you report and write, the better at this you'll become. But that doesn't get you out of the hole now, does it? So, where to begin?

First, ask yourself, "What is this story about?" Then, discard any information that does not advance the theme of the story. Don't feel territorial about the information you've collected. If you've done an adequate job of reporting, you'll have far more data than you can or will want to use.

Second, ask yourself, "What part of this story will be most interesting to the readers? What will be something my readers don't know? And even if readers know a little about it, how can I tell this story in a way that will make them want to know more?"

Consider the story on page 14. The author, Leslie Courtney, did not conduct a flash interview with Shaffer and then whip out the story. In fact, Donya Witherspoon, the adviser of the paper, said the first draft was a rather dull, quoteless story.

"Nathan Shaffer was a student of mine so I reinterviewed him in front of the journalism

THAT'S 'MISTER' TO YOU

Each staff should either develop its own style manual or keep a copy of a style manual close at hand and refer to it often. Highly recommended: The *Associated Press Stylebook and Libel Manual* and the *Quill & Scroll Stylebook*.

Common style errors often involve the use of titles. Here are a few basic rules.

■ Use of courtesy titles *Mr., Mrs., Ms.,* and *Miss* are optional. Be consistent. Some publications opt to drop all titles to avoid age bias so that all sources—teens and adults—are treated equally.

❑ Confine capitalization to formal titles used directly before a person's name.

■ A formal title is one that denotes a scope of authority, professional activity or academic accomplishment so specific that the designation becomes almost as much an intergral part of an individual's identity as a proper name itself. For example: *President Clinton, Gov. Mario Cuomo, Lt. Col. Oliver North, Pope John Paul II, the Rev. Billy Graham.*

❑ Most school personnel need not have their titles capitalized. Exception: *Superintendent* John Woolridge, *Principal* Mary Roberts.

■ Most school titles serve primarily as occupational descriptions. Example: *head football coach* Bill Smith; *band director* Richard Murray; *assistant principal* Roland Hayes.

❑ Avoid double titles such as *Mr. John Woolridge, superintendent.* Instead, on first reference, identify him as *Superintendent John Woolridge.* Also, other administrative titles: Dean, assistant superintendent and assistant principal.

■ Titles that are not used with an individual's name should be written in lower case. For example: The *superintendent* issued a statement.

❑ On initial reference, place complicated occupational titles after the person's name. Also, place the verb *said* before the source.

WEAK: "Heads will roll," *assistant superintendent for instruction* Richard Bates *said.*

BETTER: "Heads will roll," *said* Richard Bates, *assistant superintendent for instruction.*

■ When using pronoun clauses, place the verb *said* before the source.

WEAK: "Heads will roll," Richard Bates, assistant superintendent for instruction, who witnessed the food fight, *said.*

BETTER: "Heads will roll," *said* assistant superintendent for instruction Richard Bates, who witnessed the food fight.

HOW DO I GET THERE FROM HERE?

Moving from one paragraph to another is called transition. Two common forms of transition are the "key word" and "key phrase." This phrase can be a repeat of specific words or a repeat of synonyms of those words.

Example (with key words and phrases in all-caps):

Word that the school's annual SPELLING BEE is in jeopardy in the name of educational reform caused a swarm of angry reaction that left the EVENT'S former sponsors mired in a spirited debate.

The Courier-Journal, sponsors of the EVENT since 1961, said the BEE'S emphasis on ROTE MEMORIZATION and competition contradicted the spirit of the state's educational reform law.

"ROTE MEMORIZATION does not emphasize the thinking skills children need," James PASCHAL, publisher of the newspaper, wrote.

PASCHAL also expressed concern that such contests put children under too much pressure.

In its place, THE PUBLISHER suggested a writing BEE that would include essays, poetry and short stories.

class to demonstrate how to interview someone and get good quotes," Witherspoon said. "Then when the reporter went to confirm some of the information with the police, they told her the defendant had taken a plea. So I helped her rewrite the story into its present state."

So what did the adviser and reporter think would most interest readers? A descriptive anecdote that ends with "Now you're going to die."

It's an emotionally-charged, powerful lead that takes the reader through the frightening experience. The lead works well because it appeals to the human desire to read stories about things we want to happen to us, such as winning the lottery, and about things we pray never happen to us, such as having a stranger in a ski mask stick a gun in our faces.

KEEP THEM ON TRACK

A compelling lead doesn't insure that the entire story story will be read. In some cases, reporters put 95 percent of their effort into the lead and skate through the rest of the story.

You want to keep the story focused and moving forward. If necessary, informally outline your story. If the lead begins with an especially dramatic moment, you must decide how to build back to that moment and then resolve the dilemma. In other words, a young man has a gun stuck in his nose. How did he get there? How does he get out?

At this stage, it makes sense to go with chronological order. Description and dialogue of the events would be balanced with direct quotes that explain what was going through the student's mind during the robbery. The success of the story will be determined largely by the writer's ability to dovetail description with analysis and/or interpretation. What happened? Describe it. What was the source thinking while it was happening? What happened next?

Keeping the reader on track is difficult but essential. If readers become confused or cannot figure out where they are in the chronology of the story, then the game's up.

A tip: use the computer to help organize the story. Type up all quotes and information. Copy and paste all related information into what you think will make the best order. Search for the dramatic statements that will make the most powerful opening or concluding direct quotes.

The process will also help you determine where additional interviewing or reporting is needed. If you want to use an anecdotal lead, it will help if you've collected a few interesting stories.

However, do not use the computer merely to transcribe your notes and stack your quotes. Work with the direct quotes. Which information should be quoted? Which should be paraphrased? Can you use a partial quote? If so, how? Most importantly, how do you combine direct quotes, indirect quotes, transition sentences, transition paragraphs and description into a tight, focused package?

Consider the following story:

By AARON BROWN
City High School, Iowa City, Iowa

SHOWCASE

"I REMEMBER going up for air once. And I remember taking a big gulp of water. And then it was black," Phil Fort, '93 said. But that wasn't all. Fort experienced more than blackness while submerged, and dead for a minute and a half, in the waters of the Coralville Reservoir.

"At first I saw a red thing, I don't know what it was, and then I saw this white light and I saw my family and my friends. It was like a dream," Fort said. "I saw my family in front and all my friends that I have ever met and talked to were right behind my family."

Fort had been working at GS Marine that Sunday. He noticed earlier, while filling boats with gas, that the pump was giving off shocks. Not strong shocks, just enough to give "a numb feeling." Later, the shock was much worse.

"At about 1:30 a boat caught on fire because

of it. The end of the nozzle caught on fire, and the tube going down to the gas tank caught on fire. I put that out.

"I was putting gas into a boat, and I felt a tingling so I grabbed the hose with both hands [to avoid another fire] and grounded myself. It blew me about three or four feet in the air and about ten feet back. I landed in the water." The shock contracted Fort's muscles, and he couldn't let go of the hose.

"I was scared when I was awake. I was really scared. I know I was saying, 'Help, get this thing off me.' I remember seeing all of that. And then I just remember taking a big gulp of water. That was it," Fort said.

"They said I was down about 10 feet. The only thing that saved my life was the fact that my muscles hung on to the hose, and that's how they pulled me out. Otherwise, I'd be lying on the bottom of the lake."

"It seemed like it took forever," he said. "It felt really good when I was in that dream. It was the best thing I've ever had. Ever. I had no more worries. No more problems.

"I think that if I'd decided, I would have stayed there." But he didn't decide. Two men pulled the hose up, and Fort's hands were still locked onto it. The men began CPR immediately.

"When I woke up, I was scared. And I didn't know where the hell I was," Fort said. "There was a guy on my legs and a guy on my face. I kicked them both off." Fort was hot while lying on the dock, but he wasn't allowed to move. The ambulance had gotten lost and took four and a half minutes to arrive.

The paramedics gave Fort oxygen; too much. He had a seizure in the ambulance and lost consciousness again.

"All I heard the nurse say was 'We're losing him.' " He regained consciousness before the 20-minute trip to Mercy Hospital was over.

"When I got to the hospital, they pushed me in a wheelchair to the emergency room. The doctor came in and looked at me and said 'You shouldn't even be alive.' "

Fort has learned from his experience. "I realize now how close I am to my family and friends." ★

Forget the inherent power of the story itself. Let's look at how Aaron Brown chose to relate the information and how he connected each paragraph to the next.

WHERE'S THE TRANSITION?

"I'd say our chances of winning are about as good as the Berlin Wall coming down," coach Ray Danson said. "No one thought it was possible but it happened.

"We know how good they are, but we're not intimidated. We think we're a pretty good team too."

The absence of closed quote marks after the first graph tells the reader that the source is continuing to talk in the next graph. Had the quote been closed after "happened," then the reader knows that the second graph is a direct quote from a new source. Of course, you want to avoid stacking quotes on top of one another. In this case, a transition sentence would make the passage clearer and more readable.

First, he used a quote lead. Quote leads are not recommended unless the statement is exceptionally powerful. This one is.

The second graph continues the direct quote. In it, he relates a near-death experience, the center of the story around which all other information evolves.

The third graph takes the reader back to the beginning. From that point, Brown allows Fort to tell his own story. Brown's job here is to keep the narrative moving and focused, which he does through the eighth paragraph. Note the delicate use of transition sentences. At this point, no one can tell the story with more power than Fort so Brown relies heavily on direct quotes.

The ninth paragraph is a transition from the accident to the rescue and resuscitation. The 12th and 13th paragraphs describe what Fort heard and said while paramedics worked frantically to save him.

The final paragraph brings the story a logical conclusion—that is, what he has learned from this experience: "I realize now how close I am to my family and friends."

It is a gratifying resolution.

HOW DO I GET THERE FROM HERE?

Transitional words and phrases are like garlic. A little bit goes a long way. Too much really stinks up the place. Avoid the stilted and pretentious words, such as "heretofore" and "henceforth," and stuffy words, such as "thus" and "therefore."

You'll find yourself using these transitional words frequently. Just remember: if every paragraph begins with "therefore," you're likely to have one bad story.

AFTER ALL,
AND
ALSO
ALTHOUGH
AS A RESULT
AT LEAST
BESIDES
BUT
CONSEQUENTLY
FINALLY
FOR EXAMPLE
FURTHERMORE
HOWEVER
IN ADDITION
IN CONCLUSION
INCIDENTALLY
LATELY
LATER
LIKEWISE
MEANWHILE
MOREOVER
NATURALLY
NEVERTHELESS
ON THE CONTRARY
OR
OTHERWISE
THEN

WE GO TOGETHER. Instead of working separately, writers, designers, photographers, artists and editors are working together to produce easy-to-consume visual packages. Little Hawk, *City HS, (Iowa City, IA)*

THE PACKAGE. Rather than producing single, long stories, staffs work to produce powerful visual packages of information. The Epitaph, *Homestead HS, (Cupertino, CA)*

PLEASE DEFINE THAT

Okay, so you're not familiar with some of the fancy terms we've used. Here are a few definitions:

SIDEBAR STORY: a minor story that accompanies a major news story. It provides a different angle or perspective on the larger issue.

INFORMATION GRAPHICS: Combination of photography, computer art and text that provide visual and verbal messages. Information that lends itself to charts and graphs is natural content for infographics. USA Snapshots in *USA Today* is a good example. The purpose of the infographic is to give readers information they want without having to read long passages of type.

SURVEY SIDEBARS: Results of a survey are used to supplement a major news story.

INDEX: a directory or summary of information. These guide readers quickly to the information that interests them.

READ-IN: also called a nutgraf, this is a quick synopsis of a story. It gives the reader an overview of the news without having to read the entire story.

MARGINAL: Sidebar information that runs down the side of a story or the page. We use them on odd-numbered pages of this book.

FACT BOXES: Sometimes called "factoids," these boxes provide details that readers find interesting and useful. For example, a fact box may tell readers where they can find additional information on a topic.

PULL QUOTES: Used to lure readers into the text, they provide interesting or provocative details. They should never be used merely to fill space.

BULLETS: little dots (•) used to organize and summarize information. They are:
- easily digested by the reader
- visually pleasing
- fun to use

BRIEFS: Short news articles, generally two to five paragraphs at the most.

ALL'S WELL THAT ENDS WELL

How long should this story be?

How many times have you asked that question? And what does your teacher reply? "Write until you've answered all the news questions."

Or "Write until you've told the whole story."

This is the journalistic equivalent to "go ask your mother." It leaves you befuddled.

When asked, "How long should this story be?" I am likely to reply, "Four hundred and six words. Half of them should be four letters or more. Concentrate on action verbs. Give me 25 action and 15 passive verbs. Now, hop to it. Scoot!"

If they want a number, I'll give them a number.

Actually, students aren't really interested in the length of the story. Conditioned by years of writing-by-rote assignments, they're really seeking permission to quit writing.

"Well, my teacher told me it had to be 500 words in length. When I hit 501, I stopped."

Right in the middle of a sentence fragment, no less. So the question arises: when to stop?

If writing the lead is the hardest part of any story, then finding a way to end it is the second hardest. Of course, the inverted pyramid offers a fairly quick and simple way to end the story: push the least important information to the end of the story. This works as long as the students are able to identify the least important information. This isn't always the case. For example:

THE TURNIP TRUCK ISD School Board met Tuesday night in the school cafeteria. School Board President E. M. Bezzle called for the reading of the minutes of the last meeting and then led everyone in the pledge of allegiance. He then asked Mrs. Elvira Doyle to introduce the members of the Future Farmers of America, who won third place in last week's potato peeling contest. "We congratulate each and every one of you," Mrs. Doyle said.

Then, the Board awarded a $150,000 contract to replace the light bulbs in the band hall to Buck Tooth, Mr. Bezzle's brother-in-law, prompting a fist-fight between Mr. Tooth and Mayor Rob Emblind, who complained that he bribed Mr. Bezzle first and should have been awarded the contract instead. The meeting was adjourned due to an explosion that resulted when an Air Force C-130 cargo plane crashed into the building. ★

Minor problems with this story aside, the hard news lead works on those fact-driven news stories in which stacking data and direct quotes is in order. Unfortunately, those stories are rarely appropriate for high-school publications except perhaps in the news briefs. Even then, the decision to use the inverted pyramid is based more on the availability of space and competence of the reporter than the applicability of a more interesting and challenging lead.

In terms of the once- or twice-a-month newspaper, almost any story would be more interesting for the reporter and the reader if approached from a news-feature, news-analysis or straight feature manner. Finding a way to end one of these as opposed to the inverted pyramid story poses altogether different problems.

Fortunately, bookstores are stuffed with old journalism texts from college professors trying to satisfy a publish-or-perish mandate, or reporters and editors in their twilight years, offering all the jewels they've gathered over the course of their careers.

These texts contain dozens of ways to end a story, including a bunch of them you wouldn't wish on your worst enemy.

One of my least favorites is the "leave them with some good advice" ending. For example: *"Snorting battery acid is really not*

YOUR LAST WORDS SHOULD NOT BE "SHE SAID"

If you end the story with a direct quote, make certain the last words are those of the source, not the writer.

For example, this three-sentence quote was used to conclude a story about an important game.

"We have a chance to make history here," coach Jones said. *"This school has never won a state championship. We plan to be the first."*

This ending would not have been nearly as effective if it had been:

"We have a chance to make history here. This school has never won a state championship. We plan to be the first," coach Jones said.

If the story ends with a one-sentence quote, it is better to place the attribution before the quote or break the sentence at an appropriate thought pause than to end with the attribution.

very good for your health," Dr. Casket said. "In fact, putting anything in your nose is pretty stupid."

So, the next time you think about popping the top off a DieHard, don't!

Readers merely dislike sermonizing editors. They absolutely detest preachy feature writers.

They don't like wiseguys either. A lot of young writers, particularly beginning sports writers, try to slip a clever comment onto the end of every article even though the comment has nothing to do with the story. I once worked with a reporter who tried to end every story with a snickering quip. In a story about an outstanding freshman golfer, he could have closed with the following quote: "It's strange beating these older guys, but it's something I'm getting used to."

Instead, he tacked on a gratuitous and dopey, "So watch out, Jack Nicklaus. You could be next!"

Resist this temptation.

The best way to end a feature story is with a strong direct quote that brings the story to a logical conclusion and leaves the reader with the feeling that the dilemma has been brought to a satisfactory resolution.

Finding this quote isn't easy, especially if you're working on a 35-inch story that contains quotes from six or seven sources. Sometimes, I'll finish the first draft and realize that I placed the quote that I should use to end the story in the fifth or sixth paragraph. So I have to perform a bit of cosmetic surgery, cutting the quote out here, pasting it in there and covering up all the scars.

Although it doesn't guarantee anything, I often informally outline my story in an effort to determine which quotes I'll use and in what order. I always look first for the zinger quote, the powerful quote for the second or third paragraph that pulls the reader into the story. Sometimes that quote comes from an interview. Sometimes, it's a piece a dialogue. Regardless, I want that powerful quote to give the story immediacy, credibility and vibrancy.

For this technique, I need several powerful quotes. If the best quote at my disposal is "If you don't look at the losses, we had a pretty successful season," then it'll be a real toss up whether to use it as the zinger or ending quote.

Even in the presence of interesting quotes, too many young writers bury them when they should showcase them. If you have a powerful quote, use it as early as possible and let the narrative flow to a logical conclusion. Don't tell the readers what happened. Let your sources tell their own stories. Your job is to string together the direct quotes in an orderly, logical and unobtrusive manner while maintaining the drama of the story. Stay focused on the subject at hand, and push the reader toward a strong conclusion.

The best conclusion is a natural extension of the story. It flows from the story as smoothly and effortlessly as the ending of a good song .

The best conclusion is a natural extension of the story. It flows from the story as smoothly and effortlessly as the ending of a good song. "Eleanor Rigby" for example.

Or so it seems. In reality, finishing a story is often as hard as beginning it. The best advice I can offer is to let the last words the reader hears come from the characters themselves. If the story is good enough, the reader will hear the voices of the people speaking rather than simply reading the quotes.

CHAPTER EIGHT

ANALYZE THE FACTS

Absolute objectivity is impossible to achieve because decisions must be made by human beings who function in a process that is quite subjective.

In traditional journalism lore, the reporter writes a straight news story without first-person references (I, we, our) or personal opinion, presents both sides of a controversial issue and refuses to participate in any news event or take a stand on a news issue.

The theory is that each story is a mirror, a reflection of the day's events. However, that theory is a myth. Certainly, reporters can write their stories without blatant boosterism. For example:

OUR SCHOOL BAND should be congratulated for winning the district marching competition. They won despite the efforts of one particularly crooked judge who was hell-bent on seeing that the top award went to our archrival, whose performance absolutely stank. Band director Sandy Dodd refused to admit it, but everyone in the stands agreed that our band was light years better than the rag-tag Clearwater outfit.

We deserved it. Congratulations, band! ★

CONVEYING A JUDGMENT

Blatant—even subtle—editorialization can be detected and weeded out. But absolute objectivity is impossible to achieve. It is impossible because decisions must be made by humans. Even when these decisions are made according to established news procedures and values, the process is not totally objective. Certainly, once the selection of what event to report has been made, reporters

can and should set aside their own opinions.

However, reporters have great latitude in selecting sources and then deciding which information gleaned from those sources to use and in what order. Simply by picking out one element to emphasize in the first sentence of a news story, reporters convey a judgment about what is important and what is not. Any time reporters decide one part of a statement should go as a direct quote and another part as an indirect quote, interpretation is taking place.

Objectivity is easier to attain in event-oriented stories: Four persons were killed in a three-alarm fire at a downtown apartment building yesterday.

Reporters talk to the fire chief, the apartment building manager, witnesses at the scene. They go to the hospital to interview doctors or nurses. They attend the press conferences conducted by the appropriate city or medical officials, then go back to the office to pound out a story.

They do not attempt to assign blame, to analyze the still-undetermined factors that may have caused the fire or to mourn the dead and injured. All statements are attributed to an authoritative source.

All of this, one might think, would demand that reporters produce nothing more than a simple, condensed presentation of facts. Not so. Consider the following story, written by Colin Nickerson and Allan R. Andrews of the *Boston Globe*.

JEAN NICKERSON sat stunned in the Salvation Army office, unable to accept the dreadful news. "No," she kept saying, shaking her head as her husband, Leslie, sobbed beside her. "No."

A block away, clearly visible through the window of the makeshift emergency headquarters in the Salvation Army office, were the still-smoldering remains of a three-story rooming house where 14 people were killed in one of the deadliest fires in Massachusetts history.

Nickerson had just been told that her two sons—Richard, 21, and Ralph, 9—as well as her 73-year-old mother, Hattie M. Whary, were among the victims who died when flames ripped through the shabby structure early Wednesday morning.

The older son lived with his grandmother, Whary, who managed the rooming house. The younger boy was there for a summer visit from the family home in Auburn, Maine. Their bodies were among the first found when firefighters entered the burned-out second floor.

Five of the dead were found in the vicinity of a second-floor fire escape. Many of the residents of the building were former mental patients.

Some of the bodies were not found until midday and had to be dug from the sodden debris. One by one, they were removed from the building in clear plastic body bags, loaded into waiting hearses and taken to funeral homes in Beverly.

The fire, which broke out at about 2 a.m., raced through the 80-year-old wood structure in a matter of minutes, gutting the second and third floors but leaving a ground-floor pharmacy and other stores relatively intact.

Firefighters said the blaze appeared to have started in a front stairwell and spread quickly through the building. Though firemen arrived within minutes of the alarm, flames could be seen at every window of the upper floors. ★

This approach captures the tragedy of the event in human terms without pointing fingers or relying on hearsay evidence. It recognizes that the drama of the story arises from the event itself, not artificial attempts by the reporters to create it.

OBJECTIVITY IS A MATTER OF PERCEPTION

Interpretive reporting has challenged the entire notion of deadpan objectivity. Many journalists today believe that the reader needs to have a given event placed in its proper context if truth is really to be served. Otherwise, journalism becomes a rather banal exercise in quoting people who are telling the truth as well as people who are telling lies.

Like politicians, journalists today face a more cynical and wearing populace. "Don't believe what you read in the newspaper" is no longer merely a sly warning to the wise. It has become a rather universal sentiment. Newspapers are seen as either lackeys of the military-industrial state or as organs of the liberal intellectual elite.

Distrust of the mainstream media has contributed to the rise of alternative journalism. While circulation of daily newspapers has continued to plummet during the past decade, circulation and advertising revenues for alternative newspapers—those which are written from a distinct perspective—have soared. Consider the sucesses of the *Village Voice*, the San Francisco *Bay Guardian*, *Rolling Stone*, and the *Texas Observer*.

In my hometown, I often have more confidence in the *Austin Chronicle*—a weekly newspaper with a distinctly cynical edge—than I do in the *Austin American-Statesman*, our local daily whose publisher is a former president of the Austin Chamber of Commerce, a group that has promoted development in sensitive areas of our environmentally-conscious community.

PRACTICAL OR PRINCIPLE?

The principles of fairness, balance, accuracy and objectivity don't always prevail. As a young reporter for an East Texas newspaper, I covered a city hall meeting at which the town council refused to issue a license to operate an ambulance service to a black-owned funeral home.

As I sat through the meetings, I became

more convinced that the council would deny the request and that their rationale for doing so didn't make a lot of sense.

Those seeking the permit asked for nothing from the city except to operate a service in a part of town that was being inadequately served by the established medical communities. Response time in the minority neighborhood was something like four times greater than it was in the white neighborhoods.

From where I sat, it looked like a case of racism, pure and simple. Of course, I could never write that, but I thought I could at least report the story from the black perspective. I wanted to take one case involving a late response and show the consequences of the city's negligence. Reporting a group's request to operate an ambulance service is a fairly dry story. Reporting the death of a young man who died unnecessarily because the ambulance arrived 10 minutes late is an emotional drama.

My editors thought the story was a great idea. Someone higher up the chain of command didn't. Not on your life, I was told. Report what happened at the council meeting. As I expected, the council cited some stone reasons for denying the permit and moved on to the next issue, a zoning change request. My story the next day stated,

AFTER MORE THAN an hour of discussion which included some heated exchanges between members, the city council voted today to deny to Pierce-Moss Funeral Home an application to operate its ambulance service on city streets. ★

PERCEPTION DICTATES OBJECTIVITY

The remainder of the story included some of the "heated exchanges" and listed the reasons cited by the council for its decision. I ended the story by reporting that the council also approved a request to change the zoning of a local warehouse from industrial to commercial. Someone wanted to open a restaurant and bar.

Now, was this an objective story? Well, it depends on your perspective. To a casual reader of the newspaper, it had all the outward appearances of being objective. But if you were a black person who had lived in the North Tyler community and had seen friends and neighbors die because of slow or negligent services, then it was blatantly subjective in favor of powerful, monied interests.

How objective would my story about someone's death have been? Wasn't I approaching this story with a large dose of unwarranted cynicism that may not have had any connection to this particular decision by the city council? Who is to say that the one example I might have chosen to showcase would have accurately portrayed a universal truth? Wouldn't some have found this story to be blatantly subjective, merely another case of a bleeding-heart liberal preaching to society?

It all depends on where you stand.

Consider, for example, the following story, by Steve Lize of Glenbard East High School in Lombard, Illinois. This feature story has a decidedly anti-military perspective.

"HELLO, BIFF? THIS IS SGT. Bob from the Marines. Now that you're a senior in high school, I understand that you have plans for college at College of DuPage or DeVry. Did you know that the Marine Corps can help you with your education and prepare you for life in the real world?" Sgt. Bob said.

As his voice reverberated through Biff's head, it conjured images of an officer from a "Ren and Stimpy" cartoon. Biff thought the Marines were honorable, but he wasn't into the discipline and physical exertion required for the status.

"Uh, I'm really not interested right now," Biff said.

"We think that the Marines would benefit from an individual with your capabilities," the sergeant said.

"But, I'm not interested so . . . ."

"If you join the Marines, we will pay for you to go to college, give you and your friends free posters and even throw in a pair of socks! It is to

THE TRUTH IS SAFER THAN A LIE

Overcoming the fear of revealing the truth is a universal struggle. Huck Finn captures the feelings of a young journalist when he labors to tell Mary Jane how two famous scoundrels, The King and the Duke, are trying to swindle her:

I . . . was in a close place. I asked her to let me think a minute; and she set there, very impatient and excited and handsome, but looking kind of happy and eased-up . . . .

I says to myself, I reckon a body that ups and tells the truth when he is in a tight place is taking considerable many resks, though I ain't had no experience, and can't say for certain; but it looks so to me, anyway; and yet here's a case where I'm blest if it don't look to me like the truth is better and actuly safer than a lie.

I'm going to chance it; I'll up and tell the truth this time, though it does seem most like setting down on a kag of power and touching it off just to see where you'll go to. Then I says . . . .

"Don't you holler. Just set still and take it like a man. I got to tell the truth, and you want to brace up, Miss Mary, because it's a bad kind, and going to be hard to take, but there ain't no help for it. These uncles of yourn ain't no uncles at all; they're a couple of frauds—regular dead-beats. There, now we're over the worst of it, you can stand the rest middling easy."

your benefit that you join the Marines, Biff," Sgt. Bob pleaded.

"Just leave me alone!" Biff commanded, slamming the receiver down. A sudden air of superiority passed over him as he realized that he told a military officer off. Little did he know that this wasn't the end of the government's pestering.

The recruiters are at it again, feeding upon the nation's youth, specifically high-school teens. They hunt for able-bodied individuals who want to "be all they can be" through methods that are considered invasion of one's privacy.

Harold Miller, parent of a Glenbard East senior, objects to the military's method of recruitment. He was angered after a phone call from the Marines. "I don't like invasion of family privacy without being invited," he said.

Because his number is unlisted, Miller wanted to know how the Marines got his family's phone number. He tried, without succeeding, to find out how the number was obtained.

"I never got a straight answer out of the guy," Miller said.

One Marine Corps recruiting station claimed that they gather phone numbers by talking to people on the street and through referrals. They also claimed to get numbers from "interest" cards that students may have filled out as far back as sixth grade when they had no idea what they wanted to do with their future.

The recruiters, Miller thinks, solicit and take advantage of minors.

"It's impertinent to ask to talk to underage individuals who haven't much experience dealing with things in life," Miller said.

Students throughout school receive flyers from the government that glamorize the Armed Forces. By the time they're seniors, students feel pressured by flyers, pamphlets and phone calls.

"I was hoping to go through all four years of high school without being pestered by a recruiter. Besides, if a guy can't handle going through training, how can I?" senior Chrissy Erickson said.

Angered students disapprove of the recruiters' phone calls.

"I don't appreciate the military knowing my phone number," Erickson said.

"If they call me, I'll tell the Army to shove it," senior Drew Ludwig said.

"The Marines always call me. Like I want to join the Marines. I can't even jog a block," senior Phil Brow said.

In their effort to find young adults, the military invades students' and their families'

privacy.

"Joining the Armed Forces should be a family decision, not a military sergeant's who is trying to fill a quota," Miller said. ★

Keep in mind that it's less risky to convey a viewpoint in a feature story than in a news story. Lize's story appeared on a page titled, "Reactions." This page was a new concept by the staff to connect news with opinions.

IT'S ACCURATE. BUT IS IT TRUE?

Sometimes, reporters pass along bad information in an unwarranted attempt to be objective. Lazy reporters get their stories by interviewing those people who are telling the truth and then interviewing the liars. The danger occurs when they present both sides as equal and legitimate.

I can be accused of this myself. As a young reporter, I was sent to report on a speech, given by the president of a power and light company. The speech was mostly gloom and doom, slamming then President Jimmy Carter, Congress, the Environmental Protection Agency, environmentalists, Ralph Nader and just about anyone else who didn't agree that big oil companies were more philantropic than capitalistic.

My lead was, "The nation's energy situation is at an all-time low. And with a little help from the government, it's probably going to get worse. That was the message brought Thursday by so and so, who spoke to more than 100 members of the Downtown Rotary Club."

The rest of the story was pretty much free public relations on the part of a company that at that moment had requested a $58.2 million rate increase—an increase that was later approved. Even though the speaker sent a letter to the newspaper's publisher congratulating me "for the accuracy of his article," I think the only thing accurate about it were the quotes. I reported what he said.

But did I report the truth? I somehow doubt that I did. In the final scene of the movie *Absence of Malice*, a reporter is questioning Sally Fields about her relationship with Paul Newman. Upon hearing Ms. Fields' answer, the reporter asks, "Is that true?"

"No. But it's accurate," Ms. Fields replies.

Objectivity demands that we be more than merely accurate. We must attempt to report the truth. Whether novices or beginners, journalists must learn to detect the biases, both subtle and blatant, of all sources. If we can't always eliminate them, we should at least learn to recognize them.

The following story, I believe, beautifully handles a sensitive topic: problem teenagers. It does so without condescending to either parent or child, without sensationalizing the subject, without appealing to maudlin emotions and without belittling the importance of the program by thinking that the reporter's own appeal for help or support would carry more significance than simply reporting the actions of the Tough Love parents themselves and letting those actions stand on their own.

BY SHERRYL MORANG
Utica (Michigan) High School

IT IS 7:30 THURSDAY night, and the Presbyterian Church of Utica is deserted except for its well-lit cafeteria.

Slowly they straggle in, singly or in pairs. They are a friendly yet haggard group, bearing the signs of a long emotional struggle.

They are the parents of problem teenagers. There are no straight A honor roll students here, no football captains or cheerleaders—only drug addicts, alcoholics and runaways.

This is the weekly meeting of Tough Love, the parent support group that has recently been started in Utica. According to Agnes Stevens, one of the driving forces behind this program, Tough Love is a disciplinary method that involves setting limits for children and making them responsible for their own actions.

"Soft Love," Agnes explains "is what most parents use. It's where you can more or less trust your kids and set easy limits. Tough Love is when you have to set harder limits. What we try to do is enforce these limits and make our kids aware that they are responsible for their lives."

The meeting begins with Don Stevens reading a blurb about problem children and the Tough Love method. The 40 or so parents are seated in metal folding chairs, smoking, drinking coffee and leaning over to exchange greetings now and again.

The Stevens are amiable hosts, quickly putting newcomers at ease. "Hey, did I tell ya' about the three young punks they had up at the police station the other night?" Don asks. "Yeah, they'd been hauled in for smoking pot and were hanging around feeling pretty loose."

"Feeling good, man," Agnes cuts in, grinning and dragging on an imaginary joint.

Don continues. "So they take the stuff down to the lab to have it analyzed. In a little bit the police officer comes back and says, 'Well guys, how do you feel?' "

"We feel g-o-o-d!" Agnes counters, "That was good stuff, man."

"And the officer says, 'That's good because we just found out that you've been smoking horse crap.' "

The laughter is uproarious, and there is a smattering of applause.

"Now," Don says, "Let's see about our bottom-lines. Does anybody have one from last week?"

Bottom-lines are another facet of the Tough Love method. At each meeting, members will hash out their problems and try to pinpoint one thing that particularly irritates them. This they try to eliminate by drawing a "bottom-line."

There is silence. Then one woman tentatively raises her hand. "My son is 25 years old," she says, "and I told him I was finished picking up after him."

The Stevens grin and call for applause. The hesitation is gone, and people are literally falling over one another to share their bottom-lines.

"What we try to do," Don explains later, "is establish a controlled crisis situation. See, most of the people that come here really have problems with their kids, and it's very difficult for them to maintain a sense of control.

"We try to pick on something that really irritates them—it could be something as simple as a messy room, but it's something that the parents feel they can control."

Agnes adds that most problems begin with a

CONCLUSIONS CAN BE MORE INSIGHTFUL THAN FACTS

Often, arriving at a conclusion is more newsworthy than the mere reporting of fact. Consider the following example:

WEAK:
The School Board appointed Mary Jones and Bill Johnson to a blue-ribbon committee studying the school district boundaries and attendance plan. Mrs. Jones is an engineer with Graves-Douglas. Mr. Johnson owns Continental Pumps.

"I am pleased to have been appointed," he said.

BETTER:
Proponents of the forced busing plan appeared today to have lost control of a blue-ribbon committee, appointed by the School Board to study the school district's boundaries and attendance plan.

Over the loud objections of the busing proponents, the panel voted 10-3 to approve a plan that would end busing in all but two junior high schools.

"Bill Jones has consistently opposed any plan to equalize education," said Ron Hicks, chairman of Equal Education for All, a group that opposes the end to cross-town busing.

poor attitude and that once you make one change, no matter how small, others will follow.

Making changes and enforcing discipline are the focus of Tough Love. This group is part of a national organization known as the Communications Service Foundation. The CSF was founded by Phyllis and David York, a Sellersville, Pennsylvania couple. The Yorks have published a pamphlet explaining the Tough Love method and have information available for anyone who would like to start a group.

There are currently 10 or 12 Tough Love groups in Michigan—five of which are in the greater Detroit area—with approximately 500 families involved.

The Shelby-Utica group, which has been in existence for about five weeks, has almost 50 members. According to Pat Hante, group supervisor, the membership has been increasing steadily. Pat and another woman, Marilyn Kalvin, plan to take over leadership of the group when the Stevens leave.

Tough Love has not gotten the outright public support it wants, but there has been no opposition. They have the full cooperation of the police department, schools, counselors and therapists.

At meetings, parents are encouraged to send their children to therapists only when necessary. The Stevens maintain that most problems are better solved at home. However, there is no hesitation to contact proper authorities if a critical situation does arise.

The parents are divided into small discussion groups. The talk goes from evicting children, to threatening them, to alcohol, parent and drug abuse, to picking up clothes. "Just keep reacting differently," she says. "Shock 'em constantly."

Someone else describes the DRUGS sign that she keeps on the refrigerator door, and there is a suggestion that everyone rotate kids on a monthly basis. The group laughs at this, and there is almost the air of a Tuesday night bridge game, rather than a meeting.

But this is misleading. These people do have serious problems. Most have children who drink, use drugs, abuse them or periodically run away.

"When people first come to the meetings," Agnes says, "they are usually very depressed. They feel like failures as parents.

"Parents suffer a lot for what their kids do, and they always try to rescue them. But teenagers are perfectly capable of making choices, and if we don't let them experience the consequences, then they won't realize if their choices are the right ones."

So parents turn to Tough Love for support. Here they can discuss problems without feeling guilty. They share experiences, offer advice, laugh, cry, comfort each other.

"We all need support, and the Tough Love groups give this," Agnes says. "There are a lot of pressures in parenting nowadays, and it always helps to have someone there who knows how you're feeling and can say, 'Yeah, I've felt that way too.' "

She stops, searching for words. Then her voice breaks, "We really love our kids, or we wouldn't be doing this." ★

CHANGING ROLE OF THE PRESS

The notion of objectivity is a fairly recent one for American journalism. In colonial times, virtually every political party had its own newspaper. Balance and accuracy were the last of their intentions.

When the Associated Press came along in the 1880s, newspapers of all political stripe began carrying the same stories so these wire service stories had to be objective. Today, newspapers continue to operate under the assumption that the content will be consumed by a mass audience, and thus has to satisfy a widely diverse readership. Given that virtually no one likes the press—liberals, conservatives alike defile it as a lackey of the other, and journalists are consistently ranked barely ahead of politicians and right behind used-car salesmen on the "most trusted" lists—it is a matter of great debate whether this is being accomplished.

On the high-school level, we should strive to see that our news stories are as fair and objective as possible, but that we opt for an interpretive or analysis approach when it is appropriate. In non-daily publications, a straight news lead may achieve little more than rehashing the obvious. However, the analysis piece may tell readers something they don't already know.

CHAPTER NINE

PUT IT IN CONTEXT

Interpretation is not editorialization. Rather, it is
the attempt to provide sufficient explanation of facts
to help readers understand complex events.

It is difficult to teach interpretive reporting to beginners who have yet to grasp the
basics of objectivity, who believe in their
hearts and souls that it's their duty to end
every sports story with, "Congratulations,
team!"

If your paper contains a lot of cutie-pie
comments such as "The Pep Squad at our
school outdid itself last week . . . ." or "Our
most excellent principal received another
honor last week . . . .," then it may be a good
idea to read the chapter on objectivity again.

At the same time, we should remind
ourselves that the most objective newswriting
always involves a degree of interpretation. By
deciding who to interview, which quotes to
use and which facts to include in the story,
the reporter judges what is important and
what is not important.

Absolute objectivity is a myth.

Responsible interpretive reporting is not.
It is the attempt to provide sufficient facts to
help readers understand complex events.
Rather than telling readers what to think or
do, interpretive reporting provides unbiased
background information that allows readers
to form their own opinions or to take specific
action based on perspective and knowledge.

Here's an example:

Objective reporting—Louisiana
televangelist Jimmy Swaggart called for an
end of sin and a return to traditional family
values yesterday.

Interpretive reporting—Louisiana
televangelist Jimmy Swaggart, who twice in
the past year was arrested for solicitation of a
prostitute, called for an end of sin and a
return to traditional family values yesterday.

Opinion—Louisiana televangelist Jimmy
Swaggart called for an end of sin and a return
to traditional family values here yesterday, a
hypocritical move for a man who has twice
been arrested in the last year for solicitation
of a prostitute.

It's obvious how the insertion of a small
bit of information can have a profound
impact on how readers interpret the news.

In the race for the Texas Attorney
General's office in the mid-1980s, one
candidate called the other a liberal, anti-gun
crusader who would force sportsmen to "jump
mounds of paperwork" to purchase handguns
and assault rifles. The other candidate
responded by saying that he had unanimous
support of law enforcement officers.

The newspaper story about these charges
and counter-charges included the results of a
survey, taken earlier that week, showing that
more than eight out of 10 Texans supported
such restrictions on the sale of certain
weapons.

Reporting the results of the survey
provides the context against which the day-
to-day political sparring is cast, giving the
story greater meaning than it might otherwise
possess.

Here's a scenario student reporters are more likely to encounter: A high school, faced with the difficult choice between raising taxes or cutting costs, chooses to scale back various programs to keep expenses under control. Over the course of several months, the school board votes to eliminate class academic and fine arts trips, freeze teacher salaries, fire special area teachers, such as art and music instructors, and cut by 25 percent the library budget. However, the board does not reduce its administrative staff, nor does it reduce the athletic department budget.

A student reporter can cover each school board action, but the true story emerges only when each action is reported in context with the others.

So how might the story have been reported?

STUDENTS CAN FORGET about that educational trip to New York or about enrollment in a music class. Librarians are going to have to try to do as best they can with the outdated books that pock-mark the shelves. And teachers are being forced to stretch their paychecks.

When it comes to the current financial crisis, the District School Board has allowed academic and fine arts programs to take the big blows while administrators and athletic departments go untouched.

In the past three months, the Board has voted to scale back academic field trips, freeze teacher salaries, fire special area teachers and cut the library budget. The decisions have prompted teachers to wonder whether the Board has lost sight of the purpose of the school.

"It strikes me as odd that academics have taken the brunt of these cutbacks," said School Board member Scott Gentry, who voted against each. "Our job is to educate students, and these actions are making it harder, almost impossible, to accomplish this mission."

Teachers say they also fear that the Board will raise student-teacher ratios and/or slash faculty rolls. The Parent Teacher Association protested the Board's decision to fire art and music teachers, and the local chapter of the American Federation of Teachers has discussed filing a lawsuit against the school district to save jobs.

School Board members are reluctant to cut athletic budgets, given the success of the school's athletic teams and the strength of athletic boosters, teachers claim. Two members of the Board are former officers of the Football Booster Club.

If additional budget cuts are needed, the School Board will almost be forced to take a close look at the administrative and athletic budgets, teachers say. Educational funds have been cut to the bone. What frightens some is that the School Board may look to the minor sports—particularly girls' athletics—for cuts while leaving the sacred cows, football in particular, untouched.

"While many schools have moved forward in developing a girls' softball program to complement the boys' baseball program, I don't anticipate any such movement here soon," said Mrs. Karen Lyle, who monitors School Board actions. "At this point, I'm willing to suggest that all of the minor sports—boys and girls—are in jeopardy."

But classroom teachers say they wish they had it so good.

"The athletic coaches are complaining that they may be hit next, but we're the ones who have taken all the cuts so far, " chemistry teacher Lanell Raborn said. "I've been told that plans to build a new chemistry lab are postponed indefinitely. I don't want this to turn into an academic versus athletic problem, but it sure looks like the School Board plans to cut us to the bone before considering any cuts to sports programs." ★

WHAT ARE THE IMPLICATIONS?

This story does not editorialize. It does, however, analyze a series of actions, comes to a conclusion and anticipates future action based on past performances.

Remember the kid who divorced his parents? What are the implications of his success in court? Mitchell Landsberg of the Associated Press analyzed the situation like this:

IF HEATHER HATES her homework, can she sue? The correct answer is that the question is absurd. But that was the sort of outlandish scenario being suggested last week after a 12-year-old Florida boy went to court to "divorce" his parents.

More sober critics warned that American

families might be threatened by less frivolous lawsuits filed by angry children who consider their parents abusive. But that appears to be a minority view.

Although legal experts mostly agree that young Gregory Kingsley's case established an important legal precedent, few expect it to have much practical effect.

"It isn't that big a deal," said Sanford Katz, a Boston College law professor who specializes in children's issues. ★

The meaning of the news

The remainder of the news analysis reinforced this point. The article then considered the political implications to Democratic presidential candidate Bill Clinton, whose wife Hillary is a former board chairwoman of the Children's Defense Fund and whose views on children's rights were an issue in the presidential election.

More than anything else, readers need to know the meaning of the news. I once worked for a newspaper whose editor dictated that any time the Dow Jones Stock Market jumped or fell 10 points or more, the story automatically went on the front page even though few people understand the importance of the stock market rising or falling 10 points or 100 points.

The "Week in Review" section in the Sunday edition of *The New York Times* is a superb source for good examples of interpretive and analytical reporting. Rather than simply describing what happened, reporters explain why it happened, what effect it has had and how much impact it is likely to have. The writing in this section illustrates how a reporter may draw conclusions based on personal observations without recommending

what should be done. That task is left to the writers of editorials and columns.

High-school reporters can and should attempt interpretive reporting in the appropriate situations as well. These pieces may be labeled "analysis" although it is not always essential. They should carry a byline.

Differing approaches

Consider these two ways to report the same story. In June, 1993, the United States Supreme Court ruled that it is constitutional for a public school district to send a sign language interpreter into a religious school to help a deaf student learn. The ruling marked the first time the court authorized a public employee to participate in religious education and the third time in a month the justices issued a decision favorable to religion. Reporters localizing this story may take a traditional straight news approach or a more challenging interpretive approach.

> Interpretive reporting attempts to provide information about current decisions and previous problems so readers can form their own opinions or take specific action based on perspective and knowledge.
>
> • • • • • • •

■ Straight news approach

LAST JUNE, THE UNITED States Supreme Court ruled that it is constitutional for a public school district to send a sign language interpreter into a religious school to help a deaf student learn. The ruling marks the first time the court authorized a public employee to participate in religious education and the third time in a month the justices issued a decision favorable to religion.

Superintendent Robert Eudy said he does not expect the decision to affect the district.

"I attended a seminar this summer in which this decision and others were discussed, and I do not believe it breaks any new ground to extend public aid to parochial schools," he said. "I don't anticipate this district sending employees into private or parochial schools for any reason. While our officials will need to study the ruling before deciding what, if any, action needs to be taken, I can tell you that providing such services for students in private schools would be costly."

For example, providing an interpreter for a deaf child could cost between $12,000 and $25,000 per child, depending on the interpreter's experience level and how much time daily he or she spends with a student, Eudy said.

Eudy said some feared the Court was paving the way for vouchers or other forms of public funds for private aid, but added, "With the seating of Justice (Ruth) Ginsburg, who appears to be a separationist, I do not anticipate this happening."

The Rev. William Perry of the First Baptist Church said he welcomed the decision but added he did not anticipate the private school asking for or receiving assistance.

"We believe in the separation of church and state, but we believe the line has been drawn unfairly," Perry said. "We welcome this ruling as a victory for handicapped students to have freedom of choice of schools and to get the services they're entitled to." ★

Let's not kid ourselves. This would be an excellent story for the high-school newspaper. However, it simply states the facts and then allows two sources to respond to the facts. It does not attempt to explain or interpret the facts in a future context.

The next one does.

■ INTERPRETIVE NEWS APPROACH

SENIOR JERRY HAMMERS is hard-of-hearing, which is not to say that he can't hear anything, only that his hearing is so bad he's categorized as legally deaf.

The school district, required by federal law to provide education for all handicapped students, pays for an interpreter to work with Jerry at a cost of more than $10,000 per year.

Jerry also attends services at the First Baptist Church and once considered enrolling in its high school.

"I might have, but my parents couldn't afford an interpreter so I stayed in the public schools," he said.

Early in the summer, the Supreme Court rendered a decision that would have helped Jerry's family, had he decided to attend First Baptist High. The court ruled it is constitutional for a public school district to send a sign language interpreter into a religious school to help a deaf student learn.

"I think it's an excellent decision, not because I want to go to private school, but because my family pays taxes just like everyone else's, and we deserve access to the same services," Jerry said.

But don't expect the school district to begin picking up the tab for impaired students at local private or parochial schools. And don't think this is just the first step toward government vouchers for private or parochial education, as some have suggested. Even though the Supreme Court gave religious groups equal access to public schools used as after-hour community centers and upheld a religious group's right to sacrifice animals during worship services, few believe the court will swing so far as to approve vouchers.

For one thing, the court is likely to shift with the retirement of Justice Byron White, who joined the majority in the ruling. His replacement, Ruth Bader Ginsburg, is believed to strongly support strict separation between church and state.

How this ruling may affect the school district will not be determined until a handicapped student attending a private or parochial school seeks district funding for a taxpayer-paid tutor.

"I don't anticipate this district sending employees into private or parochial schools for any reason," Superintendent Robert Eudy said. "While our officials will need to study the ruling before deciding what, if any, action needs to be taken, I can tell you that providing such services for students in private schools would be costly."

For example, providing an interpreter for a deaf child could cost between $10,000 and $25,000, depending on the interpreter's experience level and how much time daily he or she spends with a student, Eudy said.

Religious leaders argue that the government should offer a neutral service as part of a general program that is not tilted toward religion.

The Rev. William Perry of the First Baptist Church said he welcomed the decision but added he did not anticipate the private school asking for or receiving assistance.

"We believe in the separation of church and state, but we believe the line has been drawn unfairly," Perry said. "We welcome this ruling as a victory for handicapped students to have freedom of choice of schools and to get the services they're entitled to." ★

Although both stories use essentially the same information, this angle better explains the decision in a local context.

WHAT DID THE ELECTION MEAN?

One of the great opportunities students had for interpretive reporting came during the 1992 Presidential election. Almost all schools conduct a mock election, and the high-school newspapers dutifully report the results. However, this reporting rarely if ever goes beyond a rehashing of numbers, supported by one or two statements of the obvious. Here's the typical story:

BILL CLINTON SURPRISED George Bush and Ross Perot in the mock election held here, in results that mirrored the national election results. Mr. Clinton won the election with 248 votes. President Bush trailed a near second with 162 votes, and Ross Perot finished third with 113 votes.

Students had varied ideas about which candidate would do the best job as president.

"I am glad Clinton won the election because he put forth the most effort," senior Mickey Mathis said. "I think he will be an excellent President."

However, others disagreed.

"Clinton is just another tax-and-spend Democrat who'll run the U.S. into the ground," junior Harry Copeland said. "Bush should have won. He hasn't done anything too wrong in the past four years."

"I believe Ross Perot should have become president because he has a lot of money and the power to make things happen, and he had a lot of good answers to all of the issues," sophomore Mike Bedford said. ★

While this story reports a fact (that Clinton won the mock election), it provides no news. But taking an interpretive approach provides an opportunity to look at the election in a much larger context, assuming that most people a week or so after the election will know who won. Note also how the story works in the results of a student mock election. For example:

FOUR YEARS AGO, students who didn't plan to attend college could expect to find well-paying jobs at one of the several manufacturing plants in the area. Today, about half of these plants are closed, and the other half are cutting back their work force, in some cases by as much as 50 percent.

A few of the plants have moved to Mexico in search of cheap labor and lax environmental laws. Others simply shut down, victims of international competition. Regardless, the unemployment rate here has doubled from 6.2 percent in 1988 to more than 13 percent today.

Also, in 1988, county residents voted overwhelmingly for George Bush. Not so in 1992. Students in a mock election last month predicted a Clinton/Gore victory, favoring the Democratic team over President Bush, 42-34 percent. Ross Perot picked up the final 24 percent of the votes.

"The economy is a mess, and all we got from the President and Mr. Quayle was a sermon on family values," said James Wayt, who has been looking for work since Reynolds Manufacturing shut down in 1990. His three children attend elementary school here.

"Winning the war in Kuwait provided people a moment of patriotism, but the war's over and we're still looking for a job. Like they say, Saddam Hussein still has a job. We don't."

Certainly, the economy was the number one issue in the campaign, local students said.

"That Clinton was able to overcome his reputation as a draft-dodger and a womanizer pretty much points out the importance that voters attached to the economy," said Buddy Pewitt, county Democratic Party chair. "People vote their pocketbook, and a lot of these pocketbooks are getting pretty low right now."

Students echoed their parents' sentiments.

"I'm graduating next year and going into one of the worst job markets in the nation's history," Carol Medlin said. "I don't have the money to go to college, and I don't know where I'll be able to find decent employment. Frankly, it looks pretty bleak right now, and I'm hoping Mr. Clinton can turn this thing around." ★

THEY'RE NOT THE BIGGEST FOR NOTHING!

Occasionally you will want to read one of the nation's most important newspapers. They include:

- *The New York Times*
- *Washington Post*
- *Wall Street Journal*
- *Los Angeles Times*

Access to these papers is restricted by circulation area, and daily subscriptions are costly. So let's not be media snobs. The nation is blessed with outstanding papers. These come to mind:

- *Boston Globe*
- *Philadelphia Inquirer*
- *Kansas City Star*
- *Dallas Morning News*
- *Miami Herald*
- *Minneapolis Tribune*
- *Detroit Free Press*
- *Detroit News*
- *Portland Oregonian*
- *Chicago Tribune*
- *Anchorage Daily News*

If you're working on a tight budget, purchase the Sunday edition only. These editions usually contain the big news stories, the special sections and the extra supplements.

Finally, keep a copy of *USA Today* around. It's easy to read and colorful. It also has that really cool weather map.

This story focuses on the news question "why" rather than restating the obvious. Instead of dishing out all the campaign rhetoric, it seeks informative direct quotes to give a sense of meaning to the election results.

Interpretive stories can also appear as sidebars to major news stories. The news story presents the latest decisions, and the sidebar places the latest event into a historical context.

INTERPRETIVE FEATURES

Interpretive angles are not confined to the news sections. One of my favorite leads comes from a story about midnight bowling, by Steve Levine of the *Dallas Morning News* (for full story, turn to page 175). It goes like this (interpretation in italics):

THE APPEAL IS NOT immediately apparent when you walk past the Camaros and vans in the parking lot and reach the front door where teenage boys smoke cigarettes *and try to impress the girls.*

Inside, it's not the too-bright fluorescent lights blinding you to young love at the shoe counter, not the dull chorus of balls rumbling down the lanes and the resulting explosion of pins. It's not even the great expanse of carpet, Formica and multicolored shoes with numbers on the back. Everything is just as it should be until you glance at a clock and see that it's past midnight.

And then glance at the lanes and see that they're all full. And glance at the shoe counter and see that all the size 9s are gone. Don't glance at your favorite video game. It probably has a waiting line.

Welcome to midnight bowling: Haven for insomniac bowlers, home for *lonely singles searching for a different kind of score* and hangout for people just looking

Midnight bowling, where you can dress up silly, act foolish and be considered normal. Where the guys slug their beer like it's the last one of this lifetime. Where foreigners test their English on teen-age girls and harried waitresses. Where gambling—bowling for dollars—is part of lane life. It is, says one alley aficionado, "very,

very different."

At least five area bowling alleys regularly offer after-midnight bowling . . . . ★

INTERPRETIVE STATEMENTS

Do you think Steve walked up to the guys at the front door and said, "I see you boys are smoking cigarettes. Why?"

"Cough, hack, gag. We are trying to impress the girls, sir," one pimply-faced sophomore said. *"But I don't think it's working."*

Probably not.

Nor did he approach a particularly lonely soul and ask, "Might you be searching for a different kind of score?"

These comments are interpretive statements that provide a context for the rest of the story. Reporters see an event, but rather than simply describing what they see, they attempt to explain what the event means. Consider the story on page 105 about a young man with cancer.

SENSE OF TIME AND PLACE

The beauty of this story lies in its fresh and original angle, its capture of detail and its sense of time and place.

A reporter rang the doorbell, hoping no one would answer. . . .

A reluctant photographer. . . sat beside her, nervously readjusting his focus . . . .

These small but hardly minor touches separate the truly gifted journalists from the formula writers.

DON'T STATE THE OBVIOUS

The two stories on page 106 show how interpretation by the reporter can turn what might otherwise be a bland, predictable story into something unique and interesting.

The first story gives us little new information. The quotes are predictable. The plot is poorly defined. There's no context for the action. Given that most persons can figure out for themselves the nature of a mock trial, it is important that the reporter attempt to

SO WHAT D'YA WANT TO KNOW?

By DIANA MOORE

Spring Woods High School, Houston

A REPORTER RANG the door-bell, hoping no one would answer. But someone did.

After a few minutes the brass knob turned, and the door swung open. A boy in his mid-teens dressed in jeans, oversized cowboy hat and faded western boots guided the reporter and a reluctant photographer through the house and into a bedroom.

On the walls were scattered posters with Bible scriptures printed across them. A bed was positioned on one side of the room, a few pieces of furniture sat on the other side, a wheelchair in the corner.

The reporter sat on the bed and skimmed over her notes, double checking her questions. The photographer sat beside her nervously readjusting his focus. The cowboy walked to the bedroom door, and the visitors waited for him to wheel in the person they had come to see. The boy they waited for had been hospitalized with cancer. He had gone through chemotherapy over the summer, and Spring Woods recently sponsored a blood drive in his name.

Instead of wheeling someone in, the boy shut the door. Then he fell back into the wheelchair and asked, "So what d'ya want to know?"

After the discovery that freshman Philipp Plumlee had no trouble walking, the interview was moved outside where the light was better. Plumlee sat on one side of the brick stairwell while his cat curled around his feet.

Since Easter he has spent most of his time at the Medical Center going through the painful procedure of chemotherapy. Before his problem was diagnosed as cancer, he was told one leg was longer than the other. Because of this, he was wearing special shoes. As part of the chemo-therapy, Plumlee was given a poison which would kill cancer. After taking it, he has to swallow glass after glass of water. Sometimes this is not enough to flush out the poison so he bleeds internally.

"Two or three weeks ago, he had a real bad reaction to the therapy," said junior Michelle Luschen, his stepsister. "His blood count went way down, and he had internal hemorrhaging.

Since then he's gotten better, but there's always a chance it could happen again."

At the time his parents were having trouble finding donors. They asked the school if it could hold this year's blood drive in Plumlee's name. The school collected 72 pints, 48 of which were donated to him.

During the summer he lived day-to-day not knowing whether his treatment would save him. At one point he was told his cancerous leg should be amputated; otherwise, he might not live. He refused the operation, and he now feels he is doing better than he has in six months.

"At the time I tried to talk him into having the operation. I thought that was the only way he could live. I'm just glad he had the strength to say no," Ursula Kerr, his mother, said.

Plumlee attributes a lot of his recovery to the support he receives from his mother and the rest of his family.

"That's the good thing about having a large family; someone is always with him. He is never alone," Luschen said.

Financially, the family has suffered in only one aspect of the treatment.

"So far, the insurance has covered everything. The part that is really costing us is Phillipp's expensive taste. I've really been spoiling him," Kerr said.

Despite the presents he has received, such as a $50 cowboy hat and a classic Mustang, Plumlee still must face the pain and loneliness of having cancer.

"I really miss the atmosphere of the school and being with my friends," he said. "The part I miss the most is not being able to be in or watch the football games."

He has spent his time at home either resting or taking trips to Galveston or Memorial City. He has also recently picked up the violin and hopes to be playing "bluegrass" with the "Dog-tooth Band" soon.

Because of his therapy, Plumlee would have to be out of school too much to return soon. But if he continues to improve as he has, he hopes to be back before his senior year.

"With the help of chemotherapy, and if God is willing," he said, "I hope to be back at school by next year." ★

DRAW A REASONABLE CONCLUSION

In **The Professional Journalist,** *John Hohenberg wrote, "Interpretation adds the factor of judgment to what is called straight news—the unvarnished recital of fact and poll taking which may or may not represent the truth. The difference between interpretation and editorialization, broadly, is that the interpreter applies the rule of reason to the news but stops short of recommending what should be done about it. The province of the editorial writer is to urge a course of action upon the reader or viewer."*

In many cases, the reporter examines the evidence and draws a conclusion. For example:

A request by seniors to travel to Miami Beach may be dead in the water, school officials said. An administrator who asked not to be named said school officials would not approve of a plan to allow seniors to take the three-day trip.

explain a bit more than what we have here:

FROM MARCH 25 through March 28, Jim Bronson's senior Government classes performed a mock trial.

According to Bronson, the purpose of the trial was to help the students understand how a court of law worked.

"He made the witnesses 'swear in' just like in a real court," senior Steve Griffin said.

Class members said that every student was involved in the trial either as a witness, judge, defense attorney, prosecuting attorney or jury member.

The case being decided that week centered on involuntary manslaughter by automobile. The defendant was charged with hitting an older lady on a winter night, after attending a party and having two or three drinks.

Chad Pitre, who played the judge, said that it was hard to decide because neither side truly proved the driver guilty or innocent.

"I had a difficult time reaching a decision," he said.

Bronson said that making tough decisions was part of the lesson.

"I wanted this to be a learning experience for my classes. This was a fun and easy way to teach this particular lesson," Bronson said. ★

What did we really learn here? Not much. The story states the obvious: if a class is putting on a mock trial, it stands to reason that students will portray judges and lawyers. Tell us something new, something we don't already know, something we can't figure out for ourselves.

Given that a specific story can take many twists and turns in the weeks between issues, it would seem that more staffs would attempt interpretive reporting. The following lead, written by Jonathan Eig of the *Dallas Morning News*, gives a deft little twist that truly captured the essence of a high-school mock trial:

THE LAWYERS DIDN'T care about money, and the journalists were all objective so it had to be a mock trial.

But if not for those nagging details, the legal drama Saturday at the Earle Cabell Federal Building might well have been the real thing. Or better.

Should Jesse Goodall, a fictional college student, go to jail for leading an environmental protest that turned into a riot? Or was Sidney Chernobyl, the nuclear-waste company official, responsible for the mayhem? And could journalistic accounts of the incident really be trusted? (The answer: Of course they could.)

More than 100 high-school students grappled with these issues at the Texas High School Mock Trial Competition. Entering evidence, grilling witnesses and swaying jurors, the attorneys did everything that real lawyers do—except bill their clients.

When U. S. Judge Jerry Buchmeyer announced the verdict in a crowded courtroom Saturday afternoon, Richard King High School came away the state champions, earning a trip to the national competition in New Orleans.

But even the students who failed to reach the final round of the tournament said the outcome pleased them.

"It gives you a chance to express yourself," said Christopher Jones, a senior at Booker T. Washington High School for the Performing and Visual Arts in Dallas. "You learn to get up and think on your feet."

In the pressure-packed finals before Judge Buchmeyer, "attorneys" Lara Hammerick and Daniel Nelson of Richard King High teamed up to defend Jesse Goodall against the prosecutors from Berkner High School in Richardson.

Anusha Chagan and Lisa Wong of Berkner tried to prove that Jesse Goodall frightened a crowd of protesters by displaying barrels full of bright green, bubbling liquids. In the ensuing panic, one woman in the fictional riot fainted and suffered a miscarriage.

But Lara and Daniel said the liquid was only anti-freeze mixed with dry ice. They said Sidney Chernobyl incited the melee by screaming and charging toward Jesse.

The same arguments were presented over and over as teams competed, but with every case came a different strategy. Sometimes, as the teams called witnesses and filed objections, the courtroom scene seemed real. Dallas-area lawyers and judges served as jurors, grading the students based on their courtroom conduct more than on the facts of the case.

To prepare, the students spend months researching the same fictional court case and

COLD REALITY. It is one thing to report the results of the big game. It's something else to report what it means. A 22-21 loss in the state championship, on a day when the temperature never rose above 20 degrees, demands an interpretive approach, both visually and verbally.

Photo by John Moore.

rehearsing their courtroom demeanor. Most of the schools get coaching from a teacher and a local lawyer.

Dallas County Criminal Court Judge Marshall Gandy, who heard one of the preliminary cases Saturday, said the students showed more poise than a lot of real lawyers.

"They're incredible for high school students. It doesn't even show," he said. "I wouldn't mind seeing any of them in my courtroom. They may even pass themselves off as attorneys." ★

The lawyers didn't care about money, and the journalists were all objective so it had to be a mock trail.

Both a clever lead and an engaging interpretive statement that plays to its audience. The success of this story is that it explains the essence of the mock trial rather than merely keeping score and listing names.

Adrian Jones of James Bowie High School in Austin, Texas captures the magic of Disney World in the beginning of a story about a student who was employed there the previous summer:

THERE COMES A TIME when the tender innocence of childhood begins to melt away. All those nursery rhymes and storybook characters give way to "real" life. The sweet memories of warm laps to cuddle in and homemade sandboxes to play in give way to conflict resolution discussions and environmentally balanced gardens.

It doesn't have to be that way. There is an escape, a place where Mickey, Donald and all the other friends come back to life.

It's a place where 100-degree afternoons and long lines are unimportant. It's a park with unusual and exciting shows, extraordinary rides and some of the most warm and fuzzy characters around.

It's Disney World, the most popular theme park in the world, and it can make even Oscar the Grouch smile.

"Smile," John-Paul Beltran said. "Always

smile. When so many people around you are smiling, you just can't help but smile along with them."

Beltran's summer was filled with smiles.

It started with an offer to audition to work as a Disney character at Disney World in Orlando.

"Everything really starts with my brother Ricky," Paul Beltran, John-Paul's father, said. "All of my side of the family, and all of my wife's side of the family, have been working at Disney World since 1975. My brother Ricky was the first one to work as a character. My other brother Freddy is in charge of the MGM stage over there."

Fred Beltran feels it is ironic so many members of his family worked at Disney World.

"When Ricky worked as a character, I used to come and see him," Fred said. "A few years later, I was a character. So it's like passing down the torch because now I'm in management . . . ." ★

INTERPRETIVE SPORTS STORIES

Sports can also be the subject of interesting interpretive pieces. This lead analyzes the effects of a defeat rather than merely reporting the fact that the team lost the game:

THE JAGUARS ARE OUT of the district race, at least for the time being. And unless Anderson or Reagan unexpectedly stumble, their hopes for a football playoff berth are practically nil.

The Jaguars dropped a 21-17 loss last week to then-winless Bowie, shattering their dim hopes of securing a runners-up playoff berth.

"We shot ourselves in the foot," head coach Cecil Plummer said. "We never got focused, and by the time we got our heads on straight, it was too late. I'm really sick about this loss." ★

Unfortunately, sports reporters are prone to sneak in an opinion or two. The following piece might have been an interesting inter-pretive feature on off-season workouts, but the writer attacks the subject with such a bias that the content of the story is obliterated.

FOOTBALL PLAYERS DON'T just vanish after a football season. Flashing their flamboyant letter jackets in the faces of other students is a common practice of the football jocks.

These jocks also appear to be buffoons by their actions and apparel resulting from the "class" which is an after-effect of football: off-season workouts.

The shabby garments worn by these beastly jocks tell the story to their animal-like personalities: sailors' caps, bandanas, florescent shorts over sweats, baby bonnets and half shirts ripped to shreds offering the sight of their hairy navels to anyone who might be watching.

An astonished passerby viewing this untamed pack of cut-throats may be tempted to turn and flee.

These ornery bandits often release their endless energy along with their obscene body odor as they charge up and down the gym floor. A different native call is shouted each time the pack tears down the floor.

An innocent mother on her way down to pick up her toddlers may catch a horrifying glimpse of this wild bunch of students tripping on their tongues as they struggle up the "hill." This infamous "hill" prompts a hot line from each agonizing muscle as it screams "Death."

"Gut check," shouts the merciless chief known to the delinquents as Coach. The mere sound of these horrendous words send the love handles of each jock into relentless spasms as they fear the grueling day.

Hours of back-breaking labor are spent in the agonizing weight room, which only these pain-enduring, ape-like creatures can withstand. This room is another room which is so unfortunately obsessed with the ungodly body odor released from the "Mama's boys." Their rubber arms and legs flex and strain at every repetition on these weights until one can clearly see each vein and

> Interpretive reporting is one of the few times when a reporter is allowed to draw conclusions based on his personal observations without actually recommending what should be done.
>
> • • • • • • •

artery in the face of these exhausted jocks. As the jocks let the last weights fall, a blood-curdling scream might be heard clear across the city as the weights crash on the outstretched, panting tongues.

These jocks drag their limp bodies, bruised tongues and whatever else may be attached to them across the gym floor in order to "punch out" the time clock.

The same time the next day, these same exhausted clowns will force their aching bodies to resume the scheduled process the next day. And all because their desire drives them to earn one more glamorous letter which will be placed on their jackets, to be plastered in other students' faces. ★

This article is designed not to analyze or interpret but rather to attack. For a better example of the sports interpretive article, look at page 110.

AVOID BLATANT EDITORIALIZATION

Personality profiles in magazines such as *Vanity Fair*, *Esquire* and *Rolling Stone* often contain generous portions of interpretation, but they avoid blatant editorialization.

Likewise, high-school reporters should avoid stories that look more like come-ons than serious journalism. As evidence, I cite the following story in a high-school newspaper:

AFTER LISTENING TO A FEW witty and varied comments on "some new England dude" who recently arrived at our school, my curiosity overcame me and I felt stirred to follow it. By that, I mean I felt the spark of challenge that most of us reporters often feel as an excuse to stick their noses into something foreign and unknown thus far.

I then commenced to meet this interesting and slightly mysterious foreigner.

The new student is a junior whose name is Brian, a quiet-mannered, 17-year-old who hails from Nottingham, the middle of England.

When I first approached him, the nervous tension that had been building up inside me was quickly dispelled as he mentally took notice of my uneasiness, smiled pleasantly and smoothly accepted giving the interview.

Brian has a relaxing presence, very much at ease with himself and those around him; surprising since it seems anyone would be easily overwhelmed and unnerved by all the attention and stares which he takes in stride.

Asked how the school courses he took back in England compared to the ones he is taking here, Brian said the classes in England are much harder with less variation for the students' pleasure. Also, the attitudes of the students there aren't quite as casual, and they are more serious minded.

When I tried probing into him about how he sees American girls and the dating scene here, he gave a big grin and replied it was all the same to him. ★

Subtle, huh? Kind of an "I'll write a story about you if you'll go out with me" approach.

The entire notion of objectivity always comes under scrutiny, but staffs on the cutting edge still want to take a shot at interpretive reporting. However, be warned: The line between editorialization and interpretation is so thin that only the most advanced reporters, working with veteran editors and advisers, should attempt to interpret the news.

COMPARE & contrast

AN INTERPRETIVE APPROACH

Laura Orr never set out to be the All-American girl. It just turned out that way. She plays volleyball because it clears her mind, she said. She's not sure why she's so good at it. "I enjoy it so I work at it a little harder, I guess," she said.

Her parents have always stressed academics so it's no surprise that she's an honor roll student. "They've never really pushed me, but I understand their expectations," she said.

Orr never ran for class officer to prove anything except that she wants to serve. Whether she set out to be a teacher's dream without being a teacher's pet is unlikely.

Still, there's no denying that Laura is something special. Last week, she was named most valuable player on the team's state championship volleyball team, and next week she will travel to Washington, D.C. as part of the school's academic decathalon team.

"I wish I could say that I've had to overcome great obstacles to attain whatever success I've had in school, but that isn't true," Orr said. "High school has been easy and fun for me. I owe a lot to my parents, who prepared me for school, and I've been fortunate to have had some great teachers."

She said she expects college to be a bit rougher. She's already been accepted to Ohio State on a volleyball scholarship, and she said she may try her hand at tennis as well.

"I plan to major in biology," she said. "I want to be a pediatrician, and since I come from a family of doctors, I know how much work is involved. Plus, sports at Ohio State is very competitive."

Not that she is intimidated.

"I enjoy a challenge," she said. "I'm ready to move on to the next big one." ★

UNRELATED STACK OF DATA

Laura Orr has been named Student of the Month. Laura is a senior and last week was named most valuable player on the state championship volleyball team.

Her favorite activites include water skiing, tennis, reading and watching movies.

"I really like Francis Ford Coppola films, especially *The Godfather* and *Apocalypse Now*," she said. "I also loved *Bram Stoker's Dracula*."

She is a senior class vice president and a member of the academic decathalon team, which will go to Washington, D.C. next week to compete in the national finals.

"I enjoy the academic decathalon quite a bit," she said. "It forces you to look at the world and understand what's going on around you."

Laura is a member of the honor roll and is a National Merit Semifinalist. She plans to major in biology at Ohio State University in Columbus, Ohio in hopes of becoming a pediatrician.

"I've always wanted to work with children," she said.

As to advice that she would give to incoming freshmen?

"Study hard, but try to have a good time in high school because the four years will pass by quickly," she said. ★

CHAPTER TEN

PULL IT TOGETHER

A unified story expresses one idea or thesis. All information
in the story develops that thesis. Of more importance,
the writing flows in a logical order.

As emphasized in Chapter 2, it is dangerous to attempt to reduce reporting or writing
to a series of steps because the process isn't
step-by-step. One element defines and is
defined by another. Theme overlaps with
angle, angle with description and so on.
Building a story is not like building an
automobile engine. The fan belts do not
define and are not defined by the manifold
intake valve. The thousand or so engine
parts are separate but replaceable and certainly not interchangeable.

In the successful story, the parts flow into
one another. It's difficult to tell when theme
ends and angle begins. Unlike an automobile
engine, which is built one piece at a time, a
story evolves from a blend of theme, angle,
focus, organization, interpretation and
description. Unity is the sum of the story's
individual parts.

A unified story expresses one idea or
thesis, and all information in the story
develops that thesis. Of more importance,
the writing flows in a logical order, with each
sentence and each paragraph continuing the
narrative, moving the story forward.

Consider the following story:

THERE IS AN ODD fellow in our town.
His name is Clarence Chapman, and he owns a
junk business. He used to be a farmer and also
worked in a foundry but had to quit for health
reasons.

Clarence is a graduate of Tamaroa High
School. He served in Germany during World
War II, then moved back here to set up business.
His wife of 30 years, Marilyn, died in 1973. "I
miss her a lot," Clarence said.

His hobbies include reading and gardening.
He also spends a lot of time in front of his house,
waving at people. Clarence does it because he
said he is afraid people had forgotten to be
friendly.

Another person who waves with Clarence is
his 36-year-old son. Sam is a college graduate in
philosophy and has been working with his father
for 10 years. Sam said his favorite philosopher is
Eugene Levy-Strauss. "I don't know why," Sam
said. "He just made a lot of sense to me." ★

STACKING DATA ON TOP OF DATA

Now, what is this story really about?
Well, it's not about anything in particular.
It's a collection of unrelated facts—a dis-
jointed piece of writing. It lacks unity
because the writer never selected a specific
theme, never explored interesting angles, did
very little research, failed to describe either
the persons or the scenes, and never placed
the action into a context. Instead, the writer
stacked one piece of data on top of another,
rendering all of it irrelevant.

So what that this guy likes to wave at
people? Who cares?

So what that he has a son? Who cares?

So what that the son majored in philosophy? What does that have to do with

anything?

Well, read the following story, and you can see how successful writers—in this case, Andrew H. Malcolm of *The New York Times*—take what otherwise may look like irrelevant data and turn it into a wonderful story.

TAMAROA, ILL.—FOR ALL but 900 people in the world, this sleepy southern Illinois community is little more than a 40-mile-an-hour speed zone on the way to somewhere else.

But back about 1970 something unusual began to happen here, something so weird that drivers would slow down and turn their heads to stare as they passed on Route 51. Some people would even drive by again or stop their cars and demand to know what was wrong.

What was happening up there on the north end of Walnut Street was that someone was waving. Just standing or sitting there in front of his place waving, like the old days.

He would wave at people in cars and trucks, on tractors and bikes—even pedestrians would get a wave.

For 12 hours every day in rain and snow and summer sun, this guy would sit in front of his shed and wave at everyone, as if he was friendly and cared about them.

Then in 1976 the unusual man was joined by his son. So there were two people waving at everyone, whether they knew them or not.

"We just decided," said Clarence Chapman, Tamaroa's first unofficial waver, "that the world had maybe forgotten how to be friendly-like, locked up in their air-conditioned cars and basements and all. So Sam and I wave. We're just saying, 'Hi. Howdy. How are you? Nice day.' That sort of thing."

The trouble is that waving friendly-like is catching. Many passersby now actually wave back. Some honk their horns. A few shout to the men they've never seen before: "Hello!" Many stop to chat or swap tall tales.

There are unconfirmed sightings of people waving in other parts of this depressed town. And if the Chapmans are a little late getting out some morning, the regulars will still toot their horns and wave back as if both men were there waving away.

At least some of them do. "Kids always wave," says Clarence Chapman. "But by the time they grow up, it seems like some of them stop waving. Oh, I guess they think it's too strange or something."

Of course, this kind of irrepressible friendliness is annoying to some motorists. Some even yell an obscenity. "We smile real big and wave back," said Sam Chapman, "and think to ourselves it's real good that some folks are just passing through."

Clarence Chapman is a 64-year-old former farmer forced out of that business by economics and out of a foundry job by asthma that still starts him coughing if he laughs too hard. He walks on a cane now, wears a thin mustache, a straw cowboy hat, a Rin-Tin-Tin string tie and whatever slacks and shirt he can find at home, across the road from his junk shop.

"We call it junk," he says. "But after you buy it, you can call it anything you want."

Sam Chapman is 36 and has been waving for 10 years, since he graduated from college with a major in philosophy. "The demand for philosophers was somewhat soft then, as now," Mrs. Chapman says. So he joined his father's junk business.

The junk business in rural southern Illinois is not a high-pressure occupation. It provides ample time, year-round, for at least one of the Chapmans to wave at every passing person.

At mealtimes, Sam and Clarence take turns going indoors so they do not miss an auto. In between, they listen a lot to the birds in the sassafras trees.

Some passersby require comment: "There goes the Knight boy home from Bible school to mow the lawn." "Old Harold must be hitting the suds already today. He's got his missus driving." "Don't know those folks. Hi. How are ya?"

The two men might even break into song, which tells neighbors that life is progressing normally. "You can hear them clear up to my house," said Phyllis Ferguson. "They're not stuck-up or anything, just old-fashioned friendly."

They don't have a phone. "Somebody wants us," says Sam, "they can come see us."

And they're too busy to watch television. "In the old shows," says Clarence, "crime didn't pay. Now, you look at TV and wonder if maybe it might."

They are not bothered by non-wavers. "It just ain't some people's way to wave," says Clarence Chapman. "But you can tell the city folks right off. They're the ones that think waving is strange." ★

Perfect balance and coordination

So what that this guy likes to wave at people? So what that he has a son? So what that the son majored in philosophy?

Are these important considerations? Of course, they are. We see a man who is conducting his own crusade against the isolation of today's world, who is clinging to an old ideal that we should love our neighbors, whether we know them or not, and who is making some progress.

We can picture him—a cane at his side, a thin mustache, a straw cowboy hat, a Rin-Tin-Tin string tie and "whatever slacks and shirt he can find at home, across the road from his junk shop" as he and his son sit on the front porch, talking about people driving by and waving at each passing car.

It is particularly important to remember that this story was published in *The New York Times*—the house organ of snooty city folks who probably think waving is strange. The story begins with an interpretation: "For all but 900 people in the world, this sleepy southern Illinois community is little more than a 40-mile-an-hour speed zone on the way to somewhere else."

It isn't an editorial comment. It's the reporter's assessment of the situation, and he's probably right. We feel comfortable with the reporter's assessment because the lead immediately presents two facts: the town population and the speed zone, simple but good reporting of pertinent details.

In a non-too-subtle dig, Mr. Malcolm rubs the readers' noses in their silly conceptions of rural folk, their condescending attitudes and their fears of strangers. "You can tell the city folks right off. They're the ones that think waving is strange."

What a perfect ending. This story embodies all of the elements. It appeals to our better instincts. It touches our hearts and funnybones. It takes us somewhere and brings us back home.

It is this type of unity—a beginning, a middle and an end, working in perfect balance and coordination—that make this story so successful.

Pulling the fact together

Consider the following situation. Texas public school students participating in a series of journalism contests were required to write a feature story, based on the following facts:

✓ SITUATION:

Janelle Klein is the drama teacher at the high school and is a member of a local comedy troupe. She has been employed at the school for 11 years. She has guided the school's one-act play to seven district championships, six regional titles and two state championships. She is married to Frank Klein, an engineer for the Texas Highway Department. She and her husband have three children.

In addition to her job at the high school, Janelle is a member of the Laff Staff, a group of improvisational comedians who work at a local comedy theatre. She also founded the Clown Care Unit (CCU), a group of comedians who visit ailing children and their parents at the city's four hospitals. The clowns' purpose is to alleviate the fear and confusion of hospital stays and to provide moments of humorous routines for sick children.

St. Michael's Hospital recently opened a new Children's Hospital for youngsters with life-threatening and catastrophic illnesses. Two or three days a week, the clowns, dressed in mock hospital garb and bearing such names as Dr. Comfort, Dr. Stubs and Dr. Funnybone, make the rounds at local hospitals to visit sick children. Usually, the clowns perform a 20-minute parody of hospital personnel, food and procedures and then make the rounds on the floors to visit children too sick to leave their rooms. You are writing for the issue of the student newspaper to be distributed Friday, April 3.

HELP ALL REPORTERS ASPIRE TO A HIGHER LEVEL

Editors are the key to guaranteeing that a newspaper or a yearbook makes unity the standard for every story.

First, their stories must be artfully written and painstakenly edited.

Second, editors must make unity a goal and requirement for all copy they deal with—whether it's the longest in-depth analysis or the shortest news or sports brief.

To this end, editors must nudge, prod and occasionally scream, whatever it takes to help all reporters aspire to a higher level. Then readers will know that the publication is always worth reading.

■ **JANELLE KLEIN**

I have enjoyed my 11 years at Leaguetown High School, and I'm going to miss the students. I can't overstate how important I think it is to continue to support the fine arts in high school. Basic curriculum in high schools is very much overemphasized. Students need a well-rounded education of core classes as well as enrichment classes. I joined Laff Staff because I enjoy performing, and I think it is good for students to know that their teachers can do as well as teach. However, this project has grown more important for me each year, and with the opening of the new Children's Hospital at St. Michael's, the need for this service is especially dire.

Clown Care got its start in 1991 when an official at St. Michael's Hospital asked if the Laff Staff would entertain at a gathering for patients and their families. A fellow member of the Laff Staff, Jeff Gordon, and I obliged. We put together a 20-minute parody of doctors and hospitals, and it was the most fulfilling 20 minutes of my professional career. It was from that experience that the CCU plan took root.

This project came out of an unconscious place in myself. After going through a lot of feelings of loss and grief when my best friend's son died a few years ago, this gave me a feeling of celebration and joy, of healing after his loss. Call it a love and caring, God, a higher consciousness—whatever—I want to give my life to this project.

The nurses and doctors have been extremely supportive of our efforts. They accepted that we were there as part of their world. I had one ugly encounter when we first started. A hospital staff member said, "Clowns don't belong in the Intensive Care Unit." So I said, "Neither do children." I won that one.

I've encountered so many extraordinary young people that it's hard to single one out, but I do think a lot about one young man named Christian, who had a chronic heart ailment and was very angry and very lonely. For more than a year, we spent time with him, trying to reach him. One day, I taught him a "mind-reading" card game, and he began to open up. He took great pride in fooling one of his real doctors with the card trick.

I later told him he was good enough to join CCU, but he said, "I'd love to, but I can't walk." I told him, "Oh, you can walk." Of course, he hadn't taken a step in eight months.

Within two weeks, he had found a pair of tennis shoes and was on his feet as a $2-a-day CCU performer. After that he blossomed, and I think it gave him the strength to battle against his mounting medical problems. He died two months after open-heart surgery, but those last few years of his life were full of joy. He didn't die a lonely and angry young man.

I've had a few rejections. But I don't let them bother me. My responsibility is not to save the children but to love them and give joy and celebration, not to make them accept it. That's their choice.

■ **DR. ALFRED NASH, DIRECTOR OF THE CHILDREN'S HOSPITAL OF ST. MICHAEL'S**

Most of us thought it was a wonderful idea, but we were not sure how it would work and if it would be accepted by the parents of sick children. But the clowns' techniques were so disarming, they captivated everybody immediately.

As hard as it is for children to be sick, it is equally difficult for parents to have sick children, and a lot of us at the hospital sometimes forget this. Indeed, we—the doctors, nurses and staff members—thoroughly enjoy the shows even when the clowns are poking fun at us.

■ **MELINDA MATTHEWS, MOTHER OF CARRIE, AGE 5, A SICK CHILD**

The clowns are wonderful. One day, we were all in the room when Dr. Stubs (Janelle) stuck her head in the room and asked, "I hope I'm not bothering you." Then, she pulled up beside the bed, pulled out several crumpled sheets of paper, a huge pencil, and began asking her, "Are you married? Any children? Does your nose ever turn red?" Then, she plopped a big red nose on Carrie. Finally, she asked, "Have you ever had a how-long-can-you-go-without-laughing test?" Carrie answered "no" to all of the questions. Stubs then took out a large wind-up clock from her bag and let it drop to the floor. Of course, Carrie giggled, and Stubs said, "You only lasted four seconds. Want to try again?" So she planted a red nose on me, and Carrie just erupted with laughter. For a few moments, at least, her mind was off the pain and trauma of being ill.

■ **EXTRA INFORMATION**

The Clown Care Unit recently received a $25,000 grant from the Charles Altman Foundation, to be used mostly for props, salaries and administrative overhead. On Monday, March 23, Klein announced that she would leave the school at the end of the school year to devote her full attention to improving and expanding the Clown Care Unit project.

THE UNIFIED STORY

To have a unified story, we must answer several questions: What is this story really about? What is the best way to tell this story? What lead will capture the reader's attention? Can we tell the story in a logical order without losing the reader? Which information do we use? Which do we omit? Which quotes are used as direct quotes, which as indirect quotes? What are our transitions? And finally, how do we end this story so that the reader is left with a sense of resolution and satisfaction?

If we can do these things, then the story will have unity. Let's see if it's possible:

THE DOCTOR DRAGGED a chair to the side of the bed, pulled out several crumpled sheets of paper and a huge pencil, and began the interrogation.

"Are you married?

"Any children?

"Does your nose ever turn red?

"Have you ever had a how-long-can-you-go-without-laughing test?"

The patient, 5-year-old Carrie Matthews, answered "no" to each question. The doctor—Dr. Stubs—then took out a large wind-up clock from her bag and let it drop to the floor.

Carrie giggled.

"You only lasted four seconds. Want to try again?"

She did. But to no avail. Doctor Stubs planted a red nose on Carrie's mom, and with that, the patient erupted into laughter.

For a few moments, Carrie's mind was off the pain and the trauma of being ill.

Since 1986, the Clown Care Unit, a group of comedians that visits ailing children and their parents at the city's four hospitals, has worked to alleviate the fear and confusion of hospital stays and provide moments of humorous routines for sick children. It recently received a $25,000 grant from the Charles Altman Foundation.

The CCU was founded by drama teacher Janelle Klein, who announced March 23 that she was leaving the school after 11 years to devote her full attention to improving and expanding the project.

"Clown Care got its start in 1991 when an official at St. Michael's Hospital asked if the Laff Staff would entertain at a gathering for patients and their families," Klein said. "A fellow member of the Laff Staff, Jeff Gordon, and I obliged. We put together a 20-minute parody of doctors and hospitals, and it was the most fulfilling 20 minutes of my professional career. It was from that experience that the CCU plan took root."

Although apprehensive at first, Klein said doctors and nurses have been extremely supportive of the troupe.

"I had one ugly encounter when we first started," she said. "A hospital staff member said,

DON'T BE AFRAID TO ASK FOR HELP

A story is a living organism. It comes to life as soon as the fingers touch the computer keys and exists as long as a reader remembers it. It cannot be treated as though it's another school assignment to be completed, submitted and forgotten.

Making a story unforgettable requires talent, skill and diligence—the constant commitment to make the story as good as it can be.

Reporters who find that their stories are "just a bunch of facts" should meet with other reporters and editors. They may propose new angles, provide tips for other areas to develop and suggest additional sources to interview.

Reporters and editors can often provide suggestions based on their own similar experiences.

"I had a situation just like that last year. Here's how I tackled it."

Or, "I read a story about that subject in *Newsweek*. Let's see how they approached it."

'Clowns don't belong in the Intensive Care Unit.' So I said, 'Neither do children.' I won that one."

Klein said she has had a few rejections.

"But I don't let them bother me," she said. "My responsibility is not to save the children but to love them and give joy and celebration, not to make them accept it. That's their choice."

Among her success stories was a young man named Christian, who had a chronic heart ailment and was very angry and very lonely.

"For more than a year, we spent time with him, trying to reach him," Klein said. "One day, I taught him a 'mind-reading' card game, and he began to open up.

"He took great pride in fooling one of his real doctors with the card trick. I later told him he was good enough to join CCU, but he said, 'I'd love to, but I can't walk.' I told him, 'Oh, you can walk.' Of course, he hadn't taken a step in eight months. Within two weeks, he had found a pair of tennis shoes and was on his feet as a $2-a-day CCU performer.

"After that he blossomed, and I think it gave him the strength to battle against his mounting medical problems," Klein said. "He died two months after open-heart surgery, but those last few years of his life were full of joy. He didn't die a lonely and angry young man."

Klein said she would miss teaching. She's proud that she proved the "those who can, do; those who can't, teach" myth wrong. But with the opening of the new Children's Hospital at St. Michael's for youngsters with life-threatening and catastrophic illnesses, the need for this service is especially dire.

"After going through a lot of feelings of loss and grief when my best friend's son died a few years ago, this gave me a feeling of celebration and joy, of healing after his loss," Klein said. "Call it a love and caring, God, a higher consciousness—whatever—I want to give my life to this project." ★

MISSION ACCOMPLISHED

This story is unified, coherent and stylized. It begins with a descriptive scene that doesn't just tell us the purpose of the CCU. It shows us.

It is as though we've walked into a hospital room and are witnessing a doctor's finest bedside manner. This anecdote sets up the statement, "For a few minutes, her mind

was off the pain and trauma of being ill."

The scenario also prepares us to meet Janelle Klein, who founded the organization.

The writer knows that the story of the organization is more important than Klein's announcement that she will leave the school at the end of the term.

However, because this story is being written for the student paper, Klein's resignation is an important news fact and must be mentioned early in the article. But we should not mistake this additional piece of information for the theme of the story. The theme should remain focused on the program and the children it serves.

The services are outlined in specific detail. We learn of the successes and failures. It is important to note that abstract statements are followed by concrete examples. Good reporting provides specific examples to support generalizations.

The story of Christian provides a perfect example of the lengths Janelle and her companions went to reach these children.

Again, this anecdote connects a name and face to the program. Remember "60 Minutes" producer Don Hewitt's comment about the difference between subjects and stories? The clown care unit is a subject. A young man named Christian, whose life was made richer by the clown care unit, is a story.

The story then returns to the present, with Janelle saying she'd miss the kids but that pursuing this dream is her destiny. Note the addition of the interpretive, "Those who can, do; those who can't, teach" statement.

Finally, the writer searches for and finds a statement that provides the reader with a sense of resolution.

We are left with a statement—"I want to give my life to this project"—that resolves the situation. This is what Janelle is doing, this is why, here are the results, and this is where she goes from here. The last paragraph leaves us with a sense of satisfaction.

WORKING TOGETHER

Keep in mind that your story will, in all likelihood, be published in the student newspaper and thus read by hundreds if not thousands of your peers as well as two or three English teachers whose day isn't made until they find a comma splice or subject-verb disagreement.

You want the copy to be flawless. But the process must go beyond a search for correct punctuation and proper attribution. Perfectly edited copy is of no consequence unless each story has substance and is unified. Achieving this demands that reporters and editors form a special relationship that goes beyond boss-employee or veteran-novice. Editors and reporters must be equal partners in the pursuit of excellence.

Frankly, it is this special relationship that exists among all members of the staff that makes being a member of a student newspaper so special.

The former editor of the Westlake High School (Austin, Texas) *Featherduster*, provided me with an excellent example of an effective editor-reporter relationship. This relationship is typical of those found on the finest newspaper staffs across the nation.

By LAURA MATTHEWS
Westlake High School, Austin, Texas

THE ONE THING that I tried most to establish as editor was a working relationship with every staffer. This did not mean being the most popular person on staff; people generally do not appreciate being reminded about deadlines even in the sweetest manner ("Bill, if you don't get that story in, I will have to hang you by two toenails instead of three").

Since on *The Featherduster* I edited the majority of the copy before it ever got to the adviser, I was the one who told the reporter that his lead was nonexistent or that he was going to have to interview someone outside the journalism staff for his in-depth story on the student drinking problem.

Obviously, this task demanded patience and courtesy, and the realization that each staffer had a different personality and had to be dealt with accordingly.

I also had to constantly remind myself, however, that the story I was editing was someone else's story, not my own. The writer might not have written the lead I would have written, but he or she had spent time and energy on the story, and deserved to be able to recognize it when it appeared in the paper.

I made a concerted effort, therefore, to edit copy with each writer rather than for them. I found that staffers responded better to someone discussing their paper on a one-to-one basis rather than to getting it back with ambiguous remarks all over it.

Working with staffers in person forced me to use more tact and to listen to their ideas, and the staffers appreciated my taking extra time to sit down with them rather than my rewriting their stories and making editorial decisions without their knowledge or consent.

When I did have to write comments on papers, I tried to illustrate what I was saying in the margins with (hopefully) funny comments and exaggerated examples. The staff as a whole also brainstormed together at the beginning of each issue to come up with story ideas and voted as a group on its stance for the editorial each issue.

Making the effort to involve every member of the staff took more time than any other aspect of my work as editor—many times it would have been easier just to do the job myself, and sometimes I did. That effort to take everyone's ideas seriously, however, gave me some credibility as an editor who cared about something other than her monthly column, and I believe it helped the staff work together as a whole so that no one can ever accuse the *Featherduster* of being an editor-adviser product. ★

EDITING IS THE FIRST THING YOU DO. AND THE LAST

Here's a story about teen crime. Rather than writing about specific incidents and persons, the reporter opened with a statement of the obvious and then followed it with quotes apparently gathered at random.

Teen crime is on the rise. According to the FBI, the rate of violent crime jumped 10 percent last year.

Why do teenagers commit crimes?

"They have bad family values," said Jim.

"They are too materialistic," said Jim's friend.

"There's nothing else to do," said someone else.

Don't confuse editing with proofreading. Editing begins with the identification of a specific theme, the development of a creative angle and the selection of the best quotes, the most interesting anecdotes and the most relevant and important details.

It ends with a careful examination of each word, sentence and paragraph for clarity, conciseness and cohesiveness.

COMPARE & contrast

✓ **AVOID THE 'BIG PICTURE'**

To most people, the holiday season is a time when their family gathers together for a holiday meal, sings holiday songs and opens one another's presents while surrounded by an atmosphere of love.

Unfortunately, this isn't always the case. And the holiday season is particularly difficult for children of divorced parents.

In a few cases, the family will still celebrate together, but many teens will divide their time between the parents.

"I plan to spend half of Christmas day with my mom and the the other half with my dad," junior Jason Kyser said.

✓ **FOCUS ON THE INDIVIDUAL**

Like most Americans, Jason Kyser will celebrate Christmas day with his family.

Both of them.

Like many students who have divorced parents, Jason finds special celebrations such as birthdays and holidays a balancing act.

"My mom and dad get along real well so it's not a big deal," he said. "But I have friends whose parents hate each other, and that really creates a lot of tension. The parents even get into fights over who spent the most on gifts. It gets pretty vicious."

The holiday season is stressful enough on its own, psychologists say. However, dealing with divorced parents and step-parents makes it more difficult.

"I'll spend Christmas at my mom's house," said a senior, who asked not to be identified. "I went to my dad's last year, and I was treated like I wasn't even there. I got the feeling that his new wife thought I was intruding or something. I swore I'd never go back, and I won't."

✓ **THIS LEAD IS TOO GENERAL**

The 26th amendment gave all eligible 18-year-olds the right to vote, but many do not exercise this right. According to Project Vote, a Washington, D.C.-based organization, fewer than 35 percent of 18-year-old eligible voters will cast a ballot in the 1992 election. Overall, 59 percent of eligible voters are expected to exercise their rights in this election.

Students say they don't plan to vote because of apathy. Others say they don't understand the issues.

✓ **REPORT IN TERMS OF PEOPLE**

Sandra Tate rolled her eyes. She'd heard this line before, and she wasn't swallowing it.

"I'd vote if I thought it'd do any good, but these three guys don't impress me one bit," she said. "I don't believe any of them really understand my problems."

Sandra is like a lot of 18-year-olds: old enough to vote but not interested. In fact, only 35 percent of the 18-year-old eligible voters are expected to cast a ballot this year.

"The issues are so complex, it's hard to know what to do," senior Kelly Brennan said. "I listen to the commercials and read the paper, and all it does is confuse me. I don't think any of them are telling the truth. And no matter who wins, I'm still living where I live today, and I'm still paying taxes."

But not all teenagers are so apathetic.

"This country needs a major change, and that's why I'm supporting Ross Perot," senior Jon Richmond said. "I think the LA riots were a message to the country that something's got change."

CHAPTER ELEVEN

SPEAK YOUR MIND

The economic realities of journalism require staffs to occasionally
cover events from a subjective rather than an objective viewpoint.
In special cases, this may be the better approach anyway.

This is how it's supposed to work: newspapers cover the news on pages one or two, and then comment on it on the editorial page. In theory, news and opinion fulfill two distinct and separate purposes. Reporters present the facts without bias. Editors and columnists comment on those facts.

It looks good on paper, but that isn't always how it works. The notion of objectivity in news is more myth than fact. Reporters choose the subject, their sources, which quotes to use, the story's angle and the lead. They select the tone of the story and, through pacing and voice, prompt the audience's response to the story. The process seems anything but objective.

Rather than worrying about objectivity, reporters should be more concerned that they are fair both to their sources and to their readers.

Meanwhile, opinion writers are expected to comment on the news—not make it. But that's a fairy tale too. The economic and educational realities of journalism today almost demand that we rethink how information is presented to our readers. Specifically, rising printing costs are forcing newspapers to publish fewer issues and fewer pages per issue while increasing the percentage of advertising space per issue. The result? More news to cover each issue but less space in which to cover it.

The answer? Abandoning the self-imposed restrictions regarding how news can be presented. In today's publications, news may infiltrate staff editorials and personal opinion columns as well as other traditional forms.

By the time the newspaper is published, an event may be old news. It may make no sense to dwell on who, what, when, where, why and how. But neither can ignoring the event be justified. Thus, opinion articles—staff editorials, feature spreads and personal opinion columns—may serve a news function. Alert staffs passionately debate how to treat issues. They ask, "Does the story deserve news, feature, editorial or column treatment? Which form best serves our readers' needs?"

This should thrill some young writers, who are in journalism for one reason and one reason only. They want their own column. It's understandable. Professional reporters covet their own columns. This may not be true for high school staffs, but it is for the daily beat reporters. Columnists are publicized by the newspaper on billboards and in house ads. Beat reporters aren't. Columnists sometimes make big bucks. Beat reporters rarely do.

So it is reasonable to want to become a columnist as long as you don't delude yourself into thinking that after writing a column for a few years, you will write the Great American novel and then get a TV show, like

Siskel & Ebert, and appear regularly on one of those Sunday morning blabfests or "The Tonight Show."

While it's not likely that you'll be chumming around with Jay Leno any time soon, it is true that the best part of being a columnist is getting your picture in the paper. Regular beat reporters don't unless they're arrested for something.

Mug shots of columnists should reflect the writers' personalities. If you scan the typical daily newspaper editorial pages, you'll see pictures of writers smoking pipes, holding their hands on their chins, looking stern and serious. Other than being unbelievably unphotogenic, what do columnists have in common?
• They are intrigued by people. Basically, they like them.
• They see ordinary events in new and unusual ways.
• They are willing to take chances. They are willing to put themselves on the line, sometimes to reveal something about themselves that is personal and sensitive.
• They consider themselves independent.
• They feel strongly about issues and want— no, need—to share their opinions with others.

Many columnists are intrigued by people, see ordinary events in unusual ways, take chances and consider themselves independent.

So why do some columnists become stars who appear on David Letterman while others are sent back to covering school board meetings after one or two attempts?

Because they have cultivated a clear and unique voice. For some columnists, the voice exploits a God-given talent or skill. Others discover their voice through a lucky break. But a lot of it is work. They have polished their craft to the stage where the average reader can identify the writer merely by reading the lead of the story.

Dave Barry comes to mind. So does

Molly Ivins. I can pick out a Dave Barry or Molly Ivins column from a stack of 1,000 imitators. No one writes about exploding cows and ear hair like Dave. And no one writes about politics with the same sense of sarcasm and bewilderment as Molly.

But that shouldn't stop you from trying. As a beginner, you should read a lot of columnists, find a few you like and learn from them. I didn't say plagiarize them. Instead, find a writer whose style and voice most appeal to you as a reader and who comes closest to representing your own writing style and voice. In other words, don't try to come off like George Will if you have the vocabulary of Jethro Clampett.

Most of the national columnists write either editorial topic, analysis, mood or humor columns. Let's look at each briefly:

EDITORIAL TOPIC COMMENT—
This column presents opinions or ideas about topics that are currently of special interest and have strong personal impact upon the readers. The form has been called the "news-behind-the-news" column.

Often, editorial topic columns mirror the staff editorial in structure: lead that introduces the situation and presents clue to stance; body that explains; conclusion that recaps stance and includes call to action.

However, that need not always be the case. Consider the tongue-in-cheek approach to a serious topic. Also notice how the writer uses two principles of effective news writing: tell a dramatic story and focus on an individual.

By MARK HORVIT
Sharpstown High School, Houston, Texas

SHOWCASE

JOE SAT IN his fourth period class staring at the teacher while his mind slipped further and further into oblivion. The droning voice over the P.A. had interrupted his classes so many times it only sent him deeper on his journey.

Suddenly the lunch bell rang, snapping him out of his trance. He collected his books and walked out into the hall. Though he didn't look like the type, Joe was the worst kind of criminal—he left the campus for lunch. Joe was a smart guy, but he couldn't understand what the problem was. He was 18, old enough to be drafted, but he couldn't go to McDonalds for lunch.

He made his way to the parking lot. He walked past the rest rooms. Since he didn't smoke cigarettes or take drugs, he had no reason to go in. As he walked past a row of lockers, several of them exploded, and smoke filled the hallway. Joe continued, oblivious to the commotion. He was used to this kind of thing. After all, he had been going to public schools for 12 years.

He passed by a classroom where an English teacher attempted to read Shakespeare while students in the back of the class were dipping Skoal and misusing pharmaceutical products. This didn't faze him either.

Walking through the patio, he watched a group of kickers ramming a freshman against a tree. Finally, he reached his car, turned the key in the ignition and headed for the exit. Right before he got there, a white car with flashing red lights blocked his way. The security man got out and walked to Joe's car.

"I hate to do this," he said as a smile crossed his face, "but kid, you're busted."

He paused for a moment, then added, "You know, it's students like you that give public education a bad name." ★

PERSONAL REFLECTION—These columns can be humorous, sentimental, melancholic or any combination thereof. Among the devices good columnists use in writing personal reflection columns are anecdote, exaggeration, puns, narrative, scene development and fictional dialogue.

While columnists may write about themselves or their experiences, the messages these columns carry are universal. When Anna Quindlen of *The New York Times* writes about her mother, she also reminds us of our relationships with our parents. When Bob Greene of the *Chicago Tribune* writes about what it was like to be a geeky high school kid, he reminds his readers, many of whom are well into middle age, what they

were like at 15.

The goal of each personal reflection column is to appeal to the reader's emotions. The reader should feel the writer's rage, sadness, joy or excitement. Consequently, the reader should also feel rage, sadness, joy or excitement.

The next column fulfills that lofty goal even though you do not know Frank. It was part of a newspaper staff's coverage of the death of a young man.

By DEBORAH GEMBARA
West Springfield (Virginia) High School

SHOWCASE

FRANK ABRUZZESE did not walk, he sauntered. He didn't talk, he mumbled. And Frank never just made eye contact, he initiated a stare down.

With Frank, the expression "what you see is what you get" held little meaning because what you saw was a wiry 16-year-old whose 5-1 frame enjoyed reclining back in its seat and allowing his long arms and legs to spill over into the aisles. Frank was a self-described "trifling hoodlum" who wore little expression but a smirk and sported a flat top which emphasized his unusually pale ears and his piercing black-brown eyes.

To understand Frank was to understand that Frank was a casework in contradictions. Understated and often reluctant to even read his own writing, Frank never turned in a column or story without a proud "check out my lead" or "my end is kickin'." One of his dreams included shocking his entire class by being named valedictorian. Nothing Frank ever turned in was less than 100 percent, which often left this editor in awe.

When it came to something he believed, he would not take no for an answer. This was evidenced in his vision for a story on basketball fashions. Although countless editors had rejected Frank's idea, he produced a list of 23 reasons why this would make a great story. Frank wrote that story, and it appears in this issue.

What Frank could not express verbally, he could express on paper. Frank was a mumbler whose closest friends often requested translations. Despite this, his writing was clear, compelling and without trepidation. It was indicative of his own straightforward manner, a manner that on occasion got him into trouble. This disconcerting

THE EDITORIAL IS MORE FORMAL THAN THE COLUMN

Whereas the personal opinion column can take any number of forms, the staff editorial usually consists of a lead that introduces a situation and tells the reader how the staff feels about it. This is followed by the body of the editorial where the staff explains its position.

The other viewpoint is then introduced and rebutted, leading into the conclusion, which restates the staff stance and tells readers specifically what action the staff expects.

In years past, the editorial was usually written in formal English using first person plural.

No longer. Today's editorial emphasizes third person, clear use of logic, a sense of style and hints or suggested solutions.

honesty for his writing allowed people to feel closer to Frank.

This was particularly true of Frank's final column, a tribute to Magic Johnson. In reading and hearing Frank's worship of a hero that appeared larger than life to him, one does not see Frank's lightly mustached upper lip or his dark, close shaven head; one sees the boyish heart that did not want to stop believing in his childhood hero even when it appeared as if the hero had fallen. One sees Frank Abruzzese turning his head and brushing roughly at the tears that threatened to spill onto his cheek as he listens as the last line of his tribute is read in class. "Call me a dreamer. Call me a fool. But I believe in Magic."

Although few outside the newspaper staff had a chance to witness Frank's amazing ability to pour images and reality into anything he wrote, all who knew Frank will not forget his ability to make people laugh. Frank Abruzzese possessed an arsenal of one liners that could take the wind out of anyone's sails. His victims usually received a characteristically mumbled "sorry" following a Frank attack.

Frank would come over to my house and I would ask him to take off his shoes before coming into my house. Frank would invariably be dressed in his Bulls jacket, a T-shirt depicting Michael Jordan, baggy jeans and black hightops. "Come on Frank," I'd say, "take off your shoes," only to hear, "No way man, someone's gonna steal them." My retort would always be, "Yeah Frank, my dad's in the closet waiting to make off with your shoes."

The shoes did come off but not without some warnings from Frank that I was "gonna need oxygen" once I smelled his feet. On the last time Frank came over though, he took off his shoes, flashed me a cheesy grin and proudly stated "I came prepared. I got me some new socks."

As hard as I try, I think it will be a long time before I enjoy another Thanksgiving. For many years to come, Thanksgiving will remind me of the wake and funeral of a 16-year-old boy, one who would never see his high school graduation, his senior prom or his next birthday.

I find only one thing more horrifying than the fact that Frank Abruzzese's life would know only 16 years. That is that Frank Abruzzese would become a part of my past, a memory. Never again would he anger me to the point of violence and slip in a quiet "sorry." Never again would we talk about the direction of his love life, and never again would I watch him, like a little boy, dissolve into laughter. ★

VARIETY—And then, there's everything else, which out of convenience, I've lumped into one category called "variety." These columns appear in the form of a list, a letter to my parents, the lyrics of a song . . . whatever.

The following column was written by a 13-year-old at a Houston-area junior high school. I have long since misplaced her name or even the name of the school. But I still love this column.

I HAVE OFTEN thought how boring life would be if I didn't have an older sister. In addition to having twice as many clothes as I normally would, I also get to bug her.

Bugging an older sister isn't simple. It takes skill, creativity, talent and the ability to look innocent when you get caught in the act. You must be cunning, devious and, above all, unmerciful. If you are just a beginner, here are a few tips to get you started:

1. When a boy calls and you answer the phone, tell him she's using the bathroom.

2. Put soap on her toothbrush.

3. Tell her dates when they come to pick her up that she even gargled for him.

4. Call her boyfriend by her previous boyfriend's name. Say "oops" and look innocent.

5. When she is on the phone, ask her if she knows she has a pimple on her cheek. Dodge the pillow she throws at you.

6. Ask her boyfriend how much he's going to spend on her at Christmas. Tell him your family thought her last boyfriend was cheap.

7. Tell your sister her boyfriend has hairy fingers.

8. Offer her peanut butter and bologna sandwiches when she's sick.

9. Tell her scientists have made an amazing new discovery that kissing guys will make hair grow out of your ears.

10. Show everyone the baby picture of her naked on a rug.

11. Ask her if her jeans are supposed to be that tight.

12. Tell her she has panty bulge when she doesn't.

These are just a few things to get you started. Once you practice, you'll find it's easy to get the hang of it. Just remember to look innocent and deny everything. When you grow up, you'll have many funny times to look back on and laugh at. It's not bad having an older sister at all—it's fun if you just go about it the right way. ★

WRITING THE PERSONAL OPINION COLUMN

- #### REPORT FIRST.

  Write second. Interviewing and observing are the most important elements of column writing. Get people to talk and use their anecdotes in your columns.

- #### TAKE RISKS

  Be willing to take risks with your writing but never with the facts.

- #### MAKE PEOPLE THINK.

  Express an opinion that will generate discussion. Take a stance on something of importance. Don't be so vague that you merely state the obvious. Make certain the column is of consequence, which means you must pay attention both to the substance of the subject and to the treatment of the subject. This one isn't.

TEENAGERS HAVE always been interested in clothes, and as the years go by, fashions have changed. No one wears Nehru jackets any more. So far this year, the most popular colors are mustard and purple. Floral and hyper-color shirts are very popular, as are Girbaud, Guess, Blue Zone and Pepe Company jeans.

Teenagers are also picky about how they wear their hair. Lots of guys are cutting their hair with a mushroom style. Girls are starting to go with the natural look.

As one walks the halls throughout the year, one will see guys and girls wearing different brands of clothes and wearing their hair in different styles, but in the end, everyone wears his or her own style. That's what makes us individuals! ★

- #### BE PROVOCATIVE.

ABORTION IS a very complex issue that the United States Supreme Court may decide this fall. Many people think abortion is murder and are willing to protest in front of clinics and even be arrested.

Meanwhile, others believe that it is the right of the woman to control her own body and that if abortion is outlawed, it will force women to rely on back-alley doctors in unsanitary conditions.

Both sides seem to have a valid point. No one really wants to see a baby aborted, but should we make abortion illegal?

It doesn't look like either side is listening to the other, and this is a battle that may be fought in the courts and legislative chambers for years as well as on the daytime talk shows.

Maybe it's time you gave this some attention. Abortion: murder or freedom? Think about it. ★

- #### DON'T CHEERLEAD.

WHAT IS SCHOOL spirit? Webster has 15 definitions of spirit, but none of them seem to apply to our school. School spirit is important for a school. If a school has spirit, it can back its team on to victory. A school with students ready to yell can help a team win.

But such was not the case last week. The Tigers lost because of the lack of school spirit. And some students have the nerve to ask, "What's wrong with the team?"

There's nothing wrong with the team that a little support couldn't cure. We have an explosive group of running backs, a punishing defense and a great coach.

So you may ask, "Why have we lost our first six games if they're so good?" Before we can totally blame the team, other questions must be asked: How many fans helped or hurt the team? How many games have you attended? Do you stay for the entire pep rally? How many times have you given a word of encouragement instead of a negative word after a loss?

Blaming the players doesn't help anything. If a team is to do well, it's going to need more than great athletes. It's time students pulled together to support the team. Maybe this way, we won't

HOW AN EDITORIAL DIFFERS FROM A PERSONAL OPINION COLUMN

So what's the difference between an editorial and a personal opinion column? Well, imagine that Mark Horvit's column (page 120) on the closed campus had been a staff editorial instead. It might have been written like this:

The school board should reconsider its closed campus policy. Most students will accept the responsibility of greater freedom, and those who do not should be punished accordingly.

A school should not deprive all students of a privilege simply because a few might abuse the privilege.

Plenty of fast-food restaurants exist within five minutes of the school so getting off campus and back in time for classes should pose no problems. And many students need these few minutes away from campus to relax.

Open campuses work for at least five other high schools in the area. It's past time to make them a reality here too.

lose our last four games.

And maybe Webster will include a 16th definition of spirit: Lincoln High School! ★

•DON'T CHAT WITH THE READER.

MAJOR YUK

HELLO ONE and all, and welcome back to Huskyland. It's time to get back to the busy schedule of attending school at 8 o'clock and working your way through the day. No more lying around the pool to get a suntan. Instead, it's sitting in a desk, taking notes, listening to lectures and cracking the books.

School is a lot of work, but it can be a blast too. School is what you make it. It's all up to you.

As your monthly columnist, I hope to be discussing many items of importance this year. This month, let's begin by discussing extracurricular activities. Many people don't get involved because everything is reserved for the so-called popular people. NOT! Maybe these popular people are the ones who are involved, but how do you think they got to be popular in the first place?

All of the extracurricular activities are for you so don't think it's always the popular people who get selected. You are only letting yourself down and maybe others if you don't try out.

Well, that's it for this month. See you next time. And remember, get involved and you will be the one who gets the praise and the glory. You may even become popular too! Like me! ★

• LOOK FOR AN INTERESTING ANGLE.

What facts might have been overlooked? New Yorker Jimmy Breslin won the Pulitzer Prize in the 1960s for political commentary. One of his finest efforts dealt with the assassination of President John F. Kennedy. But he approached the story from a different angle. While the world's media assembled outside the rotunda of the Capitol in preparation for the burial, Breslin stood in the cold, talking to the man who dug the grave. While others covered the global implications, Breslin reported what Kennedy's death meant to one man—a man not much different from all of us.

• LOOK FOR IRONY OR SYMBOLISM.

In one of her short stories, novelist Joan Didion wrote about the 1968 riots in Berkeley, California. She found irony in the fact that several members of the Black Panthers—a radical, anarchist group—were also enrolled in a local hospital health plan.

• TARGET AN AUDIENCE.

For example, Erma Bombeck has had a long and successful career writing for and about middle-class suburban housewives.

At the same time, remember that columnists best succeed when they reach beyond members of their own clubs or cliques. The best columns speak to all students—not only athletes, honors students or musicians—and deal with universal themes and subjects. A column about the "date from hell" will be enjoyed by the National Merit scholars as well as the so-called "at risk" students if it is clever, insightful and realistic.

• DEVELOP A VOICE.

Your column should reflect your personality. What can we tell about Richard Kirkwood from the following column?

SHOWCASE

By RICHARD KIRKWOOD
Northside HS, Roanoke, Virginia

WELL, THE YEAR is teetering on the brink of summer, and seniors all across the land are dancing in the streets at the thought of finally leaving high school. This is the wrong attitude. I know most of you are thinking, "Well it's my last year and then it's Good-bye Gulag!"

Remember, with fall comes college. Let's capitalize it: College. The applications you've already filled out have probably given you some idea of what's in store for you, with questions like:
1. What's your name?
2. What're your grades like?
3. Staple check here.

After a year at college I have become a much more stable and calm human being, and I have reached this state through a carefully kept college student secret of inner bliss: wrecking bathrooms.

If you are pushed down to the wire on a term paper, or exams are hemming you in, or if you've been arrested or any of a thousand common stress points for college students, there is nothing more relaxing than finding a good bathroom and wrecking it. Paper towel dispensers are easy marks and can be removed with little effort, but wall-partitions pose some difficulties and should be saved for events such as expulsion or flunking a course. Warning: Do not attempt to uproot major plumbing unless you are in good health and wearing old clothing.

Actually, anyone can deal with college simply by following a few guidelines:

Do not eat in college cafeterias. Once or twice may not cause any permanent damage, but any more than that and your stomach lining is grass and reheated fish-sticks are the lawnmower. If you insist on following this dangerous practice, memorize the route to the infirmary and take up jogging.

Order pizza frequently.

Do not borrow money from other students! (What are parents for, huh?)

Keep up with your schedule. This isn't too hard. One of the greatest things about college is that you have time between your classes! No tardy bells here! Between any two given classes you can have time to stop, walk around, enjoy the beauties of nature, get a soft drink, play a game of pinball, look at your watch and think "Gosh, I'm late," and then go order pizza.

Of course, you should always be punctual and attend classes. There is no excuse for missing classes, except for these:

a. You're sick.
b. You're dead.
c. It's really a nice day.
d. The pizza you ordered in the last paragraph hasn't arrived, and it would really be quite rude to go off before it comes—and then you'd better eat it before other ravenous college students notice and pounce on it, by which time you'd only get to class in time to hear: "Test on Friday. Class dismissed."

Other guidelines: Always attend exams, or they'll count off; checks for teachers' bribes must be made out to "cash"; clean out your dorm rooms if EPA inspection seems imminent; attend poetry readings for free food.

Sure, it's a lot to remember, but it'll be worth it. Remember, college is your ticket to better jobs, a higher life-style, lasting friendships. It also gives you the opportunity to revisit your old high school, look around at the new students, America's future and the pride of the country, and, with a tear in your eye, laugh hysterically. ★

Traditionally, these columns would appear on the editorial page. So forget tradition. Comment need not be confined to the opinion page. The page one coverage of a news event or issue may take the form of an opinion, or at least a free-form writing style that allows the reporter to interpret an event, issue or trend in a highly subjective manner.

The Glenbard East (Illinois) staff covered the debate surrounding the release of Spike Lee's movie, *Malcolm X*. In addition to a review of the movie, one editor wrote an article about how the film reflects a trend of movies that transcend the barriers of cinema and become social statements. This alone was a provocative issue for a student journalist.

Accompanying the article was a sidebar column examining the commercialization of Malcolm X's legacy. The free-form writing style uses both news and opinion elements.

SHOWCASE

By JEFF SARMIENTO
Glenbard East (Illinois) High School

X. NEVER IN history has the 24th letter in the alphabet stirred up as much of a following as it has in today's pop culture.

From the seemingly ubiquitous X-cap to the "By any means necessary" portrait T-shirts, a fashion statement has emerged from a 1960s social statement.

Before the filming of the much-hyped Spike Lee movie, Lee and other celebrities such as Michael Jordan began sporting the X-cap to popularize a fad that had already festered in Chicago. The X pays tribute to Malcolm X, a black civil rights activist of Martin Luther King's day. Malcolm led a militaristic black Muslim movement and became a martyr for his people.

This symbol of black pride caught on and gained popularity among urban youth. X jackets, T-shirts and boxer shorts find a place in sports-wear and fashion wear stores.

The average shopper is likely to see as many

FIVE WAYS TO CHOKE ON YOUR OWN WORDS

- Gossip. Go ahead. Try to slip something past the adviser. There are lots of unemployed lawyers out there looking for an easy bundle.
- Slang. I can see on the horizon a ton of Beavis and Butthead columns. *"Do you have school spirit? You should. School spirit is cool. NOT!"*
- Play on words that border on profanity such as "bull sheet" and "jock shorts." Grow up.
- References to bodily functions. We don't want to hear about them.
- Religious comments, especially those that attempt to promote or inculcate religion. It's not the purpose of the student newspaper to save souls. Nor should it belittle religious convictions.

different styles of X-caps as Sox caps. The colors of the apparel usually include black and white, shades easily matched with nearly everything in urban fashion.

Street wear trends drift out of the city and eventually land in affluent suburbia, where teens exploit it.

"The X fashion started when Cross Colours got popular over the summer," senior Waleep Burrell said. "You can find X stuff at stores such as Journeys."

Students understand that there is more to X wear than black and white stitching, and they maintain the image of their hero.

"I think they show pride in their heritage," freshman Reyes Moreno said.

"People who don't know about Malcolm should quit perpetrating," said junior Ty Cockrell, who owns a pair of X earrings as well as several T-shirts.

However, the "statement" has lost some of its meaning because a tribute to the activist has faded into another way to make a buck.

"I think that the T-shirt designers make them half for the message and half for the profit," freshman Jon Woodall said.

"The designers should put the profits into helping the homeless and not just put it in their pockets," Burrell said. "I know that's what Malcolm would do with the money."

Junior Fred Hall, who refrains from wearing X paraphernalia, claims that people do not understand Malcolm X enough to pay tribute.

"People disrespect him when I see them tipping their caps left or right and banging with them," he said.

Hall suggested that students should spend their time finding leaders in their own generation instead of wearing out the leaders of another time.

"Malcolm was a bold leader and he did what he did, but it's over," Hall said.

Burrell thinks differently. "We do have good black leaders who serve as role models, such as Michael Jordan and Jesse Jackson," he said.

Others think that the X phenomenon is simply a passing fad.

"It's the same as the African necklaces people wore two years ago," sophomore Fawne Hall said.

However, the X-wear symbolizes a newly found black pride. Burrell sports a thick X medallion around his neck. "I'm proud to wear it because kids can look to see what I stand for," he said.

The statement also extends across color lines as non-black students have also caught on to X-fashion.

"It bothered me at first," Burrell said, "but it's their choice to wear what they want."

Woodall suggests it is not a racial issue. "It's just a letter on a piece of clothing."

Relating the X craze to the yearly demand for the latest Air Jordan shoes, freshman Ivin Dionte said, "It's more of a fashion statement. Once something new comes in, X will play out." ★

WRITING REVIEWS

My 10-year-old daughter and I have an agreement. If I'll shell out $6 for her to see a movie, she'll say it was awesome. *Jurassic Park* and *Ernest Saves Christmas* were equally awesome in her opinion. This says a lot more about 10-year-olds than it does about either movie.

High school students are a little like this. After shelling out a week's pay for a dinner date or concert ticket, students expect the experience to be awesome, and, at least in terms of concerts, as long as the band lays on the requisite amount of smoke and lasers and cranks out the maximum level of sound, it usually is, at least by teen-age standards.

At least, that's the impression I get from reading the concert reviews in student newspapers. Students have limited funds so they carefully spend their money on the events they really want to see. Given that they can afford to see only so many concerts, teens are likely to select the ones they expect to most enjoy. The concert reviews reflect this reality, and I don't have a problem with their verdicts.

But I do have a problem with the tendency to rehash the program rather critique the concert. Instead of reviewing the performance, young critics too often recite the order in which the songs were played and what the performers were wearing. How often do we need to hear that rock and roll musicians wear ripped blue jeans and spandex? How surprised can we be that the show included lasers and smoke? Or three encores?

Evaluate the performance in context to the entertainer's career and hype. A U2 concert will generate phenomenal publicity. Was the performance equal to the hype? If so, why? If not, why? Don't just rehash the play list.

The same is true for movie reviews. Too many provide little more information than is available in the final credits. For example:

JEAN CLAUDE Van Damme's *Hard Target* is probably his best movie since *Blood Sport*.

Van Damme plays a Cajun veteran who wanders around New Orleans. He rescues a girl from thugs, and action starts. He is pulled into an operation where people pay to hunt humans. When one of Van Damme's homeless veteran friends is killed, the hunt begins.

Like all of his movies, *Hard Target* is full of action scenes, fighting, special effects and stunts. It's a must-see for action movie fans. ★

Has the typical Jean Claude Van Damme fan learned anything from this review? Probably not. Van Damme isn't likely to be making romantic comedies. The writer recommended the movie, but we have no idea what he liked about it.

Now, compare this review of *Hard Target* to the following review:

By JASON HAWVER
Carrollton (Texas) High School

TAKE THE ACTION of Arnold Schwarzenegger's *Terminator* movies. Add the futuristic aspects of Harrison Ford's *Blade Runner*. Put them in a blender. Turn it on high, and what would you get? Probably a bloody mess, which is one way to describe Sylvester Stallone's violent new sci-fi adventure film, *Demolition Man*.

While some parts of this film by Marco Brambilla are entertaining, *Demolition Man* is a movie laden with problems.

First, Mr. Brambilla has an almost amateurish style of directing, using rapidly shifting camera angles and flashing lights in a futile attempt to build suspense.

Second, Wesley Snipes (*Jungle Fever, Passenger 57*) gives a completely unbelievable performance as the psychopathic Simon Phoenix, a villain so laughably over the top that he completely fails to inspire any fear.

My final problem with *Demolition Man* is the plot. A wrongly convicted cop, John Spartan (played surprisingly well by Mr. Stallone) is taken out of his cryogenic prison to solve a special case.

This essential plot is virtually identical to the basic premise of author William (Captain Kirk) Shatner's Tek novels. Mr. Shatner may have grounds for a plagiarism suit.

The most enjoyable aspect of this film is its comic elements. *Demolition Man*'s vision of the future is often humorous and sometimes slapstickish. Also, Spartan's relationship with his new partner (excellently portrayed by Sandra Bullock) and the world of 2032 in general will leave you laughing.

The special effects are also superb. But these elements don't make *Demolition Man* worth the price of admission. A definite "wait-till-it-comes-out-on-video" movie. ★

Why does this review succeed where the other failed? First, it is obvious Jason Hawver knows a lot about science-fiction movies and books, and this knowledge allows him to compare and contrast the movie to others in the genre. Bluntly speaking, he is a credible authority on the subject.

Second, the review is written with great style and confidence. He doesn't rely on catchy one-liners or clichés. It's authoritative and legitimate without being pedantic or preachy.

A review—whether of a book, film, album or restaurant—should attempt to convey an honest and fair criticism, pro or con. This criticism is gained through accurate observation and appropriate reporting. In almost all cases, this reporting involves listening, reading or viewing the performer's full body of work. It isn't fair to either reader or performer to judge the performance in a vacuum. So if you're reviewing the latest John Grisham novel, tell the reader how it compares to his earlier books as well as to

MORE WAYS TO CHOKE ON YOUR OWN WORDS

• Comments that poke fun at an individual's disabilities, infirmities or physical conditions.

• Columns that call attention to themselves, such as the "Letters to me" when columnists answer letters so that they'll have the last word on the subject.

• Rip-offs, such as imitations of Ann Landers or Dr. Ruth.

• Horoscopes unless you can provide specific information such as winning lottery numbers.

• Comments that are intended to offend. One student, in what was supposed to be an analysis of the U. S. policy in Somalia, described starving Africans as looking like "chocolate-covered skeletons." Thankfully, the obnoxious statement never appeared in print.

suspense novels of other writers?

If you're reviewing the latest Paul McCartney album, how does it compare to his music when he was a member of the Beatles or Wings? How does it compare to his most recent work? Consider this review, written several years ago by a 15-year-old, of McCartney's album *Pipes of Peace*:

YOU GUESSED IT: *Pipes of Peace* is a spotless collection of well-rehearsed melodies and vocals from a qualified expert. Unfortunately, Paul McCartney also knows how to overdo his pop.

Sure, there are some good songs on this record, but *Pipes of Peace* sounds more like a financial proposal than a musical work. The two duets with Michael Jackson are competent, and "Keep Under Cover" is great, but songs like the sappy "So Bad" shouldn't ever have made it past the "flip-side-of-a-single" phase. Last year's *Tug of War* was much better, but the superstar's effort this time around makes the listener feel as if he's drinking a tall glass of maple syrup. ★

The author, David Arnold of Houston, combines elements of feature and opinion writing. The review is a punchy, powerful and fair.

To become a critic rather than simply a writer, heed these additional tips on writing reviews:

• Avoid the first person singular. Keep yourself out of the article. Rather than "I enjoyed the concert," write "The concert was superb." And explain why.

• Don't rely on quotes from other publications. In particular, don't pilfer direct quotes or critical comments from magazines. Students often lift quotes from *Rolling Stone* or *People*.

• Make certain the review carries a byline and is clearly labeled as opinion.

• Don't try to impress the reader with your knowledge of jargon. Write for the average reader, not the studio president or movie director. Be considerate of those not familiar with the work or the jargon.

• Don't show-off your knowledge of cultural esoterica. In other words, don't compare Steven Seagal's latest romper-stomper to those of a little-known 1950s Japanese film director.

• Avoid clichés, such as "I laughed. I cried. I experienced the full range of human emotion. I was completely carried away . . . ."

• Work to convince the reader. Make the reader feel, "Hey, that's how I felt." Even if readers disagree with you, they should respect your point of view and opinions.

Note how the following column incorporates all of these suggestions to create a convincing argument.

By LAUREN JAGNOW
Glenbard East (Illinois) High School

SHOWCASE

GENGHIS KHAN, notorious conqueror of Asia, has gone into the restaurant business.

Well, not really. However, the Mongolian restaurant at 2942 S. Finley Road in Downers Grove, has chosen to name its establishment after the most famous Mongolian who ever lived.

Though you may not expect hospitality from a restaurant named after a barbarian, Genghis Kahn offers exotic, inexpensive food and quality service as well as a unique atmosphere.

The food is served buffet style with a variety of meats, noodles and vegetables that are stir-fried before your eyes by two skilled chefs using long wooden sticks to flip and stir the food on a sizzling grill.

Mongolian cuisine differs from Chinese food in that it is considerably spicier. A seemingly innocent plate of noodles and beef should be eaten with a glass of water close at hand.

Not all the food is spicy though. Combinations such as pork with pineapple chunks and peanuts taste sweet and juicy.

There is enough variety on the buffet table that you can create mild entrees or those that will generate tears. The choice makes it possible for all diners to please their palates.

There is also a prepared food buffet that offers spicy Sesame beef and fresh seafood such as Alaskan crab legs and jumbo shrimp as well as rice, stir-fried vegetables and slightly sour but tasty Mongolian bread.

The atmosphere at Genghis Kahn is relaxing and pleasant.

Careful though, you could become hypnotized if you stare for too long at the two panes of water filled with moving bubbles.

With a pot of tea in front of you and a plate of appetizers ranging from pickled cucumbers to egg rolls, your meal at Genghis Kahn is like eating with Genghis Kahn himself.

Only you won't have to worry about getting clubbed during dessert. ★

It is important to distinguish between the staff editorial and the personal opinion column. The staff editorial stands as the statement of the newspaper as an institution—not that of the individual writer.

While the purpose of the staff editorial may be the same as the personal opinion column —that is, to praise, criticize, defend, endorse, etc.—the style is different. In most cases, the staff editorial is written in formal English. Conjunctions and sentence fragments (a.k.a. "minor sentences" when used for stylistic or rhetorical effect) are avoided.

In many cases, the staff editorial follows a specific formula:

- introduction of problem
- statement of staff stance
- supporting evidence for staff stance
- introduction of alternate point of view
- rebuttal of alternate point of view
- summary remarks
- call to action

This formula is much too rigid for personal approaches. While it's probable that staffs are covering news with personal columns rather than with inverted pyramid stories because of time and space restraints, it's equally probable that staffs are choosing the personal writing because it allows writers to provide new insights and to tell the story in a dramatic way. The inverted pyramid prohibits reporters from editorializing. Occasionally, this prohibition sucks the life out of a story. Personal writing is an effective way to convey the emotions of the news.

While this style allows the reporter to break a few of the traditional rules of news style, it does not allow the reporter to do a lazy or flippant job of gathering information. Quite the contrary. The personal approach requires an even greater attention to detail and context. Anything short of a concentrated effort can lead to charges that the coverage is unfair, biased or irresponsible.

While the writing of the column or personal opinion feature may look easy, it is actually more difficult and works best when handled by students who have had experience reporting and using more traditional forms.

FIND THE PERFECT VOICE

No one sings like Frank Sinatra, not even Harry whatshisname? Old Blue Eyes has a voice and a style all his own. The same may be true for a few of the more contemporary singers, although I haven't heard enough of the current crop of teen heart-throbs to name names.

Like Sinatra, successful columnists have a voice and a style all their own. It is important to note the difference between voice and style. Voice is the tone of your writing. In one article, your voice can be angry or sarcastic; in another, nostalgic or sentimental.

Style is the composite of content, diction, structure and mechanics. It is not something you can teach apart from the other elements. It is based on individual choices in terms of words, rhythms, constructions and forms of expression characteristic to the writer. It gives the writing energy, emotion and individuality.

How can you develop your own voice? First, by realizing that when it comes to writing columns, there are no etched-in-stone rules.

Voice allows the reader to hear an individual human speak from the page—to

I'M GOING TO WRITE A LITTLE LETTER . . .

I love to read the letters to the editor. Unlike talk radio, the opinions expressed usually reflect a high degree of knowledge, wisdom and reflection. This is as it should be.

You should encourage readers to write to the publication. Print in every issue of the newspaper the policy for accepting letters. The policy should deal with length, deadlines and what may and may not be printed.

At the same time, you must take equal pains to make certain that any letter published is authentic and legally protected. Every letter must be signed, and it is wise to check personally with individuals to guarantee that signatures are not fakes.

Finally, letters must be free of content that might be libelous, obscene, slanderous or potentially disruptive of the educational process.

Remember: If it's printed in your newspaper, you're responsible for it.

establish confidentiality between the writer and the reader. It sets the illusion of a private conversation with the writer.

As mentioned previously, each writer has a number of voices. Consider how you speak differently to your parents when you're trying to explain why you're 30 minutes past curfew and when you're insisting that you cannot baby-sit your younger sister. The way writers use voice tells the reader how they feel about a topic. This succeeds so long as the writer is honest, neither too cute, too sophisticated or too sentimental. Honesty alone—not superficiality and not artificiality—convinces.

Though hard-and-fast rules on writing don't exist, you can learn from time-tested advice:

• BE CORRECT.

Get the story right both in terms of detail and context. Look for and capture the significant detail, the revealing anecdote and the prevailing mood. Make certain the tone and style of the story match the mood. Finally, edit closely so that the story is structurally, mechanically and stylistically correct.

In particular, pay attention to verb tense and parallel structures. For example:

WEAK: After leading cheers at the homecoming pep rally, senior Pearly White met her boyfriend in the parking lot, kisses him on the lips and then blushed while her friends squeal and swooned.

Note the tense inconsistency (see changes in italics).

BETTER: After leading cheers at the homecoming pep rally, senior Pearly White *met* her boyfriend in the parking lot, *kissed* him on the lips and then *blushed* while her friends *squealed* and *swooned*.

Another common problem is consistent point of view. For example:

WEAK: Swimming instructors must be patient if they work with children. You must acknowledge that some children have never swum before, and you must acclimate children to the water.

BETTER: Swimming instructors must be patient if they work with children. *Instructors* must acknowledge that some children have never swum before, and *they* must acclimate children to the water.

• USE YOUR OWN WORDS.

If you're describing Mortal Kombat, don't write: *Imbued with a veritable plethora of emotion, Joe depressed the button, thereby eliminating his video adversary.*

• BE CONCISE.

WEAK: The car we were looking for was a van that we planned to use on our vacation.

BETTER: We searched for a van to use on our vacation.

WEAK: The 6-11 center lowered his head and walked into the journalism classroom.

BETTER: The 6-11 center ducked into the journalism lab.

• KEEP IT SIMPLE.

A forceful sentence relies on a subject, a verb and an object. But additional phrases and clauses often add helpful details. The length is unimportant as long as each sentence is straightforward and clear.

• USE DYNAMIC NOUNS AND VERBS.

Any time you have a choice among words, choose the one with the narrowest meaning. The power of your writing will come from the ability of your words to evoke images and emotions.

WEAK: I could tell by the funny look on her face that she was mad.

BETTER: I could tell she was mad by the way her face turned blood red and the veins in her forehead stretched like a cheap pair of double-knit slacks. The meat cleaver that she clutched as she shrieked, "Prepare to meet thy doom!" was a dead giveaway too.

• SPICE IT UP.

The writing must have rhythm. Sometimes it should gallop. Other times it should trot. The pace varies according to the subject and the mood. Political differences aside, from whom would you rather hear a speech: Jesse Jackson or Al Gore?

While I admire Mr. Gore, he's a bit of a technocrat and a stiff. Mr. Jackson, on the other hand, knows how to give a speech. He peppers his speeches with anecdotes. He knows how to use colorful touches such as hyperbole, alliteration, allusion and personification. His "Keep hope alive" speech sent shivers down my spine.

Jackson's speeches are a reflection of his personality. Unfortunately for Mr. Gore, the same cannot be said for him.

Consider the difference in the two excerpts from the 1992 Democratic National Convention:

Mr. Gore: "We are part of something much larger than ourselves. All of us are capable of imagining. And, my friends, if you look up for a moment from the rush of your daily lives, you will hear the quiet voices of your country crying out for help. You will see your reflection in the weary eyes of those who are losing hope in America. And you will see that our democracy is lying there in the gutter waiting for us to give it a second breath of life."

While this prose is nice, it's no match for the power of this excerpt from Jackson's speech:

WE HAVE A president who has traveled the world, but has never been to Hamlet, North Carolina. Yet we must not overlook Hamlet.

It was there that 25 workers died in a fire at Imperial Foods, more women than men, more white than black. They worked making chicken parts in vats heated to 400 degrees, with few windows and no fans. The owners locked the doors on the outside. The workers died trapped by economic desperation and oppressive work laws.

One woman came up to me after the fire.

She said, "I want to work. I don't want to go on welfare. I have three children and no husband. We pluck 90 wings a minute. Now I can't bend my wrist, I got the carpel thing. Then when we're hurt, they fire us—and we have no health insurance and no union to help us. We can't get another job because we're crippled so they put us on welfare and call us lazy."

I said you are not lazy, and you are not alone.

Her friend, a white woman came up and said:

"I'm seven months pregnant. We stand in two inches of water with two five-minute bathroom breaks. Sometimes we can't hold our water, and then our bowels, and we faint."

We wept together.

If we keep Hamlet in our hearts and before our eyes, we will act to empower working people. We will protect the right to organize and to strike. We will empower workers to enforce health and safety laws. We will provide a national health care system, a minimum wage sufficient to bring workers out of poverty, paid parental leave. We must build a movement for economic justice across the land." ★

No doubt, the power of this statement comes not only from the writing but from Mr. Jackson's delivery. Still, I believe its ultimate power stems from the fact that it focuses on specific people rather than political rhetoric and speaks to the heart and to the mind.

• BREAK THE RULES.

Occasionally. And know why you're breaking them. Good writers break rules to achieve a stylistic or rhetorical effect.

To vary your rhythm, use a sentence fragment occasionally. I'm not suggesting that you should omit a noun or a verb arbitrarily. But there are times when a sentence fragment works quite well. Like right now.

And don't get too hung up on mechanics. Too many teachers worry about mechanics to the exclusion of the more important content. Concentrate first on what you have to say. Worry second about whether you dotted all the i's and crossed all the t's. Your editors and adviser will help you with this.

BUT WHAT IF NO ONE WRITES?

Okay. So no one writes you a letter. Big deal. If the readers won't come to you, then go to them by conducting surveys and printing the student comments.

• You must ask an intelligent question about an important issue or event. "What is your favorite color?" doesn't qualify.

Many staffs connect the survey to the lead editorial.

• Carefully word the question so that students can understand it and respond to it.

• Avoid asking more than three questions per survey. The first should be a warm-up question to help readers begin thinking about the real questions you expect to use.

• If you want 10 or 12 usable responses to print, you need to survey at least 100-200 persons.

• Print only those comments that lend insight and information to the issue at hand.

• MATCH YOUR TONE TO YOUR PURPOSE.

If you're writing about a serious topic, take a serious approach. If you're writing about something odd or funny, take a witty or satirical approach.

Master the use of words. Find new and more precise words with which you're comfortable. But if you want to say "help," don't say "succor." If you want to say "agree," don't say "concur." If you mean "clear," don't write "lucid."

In addition, avoid colloquialisms, slang, jargon and clichés. Down South, we like to say "I'm fixing" when we mean "I am about to." For example: "I'm *fixing* to watch the Cowboys beat the Redskins like a stepchild."

The cliché "beat 'em like a stepchild" always sends the politically correct crowd through the roof, but that's not reason enough to use it. Avoid clichés. Like the plague.

• BE PRECISE.

Say what you mean, and mean what you say. In one column, a young woman was writing about her experience as a teen mother. In what was otherwise a thoughtful and poignant column, she wrote, "I got pregnant in December *while I was playing basketball.*"

I've heard of man-to-man defense, but that's going too far.

Use only relevant information and in a logical sequence.

WEAK: Coach Linda Sullivan, who is a deaconess at the First Baptist Church, said the team is not in the same class as the top-ranked Tigers, whom they play Thursday night.

Now, what does the fact that she is a deaconess at the church have to do with her predictions about the Thursday night game?

It might be possible to use the fact that she is a deaconess as part of a play on words.

BETTER: Coach Linda Sullivan, who is a deaconess at the First Baptist Church, said the team doesn't have a prayer against the top-ranked Tigers Thursday night.

• KEEP IT SHORT.

Focus on a narrow topic. Write about people, not subjects. If you write about an issue, do so in terms of people. Rather than a column that preaches on the evils of cigarette smoking, write one that analyzes or interprets the actions of a person who is trying to help teens kick the habit.

It bears repeating: Be true to yourself. Stretch your talents. Explore. Take risks. But don't try to be someone you're not.

• READ.

I realize that "dictate" is a strong word, but you can never expect to become a competent writer unless you read extensively. Your development of diction and your understanding of rhythm can come only from reading widely and deeply. Then, compare your columns against the best you can find. Begin with those on the next two pages.

ABSENCE MAKES LOVE GROW STRONGER

By CLARE BUNDY
Duncanville (Texas) High School

"CLARE!"

Her voice filters through two insulated walls, three doors and a mirror.

And it's still loud enough to abuse my ears above the running shower water which, five seconds ago, was blissfully peaceful.

I turn off the water.

"What?" I scream back.

"Come HERE!"

I trudge into the hall from the bathroom, dripping all over our 'universal rust' carpet.

Entering my room, I sight the source of the formidable voice. Lillian.

Lillian is half harpee, half vulture. Lillian is angry. Lillian is my 18-year-old sister.

I peer over her shoulder to see what the reason for her wrath is.

An eyeshadow applicator.

She fingers the spongy end, whips around and wipes her hand on my white terry cloth robe.

"That's BLACK, Clare!"

"Thank you. You're very observant, Lil."

"I get out a *special applicator* every morning so you won't use it for that black crap you put on your eyes, and what do you do? You *use* it, and now it's black, too! You *know* I only use brown!"

And she storms out of the room, leaving me with ringing ears and a severe case of the "So what's!"

I return to the bathroom to blow-dry my hair. Lil's leaning over the sink, using a new applicator on her eyes. I roll mine, and they automatically stop at a light pink scar on her tanned back; an arc starting up near her left shoulder and trailing off at her right shoulder blade.

My brief anger at being verbally abused disappears, and I flash her my brief "Good-morning-to-you" smile.

I don't know what the scar means to her. I've never asked. Not that we don't talk; many a night she's crept into my room at 1 A.M., pushed under the covers, and whispered, "Clare . . . .you up?" And we launch into a one to two-hour discussion on guys, our parents, our feelings. Life.

But we don't talk about the scar, or its origin: a tumor, the size of a grapefruit, that was on her lung when she was only 7 years old. We don't talk about the specialists flown in, the risky operation performed or the roll of film our father dedicated to taking final pictures of the little blond girl he expected to lose.

We don't talk about it, but I haven't forgotten. Every time Lil turns her back, I remember when she came back home to us. Changed by the pain of 52 stitches and blood tests twice a day, doctors shaking their heads and a morbid hospital atmosphere, my sister returned a different person.

She came back an angry child I didn't much care for because my 6-year-old mentality couldn't possibly understand. My 17-year-old mind can. And does.

Yet my brain is often distracted by her 15-minute oratories on "Why Clare shouldn't borrow a shirt without asking" or "The advantages of good housekeeping." She is a neat nut. And she has a temper. These two traits do not mix so well.

She once got so mad at my little sister, Terese, for leaving an uneaten plate of spaghetti in the spotless kitchen that she chunked that plate, along with its cold, congealed contents, right into my younger sister's room. Terese yelled upon finding it, huffed and puffed while she cleaned it up, and rolled her eyes at me as we passed in the hall.

"I can't wait until she goes to college," Terese said.

"Yeah," I agreed with a grin.

But it's not exactly true. Lil's yelling, but she's alive. Really alive. And now that her bed's empty, my sleep's not being interrupted at night, and I'm not being hollered at for a lost earring, I kind of miss it. But she won't be gone for good. She was almost gone forever.

I'll keep in mind the scar: a symbol for me, of good fortune and a "Gee, it's great to be alive!" outlook. And I'll keep in mind the talks about guys, our parents, our feelings.

Life.

Ain't it grand! ★

HELP ME PICK A NAME FOR MY COLUMN

By LAUREN FLANS
Staples High School, Westport, Connecticut

WELL, IT'S finally happened. For many—OK, for a few of you who actually read my articles—your worst nightmare has come true. That's right, the kind, generous, caring, compassionate, superior people at *Inklings* (i.e. my bosses) have decided to give me a monthly column.

For those of you who are aware that my sole talents are falling asleep at various times during the day and being able to produce "handwriting" that even skilled archaeologists have trouble deciphering, this news will come as quite a shock to you.

But I assure you, it is true. From this point on, in every issue of Inklings, I will be given a small section of the paper (technically referred to as "filler") in which I will be able to gripe about whatever happens to be bothering me that month (I keep detailed lists).

However, in this first column, I will not be voicing my various complaints. Rather, I will be relating to you, my readers, a grave problem that I encountered after finding out that I had been given a column: namely, what I should call it.

Now, for those people who have graceful, elegant, musical names such as Erma Bombeck, this poses no problem. I also thought about using some zippy rhyming title. However, since just about the only things that my last name sort of rhymes with is "clams," I obviously encountered some difficulty.

This is precisely the reason I took a significant portion of my computer literacy class attempting to think up some snappy names for my new column. So for those of you who are still conscious and still reading this, I now present:

Possible names for my column!

• Ideas that I get after I haven't eaten for about 10 hours.

• Thoughts I have that really worry my parents.

• The kinds of ideas that a troubled childhood can cause.

• Why are you looking at me like that?

• No, I don't have a past record of mental illness. Why do you ask?

• Shut up or I'll hurt you (I really liked this one).

• Conan O'Brien would pay Millions for this stuff.

Well, there they are. After coming up with these brilliant insights, despite the fact that I obviously have way too much spare time, I had a great deal of trouble deciding which one to use as the title of my column.

That is why I am now officially conducting the "Help Name Lauren's Column Survey."

Basically the role that you, the reader, will pay in this exciting new venture is to send me a postcard with your choice for what my column should be called. The role that I will pay will be to read your responses while stuffing my face with Oreo cookies and watching Tiny Toons (my dedication to my art knows no bounds).

I realize that most of you probably have about as much interest in this survey as you do for the plight of the spotted owl, but I am attempting to interact with my readers.

In fact, beginning with my next column (in which I will also reveal the startling winning title), I will be asking readers to also send me letters as well as articles from respected publications such as the *Weekly World News* (the first paper to break the fascinating story of Elvis and JFK's joint bungalow in the Berkshires) because I like getting mail. No! Just kidding.

Based on what you write and send me, I will choose the subjects from my various columns. This is actually a technique that a very talented humor columnist named Dave Barry uses, and he has his own TV show and makes lots of money (call me ambitious).

Anyway, you can write me. I am fully aware that a great deal of you have better things to do with your life than write me. However, please take the time that you could be using to do something important, and send me stuff instead.

If I use part of a letter or an article that you have sent me, I will publish your name in my column (not only is this the very definition of incentive, but it can also be referred to on college applications).

So please take the time to tell me what's on your mind (unless it in any way involves gerbils). I really need to hear from you. I really need to know what you want. I really need something to do while I watch Tiny Toons. ★

CHAPTER TWELVE

CLEAN IT UP

Proofreading is one thing. Editing is another. While proofing is searching for the typos and style errors, editing involves careful examination of word choice, pace and tone.

Editing is a matter of balancing standards and personal whim. Too often, students get the wrong impression that reporters dash into the office, rip off 10 or 12 pages, zip it past a copy editor and wait for the Pulitzers to roll in. That isn't how it works. Reporters labor over their leads; they juggle parts of the story, cutting and pasting on the computer to create a piece that balances message, tone, pace and clarity – at least as perfectly as their skills permit.

Consider the following story:

THE CHS MIGHTY Marching Bulldog Band raised over seven hundred dollars selling Christmas trees last month. The money is part of their fundraising effort to go to the Orange Bowl Parade of Bands next January.

"We have wanted to go to this festival for several years but could not afford it," according to band director Jerry Downs. "If we stay on target, we will have sufficient funds to afford this trip."

Brad Nichols, Band President, said hauling the trees was very hard work but also said, "It will be worth it because everyone is looking forward to going to Miami. It'll be great to be on the beach. I am proud to be a member of the band." ★

Now, let's proof the story (corrections in italics. Also, notice omissions.).

AS PART OF ITS fund-raising effort to go to the Orange Bowl Parade of Bands next January, the band raised *more than* $700 selling Christmas

trees last month.

"We have wanted to go to this festival for several years but could not afford it," band director Jerry Downs *said*. "If we stay on target, we will have sufficient funds to afford this trip."

Band president Brad Nichols said hauling the trees was hard work but *added*, "It will be worth it because everyone is looking forward to going to Miami. It'll be great to be on the beach and away from this cold weather." ★

Begin by dropping all the adjectives (the CHS Mighty Marching Bulldog . . . .)

The band is an it—not a "they" so we've changed "their" to "its." When dealing with numbers, use "more than" rather than "over," which is used when referring to crossing a barrier or intervening space, as in "The cow jumped over the moon."

Some would argue that "band director" preceding Jerry Downs should be capitalized. However, band director is a position—not a title. The same goes for "head football coach" and "band president."

When in doubt, consult the *Associated Press Stylebook and Libel Manual.*

Delete "very."

Now that the story's proofed, we can see that we still have a pretty bland although polished story. It's time for a serious editing job. First, let's determine what part of this story our readers will most likely care about.

Do readers care that Brad Nichols is proud to be a member of the band? I doubt it. For my money, a bunch of young people risking frostbite is much more interesting than the fact that they raised $700 to go to Miami. So let's develop that angle by asking a few questions.

"While you were freezing, what did you say to each other?"

"Did people get into arguments?"

"How did your hands feel?"

"What did they look like?"

With this information and more, you can create a much more compelling story. For example:

HUDDLED AROUND A SMALL heater, four band members waited for the next customer and argued.

"I'm not going out there again. I waited on the last guy," junior Roger Wharmund said. "It's your turn."

"No way. I'm freezing," senior Angel Walker answered. "Let Ann go. She hasn't been out in an hour."

"I can't go. Look at this blister," sophomore Ann Hughes said. "My hands will never recover."

"You should have worn gloves," senior Brad Nichols answered. "What did you expect? That unloading Christmas trees would be fun?"

These students and others spent Friday hauling Christmas trees from a refrigerated truck to an outside lot, where the fog and snow gave the event a festive holiday atmosphere that lasted only until the students started shivering.

Why all this? The band members are part of a two-year effort to raise money for a trip next January to the Orange Bowl Festival of Bands in Miami, Florida. Still, the thoughts of sunny beaches did little to warm the band members as they braved the bone-chilling weather.

"It was fun at first, but after a while we all got tired and cold," Hughes said. "We tried to break up the boredom with a little snowball fight, but even that didn't help." ★

Here's another example: the first game of the season. In this case, it's football, but it could be any sport. Too often, sports is even more carelessly edited than news or features.

EDITING CHECKLIST

As a rule of thumb . . .

✓ Use active voice and active verbs.

✓ Avoid "to be" verbs. Rather than "Mr. Jones will be leading. . . .," write "Mr. Jones will lead . . . ."

✓ Avoid sentences that begin with A, An, The and There.

✓ Avoid meaningless words, such as very, many and really.

✓ Keep sentences short (25 words or fewer).

✓ Keep paragraphs short.

✓ Keep subjects close to their verbs.

✓ Limit the number of dependent clauses and prepositional phrases in each sentence.

✓ Use first and last names in first references, and identify each source by title or position.

✓ Be consistent in style on capitalization, especially for titles of positions and groups, as well as on punctuation and on abbreviations. For example: F.H.A. or FHA?

✓ Avoid clutter, such as "order up," "go and attend," "smile happily," or "tall skyscraper."

✓ Avoid misuse of the apostrophe, especially in its/it's.

✓ Use anecdotes and examples frequently and effectively.

✓ Use direct quotes that provide meaningful information rather than clichés or predictable data.

✓ Say as much as possible in as few words as necessary.

✓ Never let personal opinion slip into a news or feature story, especially in transitions and conclusions.

✓ Maintain a consistent and appropriate tone.

✓ Answer all news questions, and never raise questions without answering them.

✓ Avoid legal, ethical, taste or fairness problems.

THE 1994-95 FOOTBALL TEAM will open their season on the home field here Friday night against the state's top-ranked team and defending state football champion, the Lakewood Panthers.

"I know their the top-ranked team in the state, but if they're not ready to play, we could surprise them," Jim Wandell, coach, said. "We have had good workouts. If the ball bounces our way a few times, we have a chance to be in the game with them. We are starting 11 new players, including eight juniors and two sophomores. I hope our inexperience doesn't hurt us too much."

"Lakewood has a great tradition, but if we play our game and give 100 percent, we stay with them," Kevin Brooks, a 6-2, 185-pound junior, said. "Our only JV loss last year came against Lakewood so we have a score to settle."

As a sophomore, Brooks quarterbacked the junior varsity to a 9-1 mark. The Panthers defeated us last year, 48-21, on their way to a perfect 15-0 season and state championship. ★

Let's clean up the really blaring errors. Note the use of transition sentences between paragraphs and the deletion of the first person reference in the final sentence. Also, young reporters often confuse there, their and they're. Watch for this.

THE TIGERS 'VILL OPEN the football season here Friday night by hosting the state's top-ranked team and defending state champion, the Lakewood Panthers, a 48-21 winner over Taft last year.

"I know they're the top-ranked team in the state, but if they're not ready to play, we could surprise them," coach Jim Wandell said. "We have had good workouts. If the ball bounces our way a few times, we have a chance to be in the game with them."

Wandell said the team is young but talented.

"We are starting 11 new players, including eight juniors and two sophomores," he said. "I hope our inexperience doesn't hurt us too much."

Among the new starters is quarterback Kevin Brooks, a 6-2, 185-pound junior who quarterbacked the junior varsity last year to a 9-1 mark.

"Lakewood has a great tradition, but if we play our game and give 100 percent, we stay with them," he said. "Our only JV loss last year came against Lakewood so we have a score to settle." ★

The edited version is clean and informative, but it doesn't capture the drama of the moment. If NBC or CBS were covering the game, you have to believe that they'd focus on Taft's youth going against Lakewood's tradition and talent. Chances are, they'd anchor the story on one or two of the first-time Taft starters and capture their anxiety and excitement. That's the real story so let's try it.

FOR AS LONG AS HE can remember, junior Kevin Brooks has wanted to play varsity football for the Taft Tigers. Tonight, he'll get his chance although he wishes it came against slightly less formidable competition: the Lakewood Panthers, the state's top-ranked team and defending state champions.

Like 11 of his teammates, Kevin is starting his first game.

"We've had good workouts so I think we'll be ready," he said. "But we're all very aware of how good Lakewood is, year in and year out. We're not intimidated by them, but we respect them a whole lot."

That respect is based on a 48-21 varsity loss to them last year. Even the junior varsity, which Brooks quarterbacked to a 9-1 mark, fell to the Tigers, although by a 24-21 score on a hotly-contested pass interference call.

"We beat them, and the officials beat us," Brooks said. "Two of our touchdowns were called back, and they got a touchdown on a very questionable call late in the game to pull ahead. I've thought about that game every day since, and I can't wait to get on the field against them Friday night." ★

Editing is more than searching for errors in facts, style, grammar and punctuation. It's searching for the heart and soul of the story, and a good editor often sends the reporter back into the field for better quotes, an interesting anecdote or descriptive details.

Journalists must become familar with the many good books on editing. Both students and teachers should have at arm's length a copy of *The Elements of Style* by Strunk and White and an Associated Press stylebook. Traditional textbooks contain a chapter on editing and all

KEEP AN EYE OUT FOR A DOUBLE DOSE

We call them "baby puppies" because one word eliminates the need for the other. Here are a few examples:

ABSOLUTELY SURE
ADVANCE ON
ANNUAL BIRTHDAY
AUCTION SALE
BABY INFANT
BRIEF MOMENT
CANINE DOG
CLOSE PROXIMITY
CO-CONSPIRATOR
COMPLETELY ENGULFED
CRAZY MANIAC
DEAD CORPSE
ENTER IN
FEMALE COW
FORWARD PROGRESS
FILLED TO CAPACITY
FOOT PEDAL
FREE GIFT
FREE OF CHARGE
GALE OF WIND
JEWISH SYNAGOGUE
KNEEL DOWN
MAXIMUM LIMIT
MUTUAL AGREEMENT
NEW RECRUIT
NEXT SUBSEQUENT
PAST HISTORY
PAST PRECEDENT
PEACEFUL TRANQUILITY
REAL EXPERIENCE
REASON WHY
REFER BACK
SAME IDENTICAL
SHARE TOGETHER
SUM TOTAL
TOTALLY ABOLISHED
TUNA FISH
VERBAL DISCUSSION
WRITTEN DOWN

of the horrors of using "which" when you meant "that" so we won't rehash every danger here, except to note a few essential guidelines:

✓ Make certain the reporter has answered all news questions. All news questions may not be equal, but all must be answered somewhere in the story, preferably as soon as possible. "When" news leads are rarely appropriate, but readers should expect the reporter to tell them the date and time of an event. It is illogical and unforgivable to make readers search for the time or place of a future event. The goal is easy access to information, not a mystery story that hides important details.

✓ Look carefully at verb tenses. Many students mix present and past tense freely. For example, one attribution may state, "John says." and the next, "Mary said." Be consistent.

✓ Don't trust the computer's spell check program. Keystroke errors can turn a sentence such as "Mothers use doctor" into "Mothers sue doctor." Big difference.

✓ Read critically. In an article about a student suspended for perpetrating some prank on the school, the reporter wrote, "The student was suspended infinitely."

That's a long time. The reporter probably meant, "indefinitely."

In another case, a reporter interviewed a student about a censorship issue. The student was a cheerleader, but that had no relevance to the free press issue. Still, the story contained the following line: "Being a cheerleader, press rights are important to me," Suzy said.

First, it's a dumb quote and should have been taken out of the story. Then, you have to wonder how being a cheerleader makes Suzy especially sensitive to freedom of expression issues.

Finally, one reporter wrote, "Sylvester Stallone was his boy hood idol."

Was Stallone a hood as a kid?

✓ Double check the spelling of every name. You can't imagine how many times a simple name like my own has been butchered. The worst was when I received a letter—no joke—from my own dear mother, addressed to "Bobbie" Hawthorne.

It just goes to show: anyone can make a mistake. Don't take chances. All factual errors are not equal. Misspelled names are the gravest of all mistakes.

✓ Make sure your verbs support your sentences. The verb is the most important word in the sentence, and no amount of padding sentences with adjectives and adverbs can replace the imaginative verb.

Rather than, "He *drank* his cola slowly," consider "He *sipped* his Diet Coke." Better still, "He *nursed* his Diet Coke."

✓ Make certain the antecedent agrees with its pronoun. Too often, students write, "The team began their season."

Team is an it—not a they. A squad is an it. So is a band, a club, a council and any other collective body of persons.

The cheerleaders are a they. The National Honor Society is an it.

✓ Watch for misplaced modifiers. "The administration has been working on developing a humane method of penalizing ineligible players for approximately eight years."

Penalizing players for eight years sounds anything but humane. A good editor will make this correction: "The administration has worked for approximately eight years to develop a humane method of penalizing ineligible players."

✓ Use your own words. In an article announcing the separation of Diana and Charles, a reporter for a Texas newspaper wrote:

CHARLES WILL LIVE during the week at Clarence House . . . . On weekends, he will continue to repair to Highrove, the country mansion and estate in the Gloucestershire Hills outside London. ★

To repair? Texans repair their pickup trucks, not themselves. Drop the pretensions. If you mean begin, don't say commence. If you mean use, don't say utilize. If you mean hurry, don't say expedite. Don't be a snob.

✔ Make certain the tone matches the content of the story. A serious topic demands a serious, sober lead. A story about a fund drive for African famine victims began, "Catching on to the latest trend is something everyone seems to know how to do, and journalism students are no exception. They started a two-week money drive with the hope of raising a substantial sum of money for Ethiopia and other poverty-stricken African nations."

Famine isn't a trend so to classify it as something like wearing your jeans backwards shows the writer is trivializing famine.

Here's another example of tone failing to match content:

"HE'S ROLLING DOWN the aisles at school every day, but it's not because of his sense of humor. Freshman James Dell is in a wheelchair. He suffered a spinal cord injury when he was a child that left him paralyzed from the waist down." ★

Being confined to a wheelchair is nothing to laugh about.

Even worse, the next paragraph of the story was a lie even though it was a direct quote that I'm certain was 100 percent accurate. Again, as mentioned in the chapter on objectivity, accuracy isn't always the truth:

"IT DOESN'T BOTHER me being in a wheelchair because that's the way I am," Dell said. "I've come to accept my life, and my friends treat me the same way they treat each other." ★

You can admire the kid's spunk, but it is impossible that he isn't bothered about being in a wheelchair. It is simply a lie, a way for the kid to handle his condition. Empathize, but seek the truth.

No one would just as soon be in a wheelchair. A good editor would have caught this.

The same is true for a similar story about a hard-of-hearing student, who told the reporter, "I want to stay deaf. I want to stay special."

Do you buy that? I don't. The young man in question pointed out the advantages of being deaf, but it's a stretch of the imagination to think that these advantages outweigh the disadvantages.

✔ Say what you mean, and mean what you say. Syndicated columnist Molly Ivins wrote about the time her newspaper published the following line: "State Sen. Roy Goodman, R-Manhattan, heir to the Ex-Lax Fortune and a usually regular Republican, voted with Democrats Tuesday night . . . ."

It's a team thing

Editing is not solely the responsibility of the editors. Reporters must make every effort to see that their stories are factually, grammatically and stylistically correct.

In the October, 1989 issue of the now defunct *Hooray for High School Journalism*, veteran adviser Bob Button of Grosse Point South High School (Grosse Point, Michigan), wrote, "Good editing starts with the assignment. Too often, a reporter has no idea what the editor wanted—because the editor never said and the reporter never asked. It should be no surprise then when the reporter fails to give the editor what he wanted."

If editor and reporter agree from the outset on the purpose of the story, the selection of sources and how the story will be used, then the final editing becomes a process of picking nits—with the understanding, of course, that any nit can make or break a story.

SURE WAYS TO BECOME THE WORLD'S WORST EDITOR

• Going it alone. Working with people is as important as working with copy.

• Revising it yourself. It may be faster, but you're better off letting reporters rewrite it themselves.

• Editing without reading. Read it all the way through first.

• Changing without consulting. Writers organize stories for a reason. Editing without asking can destroy a story.

• Going out of style. Editing in words that are inconsistent with the style or tone of the story, or the rhythm or mood.

• Playing bully. Work with reporters. Be a leader, not a boss.

• Bogging down in the stylebook. Don't edit only for mechanical precision. Edit also for theme, focus, organization, readability, thoroughness and accuracy. Ask: What's missing? What's wasted? What's confusing?

• Overplaying your hunches. Avoid making too many changes for which you cannot cite a specific rule or offer a succinct explanation. "It just doesn't sound good" is a weak explanation. There should be a reason. This is a subjective business so realize that you don't have to win every time.

SEND EDITING HELP IMMEDIATELY!

The following sentences were culled from high-school newspapers. Edit them for style, punctuation and grammar. No fair peeking on the next page.

■ 1. There will be a meeting of the Oak Bluff High School Student Council on Monday afternoon at 2:30 P.M. during which they will discuss Homecoming.

■ 2. Participating Wednesday in the Rotary Club's first annual speech contest will be Jim Daniels and Gloria Bailey.

■ 3. Bill Thomas, who is a senior here at Oak Bluff High School, took top honors in the Student Journalist of the Year Contest, which was sponsored by Quill and Scroll.

■ 4. Last Saturday, the OBHS French Club held a fundraiser. The Club raised more than $400. The money will be used to defray costs of a trip to Paris over spring break. The fundraiser is part of a two-year effort. The Club raised money by selling croissants.

■ 5. When asked about the game next week, Coach Morgan said he feels the team will be ready to battle their opponents, the Winter Park High School Panthers.

■ 6. At the present time, the Oak Bluff High School civics class is studying the past history of English common law.

■ 7. The Wildcats won the game that they played last Saturday against the Winter Park Panthers by the final score of 31-10.

■ 8. The Art Club will hold a meeting next week during which they will install new officers who were recently elected.

■ 9. The 1995 Oak Bluff High School Debate Club competed in the Garden City Debate Tournament and placed second. The tournament was held Friday in Garden City. Joe Smith was named the tournament's top debater.

■ 10. The Oak Bluff High School Band will hold their annual Spaghetti Dinner Tuesday. The dinner will be held in the school cafeteria from 6:00 P.M. to 9:00 P.M. that evening.

■ 11. The 1995 Oak Bluff High School Student Council held their first meeting at 2:00 P.M. Wednesday afternoon in the library. At the meeting, the members of the council voted to cancel the homecoming dance. They voted to do this because of low attendance at the dance the last two years. The dance was originally scheduled for the first of November.

EDITING HELP HAS ARRIVED (FOR PAGE 140)

☐ 1. *The Student Council will discuss the Homecoming dance at 2:30 P.M. Monday.*
☐ Avoid "There will" or "There is" sentences. Begin with the noun. Students know the name of their school. Time precedes date, and p.m. denotes afternoon.

☐ 2. *Senior Jim Daniels and junior Gloria Bailey will participate Wednesday in the Rotary Club speech contest.*
☐ Begin with the noun—Jim and Gloria. An event cannot be the "first annual." If it's the first, then it hasn't had time to be "the annual." That comes the next year.

☐ 3. *Senior Bill Thomas won Quill and Scroll's student journalist of the year contest.*
☐ Avoid the overuse of relative pronouns, in this case "who" and "which."

☐ 4. *To help defray costs of its planned spring trip to Paris, the French Club raised more than $400 by selling croissants last week.*
☐ Avoid date leads, particularly those that refer to past events. The infinitive phrase "to help . . ." explains why the club held the fund-raiser.

☐ 5. *Coach Morgan said the team will be ready for the Panthers. Or: The team will be ready for the Panthers, Coach Morgan said.*
☐ Avoid "when asked." If you provide the quote, the reader will understand that the source was asked the question. You can feel an emotion but not a quote.

☐ 6. *The civics class is studying the history of English common law.*
☐ "Is" implies "at the present time." All history occurred in the past.

☐ 7. *The Wildcats crushed the Winter Park Panthers, 31-10, Saturday.*
☐ If they won the game, they must have played it, and if they won it, they won it "by a final score of . . . ." Also, look for a more precise word than "beat." A team can "beat" its opponent by one or 100 points. Pick the verb that best describes the outcome.

☐ 8. *The Art Club will install officers next week.*
☐ Installation implies "new" officers, and it's easy enough to assume that since officers have not been installed, the election was held recently.

☐ 9. *Ginger Robbins was named top debater, and the Debate Club took runner-up honors at the Garden City Debate Tournament, Friday.*
☐ That Ginger was named top debater is the most important fact. It should lead the sentence. Again, if the club placed second, it must have competed.

☐ 10. *The band's annual spaghetti dinner is set for 6-9 P.M. Tuesday in the cafeteria.*
☐ The band is an "it"—not a "they." Note: 6-9 P.M., without all the 00s.

☐ 11. *Citing poor attendance the past two years, the Student Council voted Wednesday to cancel the Nov. 1 homecoming dance.*
☐ It is not important that the Council held a meeting. That the Council voted to discontinue the dance is important. Note the use of the present participle lead, which answers the all-important reason "why."

THERE MUST BE A BOOK ON THAT!

There probably is. A well-stocked journalism classroom should contain one or all of the following reference books:

• A good dictionary is absolutely essential. It should be the most used book in your publications lab.

• A thesaurus comes in handy, especially for headline writers. Roget's is the most popular, but the *Webster Book of Synonyms* is quite handy.

• The *Associated Press Stylebook and Libel Manual*. Most students are shocked to discover the wonderful sections on sports, libel and caption writing.

• *Grammar for Journalists* by E. L. Callihan is indispensable. It is available from the Chilton Book Company in Radnor, Pennsylvania.

• Don't hesitate to call upon the reference librarians at your school or public libraries. They are willing and trained to check a specific fact. Get to know them.

• As the information highway becomes more of a reality, it will be helpful to learn to use computer networks such as the Internet and America On-line.

In addition, many specialists provide information via 1-800 numbers.

This article, by Rachel Seewald, a young journalist with whom I work, was written from the same fact sheet that is provided on pages 114-115.

I've edited her story by striking out unnecessary or inappropriate words and sentences and placing changes in italics. Note that it required little proofing.

At the same time, compare the angle and tone of this story to the story on pages 115-116.

In all fairness to Rachel, I did not direct her in any way so her story takes more of a news than a feature angle. This is the angle that most beginning student journalists would take, but not necessarily the one that I would recommend.

Janelle Klein, Leaguetown's drama teacher for the past 11 years, announced March 23 that she would leave the school in May ~~in order~~ to devote her full attention to improving and expanding the Clown Care Unit project.

The Clown Care Unit, founded by Klein in 1986, consists of a group of comedians who visit ailing children and their parents at the city's four hospitals. The project began when an official at St. Michael's Hospital asked ~~if~~ the Laff Staff, a group of improvisational comedians who work at a local comedy theater, ~~would~~ *to* entertain at a gathering for patients and their families.

"A fellow member of the Laff Staff, Jeff Gordon, and I obliged," Klein said. "We put together a 20-minute parody of doctors and hospitals, and it was the most fulfilling 20 minutes of my professional career. It was from that experience that the CCU plant took root."

St. Michael's recently opened a new Children's Hospital for youngsters with life-threatening and catastrophic illness. The clowns' purpose is to alleviate the fear and confusion of hospital stays and provide moments of humorous routines for sick children. Alfred Nash, director of the Children's Hospital at St. Michael's, *said he* wondered how parents of sick children would react. After watching one of the shows, *he said* he knew the project would work.

"Janelle's and other clowns' techniques were so disarming, they captivated everybody immediately," Nash ~~stated~~ *said*. "We—the doctors, nurses and staff members—thoroughly enjoy the shows even when the clowns are poking fun at us."

Although Klein *said she* receives much support from doctors and nurses, she has ~~had to face~~ *faced* ~~some~~ rejections as well.

~~Klein comments,~~ "I don't let them bother me," *she said*. "My responsibility is not to save the children but to love them and give joy and celebration, not to make them accept it. That's their choice."

During her 11 years at Leaguetown, Klein guided the one-act play to seven district championships, six regional titles and two state UIL championships. She *said she* hopes that strong support will continue for fine arts in high school.

"I have enjoyed my 11 years at Leaguetown High School, and I'm going to miss the students," Klein said. "Basic curriculum in high schools is very much overemphasized. Students need a well-rounded education of core classes as well as enrichment classes."

It is not easy for Klein to leave, but she admits she is ready to move on.

"This project has grown more important for me each year, and with the opening of the new Children's Hospital at St. Michael's, the need for this service is especially dire," Klein said. "Call it a love and caring, God, a higher consciousness—whatever—I want to give my life to this project."

The Clown Care Unit recently received a $25,000 grant from the Charles Altman Foundation, to be used mostly for props, salaries and administrative overhead.

~~Klein is married to Frank Klein, an engineer for the Texas Highway Department. She and her husband have three children.~~ ★

CHAPTER THIRTEEN

PUT IT IN THE BOOK

Photographs alone cannot tell the story of the year. Yearbook copy should focus not on the events themselves but rather on how students will want to remember the events.

In high school, I was a starting defensive back and wide receiver for the White Oak Roughnecks, a 13-1 state semifinalist from Northeast Texas.

I hadn't thought much about this until recently, when the local newspaper, the *Austin American-Statesman*, published a story about the Pflugerville Panthers, one in a series of articles about championship teams from Central Texas. Pflugerville, then a small farming community north of Austin but now a suburb, is the reason we weren't state finalists. They beat us, 7-6, on a bitterly cold December night at Wildcat Stadium in Temple, a city of 70,000 located half-way between Austin and Waco.

It broke our hearts. I can still remember how we sat in our uniforms and cried—even Danny Denton, Mr. Cool—as our coaches treaded their way through the crowded dressing room after the game to try to console us. I'm certain two or three of them were as broken up as we were.

But time and life go on, and, as I said, I only think about that game when I'm forced to drive by Wildcat Stadium—it's right on Interstate 35—en route to Dallas or to visit my family back in East Texas. Seeing that stadium is like looking at a tomb.

The story in the *American-Statesman* brought back a lot of memories. The reporter, George Breazeale, interviewed Pflugerville players and coaches, who gave the game a sense of historical perspective. It was as cold to them as it was to us. They were as thrilled in victory as we were devastated in defeat. Strangely enough, they said they better remembered their win over us more vividly than their 45-7 loss to Sonora the following week in the state finals—just as I have over these years preferred to remember our quarterfinal, come-from-behind win over Barbers Hill.

So what?

The reporter's article reminded me of the power of writing to rekindle emotions, and it made me wonder why yearbook reporting—particularly sports reporting—doesn't attempt to concentrate on the sensory aspects of teenage life. Certainly sports embodies and magnifies all of the trials of adolescence, but coverage too often consists of a collection of data: scores, season records and obligatory, as well as largely meaningless, quotes that never capture the essence of either a game or season.

For example:

THE BASEBALL TEAM ended its season with a 10-9 record. The district record was 6-4. Thirteen boys comprised this team with four managers, two bat girls and two coaches.

"We had a good season, but I would have preferred that we win more games," said Coach Bill Smith. "The highlight of the year was our win over Clear Creek, and the low point was the loss to Madison."

Joe Small was named first team all-district short-stop, and Jerry Kiner was chosen second team catcher.

"We are certain to win a district title next year," Kiner said. ★

This copy doesn't capture a moment. It doesn't appeal to the emotions. It merely transacts data. And this isn't enough, for either the fan or the player. Successful yearbook sports copy gives meaning to the scores, the statistics, the post-season honors. It records the season in human, not numerical terms. It seeks to do more than tell the reader what happened. Instead, it attempts to show why and how the events happened. It tries to capture what it was about the game or the season that the players and spectators will most likely remember.

How is this done? Through observation, interviewing and interpretation.

First, the reporter must witness the event. That means attending practices and games, even pre-game skull sessions and post-game locker-room talks. You cannot get a feel for the team—its expectations, its personality— unless you are there, and you cannot successfully tell the story of the year unless you show how the team met, failed to meet or surpassed its expectations.

You cannot report from a distance. Sportswriters covering professional football teams often travel with the team, eat with the players and play poker with the guys. They get to know the athletes as something more than stuffed jerseys.

For Hunter S. Thompson to write about the Hell's Angels, he had to ride with them, even if it meant risking his life, which it did. In *Paper Lion*, George Plimpton became a quarterback for the Detroit Lions to understand what it means to be a professional football player.

For you to tell the story of a team that surpassed its wildest dreams, you must be there at the moment of victory. But of more importance, you must have been there when

that moment was nothing more than a wild dream to appreciate how meaningful it would become.

It is not enough to write, "They surpassed their wildest dreams." You must show what that means by providing specific examples and poignant anecdotes that make an abstract statement such as "They surpassed their wildest dreams," something real and meaningful.

For example, which of the two stories more successfully captures the essence of victory?

PLAYING IN NEAR-FREEZING weather, the Lions stopped a late-fourth quarter drive to preserve a 14-7 victory over Jefferson in the state championship game. The Lions finished the season with a 14-0-1 record, the best mark in the school's history.

"The kids surpassed all of our expectations," Coach Ernest Buckner said. "More than a few times, they could have given up, but each time, they reached down deep and found the character to win."

The season opened with a 20-17 win over Roosevelt, followed by consecutive wins over Glenview, 14-10; Kennedy, 28-24; and Taft, 17-7, with the lone blotch on an otherwise perfect record being a 24-24 tie with Parkcrest. ★

The remainder of the story lists scores, statistics and highlights, without attempting to humanize the story other than attaching a name to a number. All data is mulched into a single story, as though it were all equally important. Meanwhile, we get no sense of who these young men are or of what they experienced. We know only that they won a bunch of games.

Chances are, the typical yearbook reader already knows that.

Now, consider the following story:

TWENTY MINUTES after the game had ended, they remained on the frozen turf of Remington field, players and their girlfriends, coaches and parents, hugging one another, slapping backs and strutting up and down the field. They pinpointed where Jeff Reymer scored on a crucial third-down fingertip catch and where Ron Vaught planted his helmet in the ribs of Jefferson's all-state quarterback Patrick Whaley, knocking the football loose to stop a late fourth-quarter drive and preserve the 17-14 win.

Long after most of the fans had escaped to their cars, they braved the 25-mile-per-hour winds and near-zero wind chill, refusing to surrender the moment and thumbing their noses at Mother Nature as only state champions can do.

"I wanted the moment to last forever," Viking senior offensive guard Billy Gammon said. "I doubt that I'll ever have as big a thrill as winning the state football championship."

The victory was a most unlikely one. Unbeaten Jefferson entered the game as the state's top-ranked team and had been touted as one of the best teams ever. In 14 games, the Lions had outscored opponents, 497-98. In the semifinals, they had routed defending champion Clearwater, 42-0, with Whaley throwing six touchdown passes.

The Vikings, on the other hand, won ugly, struggling in game after game, getting the big break that kept the season going. In the semifinals, Randy Kane blocked an extra point to save a 21-20 win over Madison.

"Whatever it took, that's what these kids did," coach Ernest Buckner said. "This is not even close to the most talented team I've coached, but these kids have character and tenacity. We were a little lucky, but we made our own luck." ★

What makes this story successful? It focuses on human emotions—"I doubt that I'll ever have as big a thrill as winning the state football championship"—rather than on scores or statistics. It embraces meaningful interviewing with specific details—"they remained on the frozen turf of Remington field, players and their girlfriends, coaches and parents, hugging one another, slapping backs and strutting up and down the field. They pinpointed where Jeff Reymer scored on a crucial third-down fingertip catch and where Ron Vaught planted his helmet in the ribs of Jefferson's all-state quarterback Patrick Whaley."

Notice that the story doesn't replace data with emotion. Instead, it uses emotion to give meaning to data.

Notice also the quality of the quotes. These are not meaningless statements of the obvious, as so many quotes in yearbooks often are. A statement such as "We are glad that we won and proud of this team. The boys played hard and gave 110 percent all the way" can be used for almost any team, any year. Instead, the coach's quote is candid and specific, more conversational than stilted, as though he were talking to the reporter rather than being stopped in the hall for a quick interview.

As important as anything, the story possesses a meaningful degree of interpretation: *The Vikings, on the other hand, won ugly, struggling in game after game, getting the big break that kept the season going.*

It then supports this interpretive statement with an example: *In the semifinals, Randy Kane blocked an extra point to save a 21-20 win over Madison.*

The reporter must have freedom to look at the big picture—pre-season expectations, injuries, weather, freak accidents, luck, team attitude, fan support and strategy changes—and then come to a conclusion as to the team's degree of success or failure. In 1992, SMU—the first and only school to have been given the NCAA "death penalty" and on the brink of having its football program abolished or de-emphasized—finished with a 5-6 season mark and its coach, Tom Rosseley, was a candidate for coach of the year. Meanwhile, the Oklahoma Sooners finished 6-4-1, and more than a few fans were calling for head coach Gary Gibbs' scalp.

A 5-6 mark isn't always a losing season, and a 6-4-1 record isn't necessarily a winning record either. It's all a matter of perspective, and the reporter must have license to interpret the meaning of the win-loss column.

This recipe of observation, interviewing, interpretation, will work for any sport—individual or team, varsity or JV, male or

STRONG COPY REKINDLES FADING MEMORIES

Basically, a yearbook is a picture book. Certainly, it serves other functions. But its primary appeal is visual, not verbal. The visual appeal does not mean that writing can be ignored. Much to the contrary.

It puts an even greater onus on the reporter to write with clarity, precision and conciseness. Over time, readers will forget names and dates. The details of the photos will soften, and the writing will fill in the blanks. So the precious space dedicated to copy must be packed with details: sights, sounds, emotions.

The key to writing powerful copy is to open with a dynamic lead, a lead that grabs the reader's attention and makes him or her want to read on for more information. Suffice it to say, you cannot achieve this by telling readers what they already know or can figure out for themselves.

The following lead and those of its kind are a waste of space:

The purpose of the Spanish Club is to help students learn Spanish. Club members included . . . .

OTHER SECTIONS

Although other styles of writing can be successfully employed, the model of writing can be used for any section of the yearbook, including theme copy, which tends to be more telescopic than microscopic in nature.

Former Texas adviser Judie Gustafson wrote, "Copy is to a yearbook what sound is to television—not a substitute for the picture but a much-needed compliment. Without a verbal report of the year, the pictorial coverage lacks meaning, depth or permanence."

The Columbia Scholastic Press Association says it considers well written copy the single most important aspect of the contemporary yearbook.

CSPA's Scholastic Yearbook Fundamentals states, "Copy should be creative (and it costs nothing extra, except blood, sweat and a few tears!). The story of the year, of the school, of the students, of the faculty, of each sport, each academic discipline and each club should reflect moods, actions and feelings, gathered through observations. Indeed, copy should take readers on an emotional roller coaster, subjecting them to ups and downs. Writers should capture the highs and lows,

female. The bottom line is not so much to record the historical data—a scoreboard can do that just as easily—but to build the story around a prevailing emotion, the one thing that people are most likely to remember.

Successful sports copy should do for the yearbook readers what George Breazeale's story about the Pflugerville Panthers did for me: it should remind them, as in my case, of how much it hurt to lose that football game or how great it was to win.

excitement and boredom, laughter and tears, and smiles and frowns."

Unfortunately, too much yearbook copy merely washes over the event, outlining the basic and most general aspects of the person, place or thing. No where is this more true than in yearbook theme copy.

First, let's understand the purpose of the theme: to tell the readers the mood the staff wants to establish, to give the book personality, to document the specifics of the year and to tie the book together, from the front cover to the back endsheet. Alert staffs attempt to select creative themes that are relevant, appealing, creative and unique. In addition, it should have graphic and marketing possibilities. Consequently, trite themes such as "Footprints in the Sand of Time" and "Magic Moments" are about as appealing as a Perry Como album.

To avoid falling victim to one of these theme clichés, the staff must ask:
• What is the mood of students this year?
• What changes have occurred since last year?
• What external factors have affected the students or school?

Problems, though, can occur because the questions are often asked during a summer publications workshop, months before anyone knows the mood of the students, what changes will occur, and what external factors will affect the students and school.

It doesn't take a rocket scientist to deduct that many themes—even those of the most successful books—can be artificial and forced. What happens to the staff that selects in July the theme "Too Hot to Handle" when the school burns down in January? What if during a summer workshop the staff selects the theme "It's all here in black and white" and then the school is rocked later in the year with race riots? How do you put a warm and fuzzy spin on that?

Because successful theme copy depends so much on placing the events of the year in perspective and capturing the tone—the spirit, if you will—of the year, it should be the last copy written. Successful theme copy cannot be written in October.

Even among the top publications, the major weakness of theme copy is its failure to analyze or interpret the events of the year. Instead, the copy gushes forth with facts that are irrelevant to the school year. Unfortunately, they lack the interpretive reporting that would give them meaning.

For example, suppose the theme of the book is "One in a Million." The typical theme copy might read like this:

THE FIRST DAY of school brought new faces, questions, anxiety and excitement. It also brought many changes. Changes were all part of the school year. New rules, policies, procedures started when students returned on the first day. Exemptions from final exams and many individual class activities pertaining to homecoming week were only some of the many activities eliminated this year. The campus itself underwent changes as a new band hall was constructed and the science wing was renovated.

Change was taking place on campus. Enrollment jumped from 1,245 to 1,513, causing overcrowding in the 391 classes held on campus. New classes in computer science were added to the curriculum while other classes were eliminated.

A proposal to close campus at lunch was narrowly defeated as was a plan to exempt seniors from final exams. Collectively, students worked to win district championships in football, girls basketball, swimming, golf and girls basketball. The academic and fine arts programs were equally successful.

The year was one of memorable changes and high academic achievements. Students adjusted to the new classes and teachers while getting involved in sports, organizations and class activities. Above and beyond it all, students worked together to make this year "One in a Million." ★

This theme copy satisfies most of the rating booklet dictates, but it is sadly uninspiring and slightly misleading. The way to upgrade the quality of theme copy is to see

WILL ANYONE STILL CARE IN 20 YEARS?

The story should not repeat the obvious. But that's just what this lead does.

Future Homemakers of America is a name of a club which denotes what its members will someday be. But what is a homemaker? The dictionary simply defines one as a person who manages a home.

When asked for her own definition, co-sponsor Rebecca Sanchez responded, "someone who spends time in bettering home and family life." This year, the purpose of FHA was to be aware of civic responsibility, learn to be part of a group and work together."

When the purpose of the club is tied in with the definition of a homemaker in the quote, the result is what FHA tries to accomplish.

How can you avoid such trite copy? By knowing about the subject fully before you begin writing, by searching for the most interesting and important infomration to pack into the lead and by empathizing with your readers so that you can provide them with the information they need and in the form and tone that they will value.

the individuals in each school. In the past, studies of high-school graduates have attempted to develop a better understanding of the impact of high school. Graduates have been asked to look back on their high-school days and answer questions such as:

• What were your happiest memories of high school?
• What were your most painful memories of high school?
• What is the biggest general problem you recall from high school?
• What changes would you make in your high-school years?
• Did any teacher have a significant impact on you?

Not surprisingly, social activities dominated the memory of the great majority of persons responding to surveys. Inevitably, the happiest moments were those spent with friends, either in school-related activities or non-school social activities.

The majority of painful memories were also interpersonal in nature. Memories of exclusion, of abandonment or loss, and of concerns about failing others permeated the data. Responses ranged from typical adolescent self-conscious embarrassment to more serious matters such as death, family disintegration and romantic loss.

The biggest problems, students said, were pressure to conform, drug and alcohol abuse, boring instruction and racism. In response to the question, "What changes would you make in your high-school years?" most students said they'd be more attentive to their studies.

Finally, the great majority of students responding to these surveys said they had been significantly affected by at least one caring and dedicated teacher.

What conclusions did the researchers draw from all of this? First, that high school is clearly the single most important factor in the lives of a majority of teenagers, whose memories of happy times do not focus on all the great ideas they learned in class but rather on school activities, athletic involvement and/or times spent with friends.

Now, why have I mentioned all of this? To prod you to begin thinking about school not as a collection of facts—how many students attended, how many classes were held, who won which championships?—but rather as a highly emotional experience. The yearbook cannot succeed unless the theme relates to the emotional experience of students. Don't ask, "What were the students doing?"

Ask, "What were the students feeling?"

What are your happiest memories?

What were your most painful memories?

What changes would you make in your high-school years?

Did any teacher have a significant impact on you? How?

Then, illustrate their answers with interpretive, descriptive reporting and writing. Yearbook theme copy cannot succeed unless it defines the events of the year in the context of students' emotional experiences. It has to plug into the collective memory bank, with all its happy and painful memories. If you can do this, then the theme copy will be cherished for a lifetime.

So, let's take another stab at theme copy, but let's abandon the dopey need to shoehorn the theme into every copy block.

NO ONE HAD to tell us the enrollment had increased by almost 300 students. We knew it every time the bell rang and we were forced to squeeze through the halls and into crowded locker areas.

"Getting from class to class was misery," senior Jennifer Cahoon said. "I finally just started taking all of my books with me every day so I could avoid the lockers. It was just too much hassle."

With more people came attempts to control them. Although attempts to open the campus at lunch failed, several homecoming activities were cancelled. Too many students. Too many risks that something might go wrong, that students would skip classes or hang out behind the gym, smoking.

Some did anyway. It was the only reason they came to school—to see their friends. But they were the exceptions. Most of us saw some reason for the endless term papers, the pop quizzes and the standardized tests even though we complained about them bitterly at the time. We knew that school was more than a place to visit with our friends.

"It all seems kind of pointless at times, but then you'll be in a class where a really cool discussion takes place and you realize that you're really interested in what caused the Civil War or how a certain poem captures the same emotions you feel," senior Dave Tabish said. "I've always said that people who think that school is nothing but a drag just aren't paying attention." ★

I could be fooling myself, but I think highly-stylized interpretive copy will be enjoyed by the readers, now and later. It's more challenging to write and much more satisfying to read. Rather than the telescopic, formula-driven theme copy that has been force-fed on staffs by rigid guidelines or outdated traditions, look instead to exceptional magazine advertising copyrighting for your models and inspirations. Read the copy in a typical automobile magazine advertisement running in *Esquire*. Note the precision of the writing, the craftsmanship of the prose. If our theme copy were written with as much care and attention, yearbooks would be more meaningful to readers, and I can't help but think that the result would be increased sales.

The following copy from a Yorktown High School yearbook (Yorktown, Indiana; Terry Nelson, adviser) goes one or two steps beyond typical theme copy. It has an edge, a personality that gives readers the sensation that the writer is speaking directly to them. The theme of the book was "Simple Pleasures."

OPENING SPREAD
WHAT MAKES you happy?

Is it getting an A on Steve York's government test you thought you failed? Or is it not getting humiliated, just getting beat by the always-tough Anderson Indians swim team?

Could happiness be the result of watching the football players come to school the day after their custom haircuts, complete with arrows, numbers and paws shaved on their heads?

SSP? No ISS? Being the only boy in FHA? Having the ability to talk in initials and still understand each other?

The feeling of relief and accomplishment after pulling off Fall Preview without the choir director, who was absent with a lung infection.

The realization that you're "in the movies" after you see your face flash in the crowd as drama club members did in the major film release of *Hoosiers*?

SECOND SPREAD
What gets you through the day?

Is it listening to the radio bursting with Run DMC to help us "chill out" during the lunchtime frenzy? Or is it the contagious laughter breaking out in a quiet classroom following a simple remark someone had made?

What about squirting those water guns to keep each other awake during choir's all-night fund raiser, Rock A Thon? Or wearing the symbolic "Green and White" on any of the numerous spirit days?

Could your boost be wandering into an informal classroom with Q-Zoo's Bob and Tom blaring on the radio? Or is it carting around that white plexiglass hall pass?

THIRD SPREAD
What makes you most proud?

Being the only tuba player in the All-State Orchestra as Senior Patty Grimes was?

Overcoming the odds of a losing season as our football team pooled resources to defeat all sectional competition with last-minute field goals?

Having a newspaper named "George Gallup" award winner by the International Society of Quill and Scroll.

Moving up a division in marching competition and still placing in the top 10 bands at the state level?

Meeting every Sunday to interview and photograph established community members in order to compile a history of Yorktown's growing in its sesquicentennial year?

Simple happenings for not-so-simple individuals. Whether it was big accomplishments or small remembrances, they all added up to a simply pleasurable year at Yorktown High School. ★

The strength of this copy comes not so

LEAD THE READER TO THE PROMISED LAND

Paul Ender, adviser of the *American*, Independence High School in San Jose, California, offers these points to be considered in writing the lead:

• Be simple, direct and concise.
• Try for 25 words or less.
• Focus on facts readers don't already know
• Feature the most important aspect of the story.
• Combine a style and grammatical approach consistent with the topic.
• Use colorful, specific, visual nouns and sensory verbs
• Avoid beginning with "a," "an" or "the."
• Avoid use of "this year," the name, initials and/ or mascot of the school.
• Avoid editorializing adjectives and adverbs.
• Use the lead to introduce a story that covers the subject deeply and with full attention to detail.

much from the strength of its details but rather from the engaging tone. The use of questions allows readers to bring into play their own thoughts and feelings. The writing allows the reader to participate in a dialogue. It turns the typically passive act of reading into an active, two-way communications experience.

Likewise, the following theme copy from a Fairmont Senior High School yearbook (Fairmont, West Virginia; Nan Cayton, adviser) has the tone of a conversation between writer and reader. All the specifics and tiny details are pulled in to give the exchange personality and timelessness. The theme of the book was "It's the Thought that Counts." Jim Burnell wrote the copy.

WELL, HERE WE are in front of the school by the gates. I wonder how long they've stood here guarding the school? Some things never change.

But a lot of things do.

You know, come to think of it, this year has had its share of unusual occurrences. Freshman Orientation was delayed until Aug. 31, and Christmas break was extended until Jan. 9 so that crews could finish cleaning out asbestos, but the teachers only got Jan. 5 off.

Speaking of teachers, we've got some pretty good ones. Math Department Head Darlene Boyles was the Science and Math Teacher of the Year. She went to Washington, D. C. —during school time? Some people have all the luck.

Anyway, teachers weren't the only ones who were recognized for their achievements. We had two Girls State officers, Governor Johnna Rizzo and Chief Justice Cara Snyder while Andrea McElroy represented West Virginia at Girls Nation.

On a more academic note, Team A took top honors at county Math Field Day while Tony Shan finished first and was a National Merit Finalist. If I had a dime for every time his picture was in the paper . . . .

How 'bout our athletes? Eric Shaffer became state golf champion, and the cross country team captured the state title with an undefeated record after two years of second place.

On Feb. 6, school was delayed two hours—

Marion Country didn't have a full snow day for two years in a row. The stretch between Christmas and Easter got on my nerves? (Of course, the Flood and Asbestos days helped.)

The senior class was the first Rivesville-Fairmont group to graduate after attending school together all four years.

Organizations were busy, too. The Encores went to Florida while the Madrigals performed in Williamsburg. At the Forest Festival, the marching band captured the title for the third time in four years, and the yearbook received a fourth Gold Crown award.

The people of Fairmont tried to save the historic High Gate mansion while voters renewed the levy and debated the construction of a new East Fairmont High School.

We cared a lot about everything we did, and when it comes down to it, it's the thought that counts. ★

Note in particular how the theme is worked into the final paragraph. But unlike much theme copy, it flows out of the copy block. It doesn't read as though it's been shoehorned in. Rather than an artificial intrusion, the theme slogan appears to be a natural, virtually indispensable, extension of the story.

Now, let's look at how Burnell continued the voice of the theme copy on a couple of division pages and on the closing spread.

STUDENT LIFE DIVIDER

If you've heard it once, you've heard it a million times. It's the thought that counts.

It really didn't matter that Mother Nature didn't deliver any snow days. There was always the negative, but we accentuated the positive.

Teachers filled out "proficiency reports" designed to congratulate us for a job well done.

And what could be more positive than avenging last year's embarrassing loss to crosstown rival East Fairmont to the tune of 20-6 and beating Elkins 35-14 to win our third consecutive homecoming game?

The homecoming dance and prom were successes as well. On Oct. 14, Cheri Warcholak was queen of the International Fiesta, and Andrea McElroy reigned April 15 during A Midsummer Night's Dream.

On June 2, the dreams of seniors finally came true as they became the 109th graduating class, but just another chapter in the school's long success story.

I'd bet if we tried to count those successes, we'd go out of our minds. ★

PEOPLE SECTION DIVIDER
NOW WHERE was I? Oh, I remember! Anyway, our success wasn't limited to academic pursuits—we often were recognized for other things. Jay Cole and Jennifer Allen spent time at Space Camp in Huntsville, Alabama. Over Christmas break, Debbie Abruzzino participated in the Lord Mayor's Westminister New Year's Parade in London, England. London, do you believe it?

A new librarian, Mrs. Elizabeth Moats, reorganized the library so students could find the books they needed for reports. Miss Linda Pinnell got a national humanities grant. Mrs. Kathy Jacquez served as president of the Marion County Education Association. Mrs. Loretta Taylor left mid-year, and Principal John D. Tennant Jr. announced his plans to retire on June 30.

Two new records were set as the class of 1989 became the last class of the 80s to graduate while the freshman class of 1992 was the smallest in the history of the school. I wonder how they figured that out? They probably did a head count. ★

CLOSING SPREAD
THE BOTTOM line is that we were held accountable for our actions and reactions. We shared the glory of the great times, and we helped each other get through the bad times.

What I'm trying to say is that things didn't always go the way we wanted. The football team compiled a disappointing 6-4 record. The basketball team lost to Brooke by one point in the state semifinals, and the Hi-Q team fell again to Philip Barbour in the first round.

Spanish teacher Loretta Taylor left mid-year while Principal John D. Tennant and senior counselor Joe Muto announced their plans for retirement. Preston Myers' accident and the deaths of Lonnie Carson and Kim Cain shook the student body.

But sometimes things worked out great. Who would forget the overtime basketball victory we snatched from East Fairmont and dedicated to Myers? Or the success of the first countywide Project Graduation? The list goes on and on.

Even when things weren't always what we planned or hoped or dreamed, we picked ourselves up and tried again.

After all, it's the thought that counts. ★

Taking greater chances with section copy also makes sense. Consider the following club coverage:

CLUB INDUCTIONS and initiations came in all forms, ranging from formal to informal, but each held a special meaning for the participants.

The Future Teachers of America held its induction at Mr. Gatti's. "Having the ceremony at Mr. Gatti's was nice because it let us go out and eat pizza," sophomore David Dixon said.

Some inductions were more formal, however. The Spanish Club held its ceremony at the Glenview Country Club.

"Being inducted into Spanish Club was special because it was the beginning for me to get involved in more school activities," junior Marc Schwartz said.

Other clubs were more outlandish. Big Sisters dressed up their Little Sisters for the day in outlandish costumes.

"My sister put me through the ultimate embarrassment. I looked really bad and had to do some crazy stuff," sophomore Tammy Tamblin said. ★

What is the theme of this piece of copy? That clubs conduct inductions? That inductions are different? Either way, the writing is boring, and the content rehashes the obvious. What have non-club members learned that they didn't know or couldn't figure out? What emotions have been captured? Will club members want to read this copy block in five or 10 years?

Probably not. So, how do we salvage this? First, redefine the theme. "Inductions are times for excitement, nervousness and, in a few cases, outlandishness."

Then, find specific examples to support this theme. Tammy Tamblin said she was put through the ultimate embarrassment. What was it? Describe it. Re-create the scene. Put it in a context. Show us what inductions mean, but make certain you do

There's no trick to writing interesting sidebars. Simply apply the same principles that have been outlined for all writing. The only difference with writing sidebar stories is that they are shorter and more precise in their focus.

While the main copy block may deal with homecoming or prom, the sidebar may deal with one person's perspective of the event. Or it may deal with an unusual element of the story.

For example, in addition to the major copy block about the championship basketball game, the sidebar may explain how the top scorer played in great pain with a strained knee.

As in all writing, the reporter must isolate a specific theme for the story, develop an interesting angle, gather information, organize the information, write, proof, edit and rewrite.

That's a lot of work for a three- or five-paragraph story. But there's no other way.

not glamorize or condone hazing.

"YOU! DOG-BREATH. Come here. My shoe's untied."

Sophomore Jason Whaley cringed. He knew the voice. It had been ringing in his ears, in his face, for days. And he knew he'd been caught again. For a moment, he considered acting as though he hadn't heard—and trying to disappear into the hallway crowd. But failure to hear the calls of senior musicians was one of the primary sins of aspiring band members—kind of a "what you don't know can hurt you." So he accepted his fate, walked over, bent down and tied—for the third time that day—Tyrone Bigg's Air Jordans.

"Thanks, Cat Barf. Now evaporate," Biggs said as his friends looked on and laughed.

Although hazing is illegal, for Jason and other students like him, joining clubs involved being subjected to one or two humiliations.

"Most of it is in good humor, but a few seniors go a little overboard," Jason said. "One of my friends had his clothes stolen while he was in gym class. And girls are pushed into boys' bathrooms all the time. It can get a little cruel."

Of course, not all inductions are so harrowing. The National Honor Society inductions are extremely formal. Held at the Glenview Country Club, the ceremonies involve tuxedos, formals and candles.

"We want members to appreciate the gravity of the situation," NHS president Barbara Richmond said. "While we don't take ourselves too seriously, we do have this one time of the year when we act with dignity and reflection."

Jason wasn't so lucky. Still, he survived the experience. And his message to next year's freshmen? "Get ready. I'm going to put them through hell." ★

✓ ACADEMIC SECTION

The typical academic section coverage goes like this: "The purpose of biology is to teach students about living organisms and the world around us. Teachers did this in a variety of ways, including a trip to the Smithsonian Museums in Washington, D.C.

Asked why students need to learn biology, Mrs. Sharon Cutworth said, "So that they will have an appreciation for all life including their own."

Classes are not important. What students learn in classes is. Occasionally, a reporter will focus on what students do in class. For example:

TAKING VITAL SIGNS, admitting patients, assisting doctors in the emergency rooms, helping maintain hospital equipment and facilities. All were experiences students in Health Occupation Students of America (HOSA) had through their health occupation classes.

HOSA is a leadership club for students in Vocational Health Occupation Education (VHOE). Through class experience and work with the club, students interested in medical careers could find out more about that career.

"The program is developed mostly for students wanting to pursue a career in the medical field," Emily Sparks, health occupation teacher, said. "The VHOE class and corresponding work responsibilities were designed to give the students some hands-on training on what a medical career is like." ★

Informative? Yes.

Interesting? Not very, which is a shame, given the powerful nature of the content. Medicine is a life-and-death career. Let's capture some of that drama in the copy. What were students' most frightening experiences? Describe the hustle and bustle of the emergency room. Tell us about the relationship between a student and a patient. Capture the sensory details and the emotions of the moment.

IT WAS 3:30 IN THE MORNING, and most of the staff on duty in the emergency room of North Hills Medical Center figured the big action for this Thursday night was over. A few had taken time to sit back, put their feet up and pull out a paperback novel. Senior Jeff Allen was sterilizing a gurney when a 1972 blue Mustang squealed into the driveway, barely missing a concrete walkway. The driver then sat down on the horn.

Racing outside, doctors found a 16-year-old boy, almost paralyzed in fear, his jeans soaked in blood. He had been playing with his dad's 38-caliber gun and had accidentally shot himself.

"The kid said his parents were out of town,

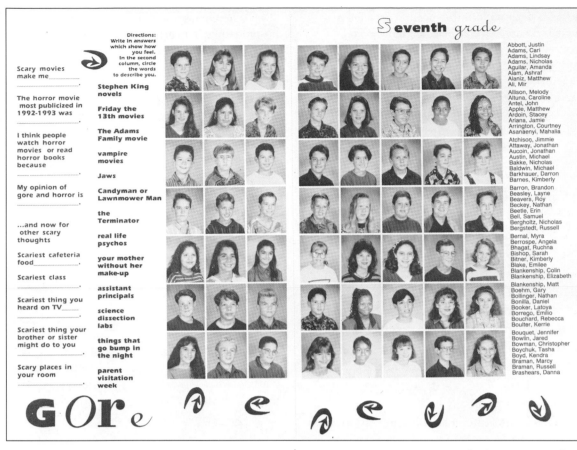

and he was too embarrassed to call 911 so he drove himself to the hospital," Jeff said. "He wanted to know if there was any way doctors could sew him up and let him go so that he wouldn't have to tell his father. He was more afraid his dad was going to kill him than he was of bleeding to death."

While brushes with life and death were rare, students in the Vocational Health Occupation Education classes got an inside look at America's health care system.

"At first, I thought we'd be doing a lot of menial labor, but that wasn't the case at all," senior Rita Martinez said. "We were in the rooms with the doctors and nurses. I helped restrain a man who had had a drug overdose. It was fascinating, and it certainly reinforced my plans to become a doctor." ★

✓ People Section

Without interesting copy, the people section quickly turns into row after row of mug shots. If you attend one of those mega-mall high schools, searching for the few dozen portraits among the thousands of faces

HAVE SOME FUN. *The Eagle* of Labay Junior High School in Houston used alternative copy blocks to appeal to young readers. Interactive copy, experts say, will become more popular with students. The adviser of the book was Kem Brossman.

can become fairly tedious in a hurry.

More than any other section of the book, the people section is the perfect place for the personality profiles and student life activity coverage. For instance, the junior section may profile an accomplished musician or actress. The feature section might look at the stress of taking driver training classes. Another section might include a feature on spring break vacations or participation in scavenger hunts.

The bottom line is this: Features must be timely, built on interesting direct quotes, descriptive and unique.

This is hardly the case with the following copy block, found on the social studies page of the faculty section:

THE STUDY of man, his past, present and

TIRED OF TRADITIONAL COPY? GO ALTERNATIVE

One of the more interesting developments in yearbook is alternative copy.

Rather than traditional lead/quote/transition formulized writing, alternative copy comes from such diverse inspirations as David Letterman's Top Ten List, Nickelodeon magazine and the typical fill-in-the-blank multiple choice test.

One of the leaders in the development and implementation of alternative copy is Kem Brossman of St. John's School in Houston.

Brossman's staffs (see example, left) have used open-ended statements, poetry, lists, how-to advice, and fill-in-the-blank sentences.

The objective is to produce copy that is highly personal, that in fact forces the yearbook readers to become copywriters themselves.

future, is dealt with in the social studies department. History, government, humanities and economics are presented to the classes. A working knowledge of these subjects is vital to a student's education.

"Those who do not know history are doomed to repeat it," social studies department chairman Ron Poling said. "Each course presents a little of all the rest as much of the information is intertwined." ★

That's it. Everything you want or need to remember about the social studies department. This copy satisfies none of the purposes of the yearbook. It serves no historic purpose. It doesn't record the facts, dates or figures of the year. It cannot be used in years to come as reference material. Nor can the school show it off as a public relations tool because it fails to show that writing or thinking skills are taking place in the classroom.

It's not strong copy.

This is. It's one of my all-time favorite features. It's from the Morgantown High School yearbook (Morgantown, West Virginia; Earl Straight, adviser). The name of the author is long lost so whoever you are, nice work.

JULIE OLSEN WILLIAMS. What a remarkable woman!

Her trauma began as a pregnant teenager in love with her stepfather, Doug, but carrying another man's child.

Addie, Julie's mother, dies shortly after giving birth to Doug's child, Hope, Julie's half-sister.

Julie, after fighting to regain custody of her illegitimate child and marrying a couple of men (both marriages ending in divorce), marries Doug, who had been in love with her all along. Hope, Julie's half-sister, now becomes a stepdaughter.

Rape now enters the picture as Julie kills the man who did it and, of course, gets out of the murder rap.

One might ask, "What else can possibly happen to a woman who's had an impossible life?"

Well, a house fire scars Julie's face and while she's being treated for the burn, she divorces Doug.

Doug remarries, and Julie returns from the hospital to be in nearly the same position she was in as a young woman—in love with a married man.

This incredible life belongs to a character in the long-running "Days of Our Lives" series, which was a favorite among seniors who spent their release time watching the soap operas.

So why do they watch these complicated stories of people with lives that are in shambles?

"Because they make my problems seem so small," senior Leslie Neely said. "I enjoy trying to figure out what's going to happen next."

Senior Amanda Gribble said she admires the action talents of the soap stars and is an avid fan of "Days of Our Lives."

"General Hospital" is Shari Miller's favorite soap.

"I've been watching it for 10 years," she said. "I used to watch it with my mother while I was growing up."

Quite a few men enjoy soaps too. Seniors Nick Blaskovics, Dave Rhudy and Alan Treat have often been found in front of the television watching "All My Children." So, join the crowd!

"The Doctors" say we've all got only "One Life To Live." Follow "The Guiding Light" to your television and enter "Another World:" the soap opera world. ★

✓ **Student life section**

Typically, students spend four years in high school, and most of it isn't spent sitting in class, participating in clubs or playing on teams. It's spent hanging out.

Student life copy should preserve the day-to-day activities, the moments that occur before, between and after the regimented activities of the school. The difficulty here is the tendency to ignore, minimize or dismiss these routine activities as legitimate copy possibilities. Students too often judge copy in the traditional news value structure—news must be about unusual or important events or prominent persons—which isn't always true. Certainly, pep rallies, homecoming, class elections, drama productions, mid-term tests, prom, graduation—the benchmark events—must be covered.

But that coverage should be balanced

against the reality that more time in high school is spent hanging out, working at minimum-wage jobs, wandering the malls, partying on weekends, driving up and down the road, and—above all—trying to woo the opposite sex. Not all students are beauty queens and National Honor Society officers, but 99.9 percent of high school students know what it's like to try to fit in, to find a niche and a gang, even if the gang consists of five geeky freshmen girls who occupy the seventh through eleventh chairs in the flute section of the concert band.

The trick to successful yearbook copy in general—and student life copy in particular—is to capture those emotions shared by all students. You can't list every name of every person who went to the prom, and you don't want to publish a lot of predictable data—the prom was held at the Four Seasons Hotel, the theme was "Midnight in Havana," the band was "The Runny Noses" and everyone had a great time. Duh!

But with a little empathy and creativity, you can capture the double-edged sword of anxiety and excitement that the prom generates. For example:

BRAD BAILEY RENTED a tuxedo, picked up his date and hopped a helicopter to the prom. "It was a blast," Bailey said.

After the prom, the helicopter flew the pair to Galveston, where they spent the weekend in a rented house with several couples—and his parents. Bailey's prom night is not as unique as it may sound. Helicopter shuttles for prom night have become more popular, competing with last year's symbol: the limousine. Some students say it's all part of the new "the sky's the limit" approach to the finances of prom night.

"I've been working for three years, saving a little here and there so that I could have the time of my life at the senior prom," said Shawn Dill, another student who rented a helicopter ride for him and his date, Andrea Faust. He said the ride alone cost $350. "The hardest part was convincing Andrea's dad that it was safe."

Of course, not everyone could afford to go to such lengths to impress their dates. Joey Moore said he didn't need expensive tricks to impress his date.

"I'm a great kisser," he said. "It's tough for a helicopter to compete with that." ★

Of course, prom is one of those "big moments" of high school. Any competent school journalist should be capable of cranking out a story that at least reports the who, what, when, where, why and how—even though that's not the real story.

But how does one report the not-so-major events—those Friday nights without dates, the five minutes between classes, the evenings at home with the family? By taking the same approach: isolate the theme, and look for the angle. As always, tell the story in terms of a specific person. Also, research, describe and interpret. For every Brad Bailey who rented the helicopter and whisked his date to the prom, there's another kid whose dreams of romance didn't come true, or at least fell far short of expectations.

For every kid whose name was on the A-list at the popular parties, there's half a dozen who spend their Friday nights flipping hamburgers or taking tickets at the local theatre. Their stories need to be told, too. And the news is not that they're holding down part-time jobs. The news is that they have dreams, ambitions, frustrations, anxieties of every nature and occasionally great triumphs. I believe that's what readers want to remember.

Your job is to help them.

THE MAGIC OF PARALLEL SENTENCE CONSTRUCTION

Eloquent sentence construction requires that the writer places ideas that are alike (parallel) in thought or meaning into grammatical forms or constructions that are alike.

The purpose of parallel structure is to unify ideas and to engage readers in an easy-to-follow thought process.

Note the parallel construction in the story at the bottom of page 144.

"Players and their girlfriends, coaches and parents, hugging . . . slapping . . . strutting . . . ."

Note how much less effective the sentence would have been had the writer ignored parallel structure:

"Twenty minutes after the game had ended, they remained on the frozen turf of Remington field, players and their girlfriends, coaches and parents, hugging one another. They were slapping one another's backs, and they strutted up and down the field . . . ."

Precise sentence construction makes or breaks a great story.

HELLO OFFICE:

THIS IS MY MOTHER, AND I WON'T BE IN SCHOOL TODAY

Sometimes, the truth resides not in a single event, but in a composite representing moments gleaned from the hundreds of hours spent in classes over the course of the year. Finding this truth requires reporters to analyze, research, observe and interview.

Keen reporters must look for irony and anecdotes. They must compare and contrast. They must keep a sense of humor and balance.

Their rewards are stories that capture the essence of everyday life in the high school classroom. This one certainly does.

By RICHARD MOON
Eisenhower High School
Lawton, Oklahoma

SHOWCASE

A GRIN CRAWLED from ear to ear. A sweaty palm was extended. Sheepishly, junior Marcus Absent awaited a small white piece of paper which meant a passport to munch Doritos, to grab a quick smoke or to take care of nature.

How did students manage getting out of class when the most exciting action was watching your next chair neighbor pick popcorn out of his teeth?

All it took was a little imagination and a non-existent conscience.

Students, pressured for an immediate explanation when asking to leave, resorted to the stock excuses known as the 'I got to's'…

'I got to go home and turn off the iron, or the house will catch fire again.'

'I got to see my counselor right now or I can't get into college.'

'I got to take my medicine right now or I might die!'

'I got to go to the bathroom … real bad!'

Sometimes these worked. Often they didn't. Students discovered that the more creative the excuse, the better the results. At least this way teachers couldn't say, 'I've heard that one before . . .' and 'Ah! That's excuse number 246 . . . .'

'There's an OU (Oklahoma University) scout waiting for me in the office. I have to meet him right now!' conned Calvin Phillips as he received a hall pass.

The 'I got to's' worked well for conning the new teacher. But how could a junior con his way out of the class of a seasoned teacher? One who had the top drawer of her filing cabinet full of excuses dating back to ones like, 'I have to leave early to help put up posters for President Taft's re-election.'

It was for this "tough" teacher, the teacher with X-ray eyes and a built-in telepathic lie detector that Red Alert, Phase Two, Emergency Excuse had to be implemented.

"I was running across the patio to get to class on time, and this herd of girls attacked me."

"This boy fainted in the hall, and I had to stand over him so nobody would step on him."

Mrs. Ginny Kish pointed out the teachers' view.

"I can recognize the creative ones after a few excuses," she said. "I just don't let them out anymore."

But teachers didn't always recognize the excusemakers. Sometimes even fellow students couldn't decipher the validity of the excuses. That is, until the student turned around quietly and with a slight chuckle mouthed the word S-U-C-K-E-R! ★

CHAPTER FOURTEEN

FORGET TRADITION

A report from the American Society of Newspaper Editors finds that the inverted pyramid doesn't reach readers. As a solution, the report encourages more storytelling in news.

Criticizing the inverted pyramid doesn't go over well with some advisers. They've surveyed the current state of journalism and don't find much to their liking, at all. News leads these days, they argue, are too chatty, too informal. They lack the discipline, the precision of the inverted pyramid.

The criticism may well be true. But the problem of undisciplined copy resides not in the structure but in the execution of the writing and editing. A narrative approach should be as disciplined, precise and concise as a straight traditional news lead.

At a summer workshop, I watched a veteran adviser sit in the back of the class and register her displeasure as I performed my dog and pony show on news reporting. As soon as it became clear that I would have little good to say about the sacred inverted pyramid, she began a slow boil. She rolled her eyes and then squinted them into tiny slits when she wanted to make certain she'd heard me correctly, as though squinting helped her hearing. She'd frown, cross and uncross her arms, and purse her lips.

I'm no expert on body language, but I could tell she wasn't buying my spiel.

After the session, she marched up to the front of the room and wanted to know upon what I based my opinion.

"I've taught the inverted pyramid for 20 years, and it's worked for us," she snapped. She did everything but wag her finger in my face.

"Our local paper has started using these feature approaches," she added. "And I don't find anything journalistic about them."

Oh, to suffer for the sins of others.

I was polite. I didn't say, "Sure. Like your hometown paper is up to its eyeballs in Pulitzers."

Instead, I told her that there will remain a place in student publications for summary leads that answer who, what, when, where, why and how in the first 25 words. The inverted pyramid shall survive, for one reason or another.

However, to answer her question: I base my opinion in part on the fact that I have judged student newspapers for 15 years and have found an inordinate percentage of their content to be boring beyond belief. So, part of my conviction results from personal observation.

Furthermore, research supports me: In 1993, the American Society of Newspaper Editors Literacy Committee released "Ways with Words," which found, among other things, "the traditional, inverted pyramid style that dominates newspaper writing does not work very well with readers."

How did the researchers come to this conclusion? On each of four days in January, 1993, the *St. Petersburg* (Florida) *Times* reporters wrote the same story in four different modes: the straight traditional mode, the narrative mode, the point-of-view mode, and the radical-clarity mode.

✓ The straight traditional mode primarily used the inverted pyramid, which places the most important facts in the first few paragraphs and moves into background and less

THE EXPERIMENT:

Testing the assumpions on which the inverted pyramid is built

The inverted pyramid satisfies the needs of reporters much better than it does readers. That's the conclusion of the Literacy Committee of the American Society of Newspaper Editors. In fact, most reporters know only one story form to report hard news—the inverted pyramid—even though other story forms are available.

The inverted pyramid allows the reporter to write a catch lead and then arrange information in descending order of importance.

The editor can then whack off as much of the end of the story as necessary, without even having to read it, because he or she assumes the reporter didn't tack on the fact that the cafeteria exploded at the end of the lunch menu story.

The problem with the inverted pyramid, Don Fry and Roy Peter Clark of the Poynter Institute claim, is that only journalists and sources can understand the information.

"Journalists put background and context in the second half of the pyramid so the reader who does not know that background cannot understand the top of the story," Fry and Clark state.

"Journalists fear any appearance of bias so they reduce people in their stories to names and titles, avoid description and hide the point of the story, or worse, write without a point.

The leaders explain that journalists also assume more knowledge than the average reader has.

"This combination of the inverted pyramid, assumptions and flat characterizations and description make stories daunting and difficult to understand for readers," they state.

To avoid repeating the same mistakes year after year, journalists could draw on other story forms and modes of storytelling in magazines and other literary or artistic publications. For the sake of the experiment, Fry and Clark created four writing modes: straight traditional, narrative, the point-of-view and radical-clarity.

These modes were tested on four consecutive days. The first story involved people returning gift pets after Christmas. Each story was accompanied by the same headline, subhead and photograph—in this case, of a cute pooch named "Jake."

important information as the story progresses.

✓ The narrative mode told a story with actions performed by characters in time sequences, including some chronological order. The story had a beginning, a middle and an end, as opposed to the straight traditional mode, which begins with the strong lead, followed by several paragraphs backing up the lead and less important information— background and context primarily—at the bottom.

✓ The point-of-view mode told a story with a viewpoint immediately clear to the reader. This story attempted to persuade by showing rather than telling, and for that reason could take any shape except the inverted pyramid.

✓ The radical-clarity mode assumed the reader knows nothing and so arranged material in an order that maximized reader understanding and explained everything the reader might need explained.

"We published the four different stories in four adjacent zones on the front page of the local section," stated Don Fry and Roy Peter Clark of the Poynter Institute of Media Studies. Fry, director of writing programs, and Clark, associate director and dean of the faculty, developed the reporting and writing techniques studied in the project. "We tried to make everything the same except the story techniques: All four were the same length and were accompanied by the same headline, subhead and photograph. We rotated the modes so that each reporter wrote a story in

By ELIJAH
GOSIER

PETS REMAIN a popular gift despite the advice of animal advocates who warn that giving pets is a bad idea. This week, like paisley ties and sweaters that don't fit, many of those pets are being returned or abandoned.

But unlike ties and sweaters, cats and dogs don't hang on a rack waiting for another buyer; many of them linger in cages waiting to be killed.

"It's not like clothes. This is not something you can return. It's a life," said Mary Chaboudy, officer manager for the Humane Society of North Pinellas.

The Society for the Prevention of Cruelty to Animals took in 14,500 pets last year. Of those, 54 percent of the dogs and 75 percent of the cats were killed. At the Human Society of North Pinellas, about half of the 12,700 animals were killed.

The county shelter gets about 15,000 animals each year, of which 6,500 are dogs and most of the rest are cats, shelter director Ken Mitchell said. After five working days, most are killed by injection of a deadly amount of barbiturates. Overall, 80 percent of the animals the shelter gets are killed.

"It's a fate that all shelters have to deal with," Mitchell said.

Processing the often doomed animals is anguishing to workers.

Chaboudy said unwanted animals start coming into the society's shelters this week when children, who are often the recipients of pets as gifts, return to school. Other experts say it takes from six weeks to eight months to see the gift pets come back. Annually, about 13-million animals are taken in by shelters nationally. More than half of those animals have to be killed.

In Pinellas County last year, the Friends of Strays, a volunteer organization that finds homes for stray dogs and cats, made 3,600 adoptions, its executive director said. Jean Bomonti said fewer than 40 of the animals were returned. She and other advocates say the successful pet placement is a result of a conscientious seller and an educated buyer.

Bomonti said her organization does not place animals as gifts. The American Kennel Club, the nation's largest purebred registry and an advocate for dogs, launches a massive campaign each year, discouraging sellers and potential buyers from giving pets as gifts, public relations manager Suzanne Lustig said.

"There has been an increase over the years in returned animals."

Luster said the AKC has no figures on dogs returned or abandoned but bases its assessment on the response from shelters and dog clubs across the country.

"As a policy, we don't endorse giving pets as gifts—as an object," Lustig said. "There are no statistics, but there is a specific cause and effect. It takes a while to sink in—maybe six or eight months—the time, the case and costs, and everything involved in owning a pet."

Advocates say the potential pet owner should realize owning a pet is a lifetime commitment. Dorothy Crockett, who runs an agency that adopts greyhounds retired from racing, said she carefully screens prospective owners. "These people come to the kennel, and I interview them and they decide what they want, and they really spend time in the kennel. Usually the dog picks the person."

She said only two of the 70 dogs she placed last year were returned, one because the dog could not be housebroken.

Advocates recognize that pets and owners sometimes will prove incompatible, and they suggest ways to improve the animal's chances of finding another home and surviving:

Give you and the animal a little time to adjust to each other; show your pet as much tolerance as you'd show a child. But don't dally after the decision is made; younger animals are more likely to be adopted. Rather than abandon the animal, animal advocates say, try to find it a good home. ★

"Ways with Words" costs $5 and is available from the American Society of Newspaper Editors Foundation, Box 4090, Reston, VA 22090–1700.

---

each mode, and each zone received a different mode each day, ultimately receiving all four."

Stories were chosen for their potential interest to readers living in all four circulation zones.

"We wanted ordinary stories, no splashy ones, hard news rather than features," Fry and Clark stated. "Because of early deadlines, we had to avoid breaking stories though all the stories were typical one-day stories and one was the morning-after report of a county commission meeting."

Each night after the stories ran, at least 220 random subscribers were questioned about their reading habits and about the four stories. They were asked:
• How much of the story they read and whether they followed the jump.
• What they learned, using true-false questions.
• How fair, balanced and well written the stories were.
• Whether they cared about the subject, whether the stories connected with their own experiences and whether the stories made them want to find out more and/or get involved.

The survey found that "writing matters to readers," according to Frank Denton, ASNE

By THOMAS
TOBIN

JUST BEFORE Christmas three years ago, Lesly Stevens was forced to play Scrooge.

But the result , she said, was a better life for Pumpkin, a 9-week-old kitten that had been found in the bushes near Gandy Boulevard. Stevens, a volunteer for Friends of Strays, Inc., fed the kitten baby formula and strained chicken soup.

Pumpkin was still a bit weak when along came a "very insistent" man who wanted to buy the kitten for his 2-year-old daughter.

"Actually they didn't like me too much because I wouldn't let them take the animal home for Christmas," she said. "I just had to discourage him because the child was awful. She was just too wild."

More on Pumpkin later.

Suffice it to say she escaped a fate that befalls many pets at Christmas time. Too often, cats, dogs and other pets are purchased on an impulse, animal welfare workers say.

Later, they say, pets often get lost in the hubbub of the holidays, and the neglect can lead to a lack of supervision. As a result, many new pets and their adopted families get off on the wrong foot, and the pet is returned.

The problem continues to grow despite repeated warnings to adoptive families to consult the pet recipient first.

"Each year it keeps getting worse and worse," said Rick Chaboudy, director of the Humane Society of Pinellas County.

Since Christmas, 15 animals have been returned to the Society for the Prevention of Cruelty to Animals of St. Petersburg, executive director Gail Rassier said.

The reasons can be found on the SPCA's return forms: "can't afford"; "the other dog doesn't like"; "needs bigger yard"; or "chewed Christmas presents."

Jake, a 6-month-old yellow Labrador retriever, was too rough with small children. Chief, a German shepherd mix, made for some exciting holiday moments when he sprang over a 4-foot fence.

Rassier said she expects the SPCA to take back up to 70 Christmas pets this month.

"It's a threefold tragedy: for the animal worker, the owner and the pet," Rassier said. "This is a very traumatic thing for them. Usually there's a lot of crying."

The county shelter gets about 15,000 animals a year, shelter director Ken Mitchell said. After five working days, most are killed by injection of a deadly amount of barbiturates. Overall, 80 percent of the animals the shelter gets are killed.

At the SPCA and the Humane Society of North Pinellas, half or more of the dogs and cats are killed.

Animal workers say they expect another increase in animal drop-offs in a few months, when the "cuteness" of holiday pets wears off.

"It's a commitment—like a child," said Stevens, the neighborhood "cat lady" who usually keeps several stray cats at her house in St. Petersburg. Pumpkin, she said, ended up as a pet for a high-school-age girl.

"She's spoiled-rotten, and she does real well."

The cat, not the girl. ★

Literacy Committee chairman and editor of the *Wisconsin State Journal* in Madison.

After crunching all of its numbers, the research team presented five major conclusions:

1. The inverted pyramid style that dominates newspaper writing does not work very well with readers. It has some strengths, fulfilling some reader's expectations of news stories, but more weaknesses, particularly with the people who are less likely to read newspapers today. Readers with less than a high-school education were especially ill-served by the traditional writing mode.

2. Storytelling techniques offer great potential for newspapers. Averaging all kinds of readers and all four stories, the narrative versions were simply better read, and they communicated information better.

3. Older, loyal readers and women are less picky; that is, they were more willing to sort out different styles. Younger and less frequent readers—those whom we are trying hardest to reach—favored the narrative and radical-clarity techniques.

4. Perhaps because it is alien to the prevailing newspaper ethic, or because it can be condescending, the point-of-view technique did not fare well among most readers and thus seems to offer the least potential. The only exception was the less-educated reader, who appeared to be reached most effectively by point-of-view.

5. Newspapers aiming at a less-educated readership should reconsider their reliance on traditional writing and experiment with other techniques, all of which worked better with such readers.

Admitting the experiment "did not achieve the kind of polarized results editors

By JENNIFER L.
STEVENSON
St. Petersburg Times

THEY ARE the little animals the holiday season purports to adore: The puppies with the big eyes and floppy ears. The kittens with the downy fur.

They're babies in a new world. And they don't mean to pull down the Christmas tree, claw the furniture or make the other dog mad. They didn't know it was wrong to eat the gifts with the shiny tags. They didn't understand that the holiday turkey was for your dinner, not theirs.

That doesn't mean they should end up in a cage. Or dead.

That's what happens to holiday pets who are returned to shelters after Christmas, like a sweater that doesn't fit or a tie that doesn't match your shirt.

Just take a peek in the Society for the Prevention of Cruelty to Animal's shelter in Largo: So far 15 pets have been returned after Christmas. By the end of January, up to 70 will be abandoned by owners who did not comprehend—or did not care—what adopting a pet really means.

Despite warnings from animal

activists that pets do not make good Christmas presents, many animals were adopted this season. And once again, many are being returned for being "too much trouble."

There's Jake, a yellow lab confined to a stainless steel cage for the crime of playing with his adopted family too much. He has lots of company: Chief, the shepherd mutt who climbed the fence, and Angie, who chewed up the Christmas presents.

"These are things animals do, but people can't deal with it," said Gail Rassier, executive director of SPCA of St. Petersburg. "Living breathing creatures carry a lot of responsibility."

And apparently, it's a chore that owners do not want to face once the excitement of a new puppy wears off.

In December, 1991, Rassier said, 290 dogs were adopted at the SPCA, most likely for Christmas presents. In December alone, people rejected 49 dogs. In January, owners gave up on another 52.

"Once it piddles on the carpet or tears up the furniture, there's a problem," Mary Chaboudy, office manager of the Humane Society of Pinellas County, said Monday. "If it's not perfect, it comes back."

Rick Chaboudy, executive di-

rector of the society and Mary's husband, said the annual parade of returned dogs always discourages him.

"You feel very sad for the puppies and very angry at the people," Chaboudy said. If you must give an animal as a present, he said, consult the recipient first. Or better yet, buy a gift certificate.

Once an animal is abandoned at the shelter, its chances at life dwindle. At the SPCA, more than half of the dogs brought to the shelter each year are killed, and 75 percent of the cats die. At the Humane Society, about half of all animals die.

For the animals that are returned to the Pinellas County Animal Control Shelter, the outlook is bleaker. That shelter gets 15,000 animals a year, of which 80 percent are killed. According to the Humane Society of the United States, once an animal is left at a shelter, its chances of survival are less than 50 percent.

That's something to think about when shopping for that special Christmas gift for Austin, Marlene or Cousin Andrea.

An animal goes back to the shelter. Just ask Jake and Chief.

They're spending their new year in a cage. ★

---

might prefer," Fry and Clark explained that the results could be interpreted to suggest uses for the narrative, radical-clarity and point-of-view modes of writing.

"Generally, reporters should incorporate narrative techniques into stories to lead readers through the whole story," they stated. "Those techniques include actually telling stories, focusing on action, characters and chronology. Narrative techniques reveal mostly by showing, with a little telling for framing."

In addition, Fry and Clark stated:
• We should encourage storytelling in news stories. Narrative techniques encourage readers to make jumps and read more deeply into stories.
• We should think of the traditional form

(inverted pyramid and AP style) as A form, rather than THE form. Reporters should keep traditional stories short because readers seem less willing to make the jump in this mode.
• We should use radical-clarity not as a story form but as a test of reporting depth.
• We should use radical-clarity for parts of stories, not the whole. We might think of radical-clarity as a sidebar form.
• We should train our reporters and editors to accept and use new forms and techniques. Even experienced and talented journalists needed retraining and coaching for this experiment.
• We should take chances, experimenting to find the forms that serve our readers rather than ourselves.

WHERE TO GET HELP

City, regional, state and national scholastic press associations provide a wealth of services. The major national associations include:

Columbia Scholastic Press Association, Box 11, Central Mail Room, Columbia University, New York, NY 10027-6969. Ed Sullivan, director. 212-854-9400; (fax) 854-9401.

Journalism Education Association, Kansas State University, 103 Kedzie Hall, Manhattan, KS 66506-1505. Linda Puntney, executive director. 913-532-5532; (fax) 532-7309.

National Scholastic Press Association, University of Minnesota, 620 Rarig Center, 330 21st Avenue South, Minneapolis, Minn. 55455. Tom Rolnicki, director. 612/625-8335; (fax) 626-0720.

Quill & Scroll Society, School of Journalism and Mass Communication, University of Iowa, Iowa City, Iowa, 52242-1528. Richard P. Johns, executive director. 319-335-5795; (fax)

By ALICIA
CALDWELL
St. Petersburg Times

IMAGINE yourself in this situation: You get an adorable puppy as a holiday gift from a well-meaning friend.

The problem is you just can't keep the lovable mutt. It would be unfair to leave the dog cooped up all day while you're at work. To top it off, he piddles on the rug. A lot.

So what do you do? Probably the same thing many others in Pinellas County are doing at this time of year. You take the little pooch to the pound.

Anguished animal workers say this week begins a deluge of returned pets, a scenario that will continue for months, despite their warnings against giving pets as holiday gifts.

Nevertheless, the holiday pet syndrome does not seem to be waning.

"Every year it keeps getting worse and worse," said Rick Chaboudy, director of the Humane Society of North Pinellas.

Animal workers say they expect another wave of unwanted pets in a few months when their "cuteness" wears off.

Each year, 13 million pets across the country are dropped off at animal shelters. Of those, 8 million are killed, according to figures from the Humane Society of the United States as quoted in *USA Weekend*.

In Pinellas, the two largest shelters are run by the Society for the Prevention of Cruelty to Animals of St. Petersburg and the county shelter.

The county shelter gets about 15,000 animals a year, of which 6,500 dogs and most of the rest are cats, shelter director Ken Mitchell said. After five working days, most are killed by injection of a deadly amount of barbiturates. Overall, 80 percent of the animals are killed.

The SPCA took in 14,500 pets last year. Just over half of the dogs and 75 percent of the cats had to be killed. About half of the Human Society's 12,700 pets had to be killed.

"It's a fate that all shelters have to deal with," Mitchell said.

Here's how to protect a pet from this fate:

✓ Don't give a pet for a holiday gift. If you feel absolutely compelled to give a pet as a present, do your homework. Make sure your friend really wants a pet. Then find out the breed, color, sex and disposition of the pet the person would like. Best of all, have the recipient choose the pet.

"I know that from personal experience," said Harvey Partridge, a St. Petersburg veterinarian. "My wife saw a little dog at the SPCA, and that was her dog. I never would have chosen that dog in a hundred years."

✓ Give the pet a chance to adjust before declaring irreconcilable differences. However, don't wait too long because the younger the pet, the most likely it will be adopted. Try to find a good home for the animal and above all, do not abandon it.

✓ Know the possible ramifications of giving a pet. If your gift pet ends up at an animal shelter, chances are good that no one will want it, and it will be killed. ★

IMPLICATIONS

The implications of this study for the student press are clear. High schools consist largely of young, inexperienced newspaper readers. The research found that the youngest group of readers learned best with narrative stories (and worst with traditional versions). Denton noted, "If an editor wants to reach young (under 30) readers, the narrative and radical-clarity stories are better read than the other techniques."

He also noted, "The least educated (without a high-school diploma) not only read radical-clarity the most and traditional the least, they also rated it the highest quality (and, again, traditional the lowest). But they learned from point-of-view and narrative (and the least from traditional)."

Whether the results of this survey can be generalized to a high-school readership is a question that future researchers may want to tackle. My gut feeling is the inverted pyramid will fare even worse among high school students than it did among the unwitting participants in the ASNE study.

In fact, the battle to win converts will not be fought on the high-school level, where readers are likely to embrace writing modes other than the inverted pyramid, but rather at the college and university level—in the offices of scholastic press associations which still place a premium on a writing form whose heyday has long since passed.

It is my hope that student editors and reporters will look beyond the current standards and conventions because we as a people cannot survive unless we are informed, and newspapers must change to serve the new generation of readers. It is this concern for their readers that is the basis for a publication's greatness, whether that publication is *The New York Times*, the *Wall Street Journal* or the *Pumpkin High Press*.

GET TO WORK

You are on the verge of a great adventure. As a journalist,
you will have a chance to grow as an individual
and to change, for the better, the world in which you live.

I hate to write, but I love to have written.

That line pretty much sums up the philosophy of many journalists. Writing is hard work. It's time-consuming, frustrating and sometimes tedious. And this comes on the heels of the hours and hours we've spent reporting—gathering facts, interviewing sources, watching and listening, thumbing through magazines or newspaper clippings for background information.

The great majority of time spent on a story involves collecting information, not writing. But as time-consuming as reporting is, it's the actual writing that most often drives us nuts. We cram all of this information into our brains and expect it to simmer until done. And when it doesn't pour out in flawless prose, we pull our hair out.

When the words won't come, when we can't remember what we want to say or how we want to say it, we question our sanity. Why did I sign up to be a reporter? Or an editor? Why put myself through this?

The thought of blowing it off zips through our minds. "Who reads this stuff anyway?" we ask ourselves. For the moment, we entertain the thought of turning in a story that isn't our best effort. But then we realize that doing so would not so much betray the subject and our readers as it would ourselves.

Ultimately, writing is a personal experience, an act of self-love. We have something to say. We want people to listen so we put ourselves on the line. We reveal our insecurities, our dreams, our passions. It takes courage and effort.

I believe it is this unwillingness to compromise our own sense of self-worth that frustrates so many young writers. It manifests itself in different ways. For example, a few former students attempted to convince me that they suffered from writer's block. I would have believed them had they written anything, which of course they had not. Rather than writer's block, they were stifled because their stories weren't writing themselves. They wanted the words simply to fly out the ends of their magic fingers.

It would have been nice, but that's not how it works. So get used to it. If you want to be a journalist, expect some pain. Buy aspirin. Find a shoulder to cry on. Be prepared to miss a few hours of sleep. I can think of nothing more torturous than searching for the perfect angle, the perfect lead.

So if someone tells you they love to write, don't buy it. If they truly love to write, then they're not working at it hard enough.

I don't say this to scare you off. Quite the contrary. I want you to fall in love with the sweet agony of reporting and writing. It can be fun, even thrilling. Too many students are turned off by teachers who think that writing is nothing more than an exercise in punctuation. I once heard an English teacher say, "I warned my students that if they used a passive verb, it was an automatic D."

I thought, "You're the kind of teacher who'd flunk John Irving."

That teacher probably used writing as a

form of torture. "Write 500 times, 'I will not use a passive verb.'"

While writing isn't easy, it brings great personal satisfaction to have written something that you're proud of, a story on which you gladly place your name. When the adviser is prodding the reporter to just get it done, it takes a special steel to respond, "Yeah, but it's my name on the story. I can't just give my readers junk."

The desire to do well comes not so much from others—the adviser, the staff, the school or the state press association—but rather from within. The standards of others may help tap that self-realization and pride in a productive way, but the desire to want to produce as perfect a product as possible must exist. Otherwise, no amount of external pressure will pry it out.

This desire to produce arises also from a need to serve. The joy of writing leads to a special result: the joy of reading. As staff members produce carefully crafted words and reflect emotions as well as ideas, readers respond. Even students who rarely read assignments will read the writing of their peers if those writers put energy and imagination into their work. At those schools, readers complain when they haven't received their paper for two weeks. "Why do we have to wait so long for another issue?" Or, "Why didn't the staff work during vacation so there would be an issue sooner?"

And though educators may not believe it, many of those demanding "their rights as readers" are the non-scholars in the school. But even students who fail courses or cause trouble in school are people too. You can speak to them in ways that show that somebody cares and that life can be interesting.

Quite simply, it's a genuine thrill to have someone you don't know—a person out of your social and educational orbit—tell you that they enjoyed reading an article you wrote. You realize that your writing has legs. It travels beyond the limits of your imagination, and you realize that you are contributing to a literacy of your world. Even better, you have helped others to be informed, to be

vital, to enjoy life on a new dimension—and to feel the joy of fulfilling dreams and the sadness of others' hardships.

I work with men and women who have graduate degrees but who are not writers. They are expected to compose at least one column each month, September through May. It's my job to edit their columns.

Only one or two of these people are naturally gifted writers, but they all have a basic understanding of the written word. The difference in the quality of the columns boils down to the amount of time each spends on his or her column. A few whip them out in an hour, columns that rehash one of two or three themes, all of which are perfunctory to the point of cliché. Participation is good. Sportsmanship is important. Rules are necessary. Blah, blah, blah.

For them, writing is an exercise no different than filling out a form.

Others spend time with the columns. They don't especially look forward to writing them. It takes time and work. It takes concentration. But they put forth the effort so their columns are an extension of their personality and character. They know they will be judged by their written comments. The publication is circulated to 33,000 teachers and school administrators in Texas alone, as well as to a few hundred others throughout the nation. The widespread circulation sufficiently scares them to do as good a job as possible.

I want you to share their fright. I want you to remember your story will be distributed to every student in the high school, every reader may take the newspaper home, every parent may take the paper to work the next day. I want you to realize every person in your community may have a chance to see your story. I want this to scare you so badly you'd never dare turning in a story that didn't receive your maximum effort and was worth reading.

Perhaps it won't be perfect. But it should be the best story you can produce in the time you're given to write it. John Lennon once said he never finished writing a song—he simply recorded the latest version in time to include it on the latest Beatles album. You should feel the same way about your stories. You will always find a better way to write it, but when the deadline rolls around, you should have produced the best draft possible.

I also want to share the exhilaration, the sheer fun of working hard on a story or column. Because you deliberately strive to provide something for everyone—from the lowly freshman to the all-powerful school board—you nap and record as many scenes of life as possible. You record the energy of Friday night parties and the acrid smell of the locker rooms to the din of the band hall. You record the moments that made the school and community proud—when the National Merit scholars are named—as well as the facts that the powers might wish were left brushed under the rug.

With so many possibilities to unleash your creativity and spirit, you and your fellow staffers will experience the rush of going from blank pages to pages bearing thousands of words and art and photos. Quite frankly, I'm a little jealous of you. You are about to have some of the most important, the most thrilling, the most painful experiences of your life. Some of this can be attributed to the fact that you're a high-school student. But much of it stems from the fact that you're part of a special collection of teenagers.

Finally, remember you're a beginner, no matter how many years you've served on the staff. You're going to make mistakes. Even though your adviser and editors are there to cover for you, mistakes will slip through. It happens to everyone. You have to learn to forgive yourself and press on.

Over the years, I've written hundreds of articles and columns. Now and then, I thumb through them. While reading these clips brings me some satisfaction, I always second-guess myself. Why did I use that lead? What did I mean by that? Who was I trying to impress when I used that word?

Occasionally, I'm embarrassed by something I've written. As a young reporter, I wrote what has to be one of the worst leads in the history of American journalism. The story involved the rewriting of Texas bank regulations, and I had interviewed at length the president of a local bank. To my eternal shame, I wrote: "In this fruit salad called life, the banker is the top banana."

It had little or nothing to do with changes in bank regulations. At the time, though, I thought it was clever. Now, it makes me cringe. I blame my editors. I was young and stupid. They should have been watching out for me. Why didn't they save me from myself?

In high school, I wrote a pre-game football story that our opponents found fit to duplicate and plaster throughout their school. They thought I had dissed them. I didn't mean to. It just came out that way. Of course, this unexpected motivation didn't please the head football coach. If we had lost the game, I'm sure he would have blamed me.

These lapses aside, I'm proud of my writing. I want you to feel the same way about yours. I hope you can pick up your newspaper or yearbook 25 years from now and read one of your stories with pride. I hope the stories entertain you, rekindle a few emotions, take you to back when.

They will if you'll put some heart and soul into them, if you'll strive for something greater than mere correctness. They will if you'll abandon the strangulating traditional writing styles in favor of more narrative, descriptive approaches. It requires more work. It takes great dedication. But the effort is well worth it.

I know. I wanted to quit writing this book months ago, to settle for something less than it is. But my editor, Howard Spanogle, refused to let me. He pushed and prodded me, embarrassed me at times, mocked me and then pampered my ego.

Now that it's finished, I can say unequivocally that I'm glad I wrote it. I'm glad I worked on it a year longer than I had expected to. I didn't love writing it, but I love the fact that it's written. I want you to experience the same satisfaction every time your words appear in print.

GUARDIAN OF ALL FREEDOMS

"A free press is the unsleeping guardian of every other right that free men prize; it is the most dangerous foe of tyranny. . . . Under dictatorship the press is bound to languish, and the loudspeaker and the film to become more important. But where free institutions are indigenous to the soil and men have the habit of liberty, the press will continue to be the Fourth Estate, the vigilant guardian of the rights of the ordinary citizen."

—*Winston Churchill
(1874-1965)*

Violence in the Classroom

DISD battles surge in attacks on teachers as counselors try to ease students' hostility

By ANNA MACIAS
Dallas Morning News

JAMES MILLER was calling roll in his first-period history class last month when one of his 14-year old students started shouting, throwing paper and walking around the room.

The Stockard Middle School teacher's cure to send him to the office came when the boy pulled a marijuana cigarette out of his pocket.

But before Mr. Miller could fill out the principal's referral form, witnesses said, the youth punched him repeatedly in the face, slammed him against a chalkboard and knocked him out.

A classroom full of stunned eighth-graders looked on as the boy kicked the unconscious teacher in the chest and fled.

Mr. Miller was left with a broken nose, loose teeth, eye damage and bruises. He has been on medical leave since the attack Jan. 7 at the Oak Cliff school.

In Dallas and other urban school districts across the nation, the safety of teachers and principals is a growing concern.

In the 1991 fall semester alone, there were 47 assaults against Dallas Independent School District staff members, district security reports show. In each of the two previous school years, the total for both semesters was about 60 assaults. Associate Superintendent Chad Woolery said the district is devoting more resources than ever before to fighting school crime and helping troubled youths.

"We're doing a great number of things," Mr. Woolery said. "The first thing is to establish safe-school committees at all schools. We've fully staffed all youth action centers with Dallas police officers. We're working on getting color-coded ID badges for all 10 high schools."

Mr. Woolery also said the district provides counseling to help troubled students. But four child psychologists were cut as a cost-saving measure this year, making the counseling staff "overworked and understaffed," he said.

District officials also are quick to point out that violence in schools reflects violence in the city.

School board president Rene Castilla says the assault problem is much more than DISD can handle alone, adding that the board would welcome help from outside groups or companies.

"The school board has stressed that we're going to protect teachers and students from abuse," Mr. Castilla said. "But we have not made any visible progress. The board has given every resource the schools have asked for. We're at our wits' end."

An update on school security is among topics planned at Tuesday's board work session.

Most frequently, teacher assaults are committed by angry teenagers who blow up at teachers after a simple reprimand or criticism, accounts in security reports show. Often, teachers trying to stop fights among students are injured.

"There's a lot of angry young people that are just mad at you as an authority," said Maureen Peters, president of the Alliance of Dallas Educators. "These kids don't see any future for themselves. Their families are scraping to make ends meet.

"There's a need for someone to help them see a future," Ms. Peters said. "If they have a sense of meaning in life, they won't have time to be mean and nasty and lash out at you."

Psychologists say the increase in violence against educators is largely due to students' inability to respect authority, handle anger and resolve problems. They describe a general trend of students, overburdened with the pressures of poverty, family and relationships, who erupt with the slightest prodding by teachers and principals.

DISD security reports show that a few teachers also have been attacked by angry parents or intruders who try to steal things from the school. The battle to secure nearly 200 campuses will cost taxpayers an estimated $6 million this year, about 1 percent of the district's budget.

Bob Baker, president of the Classroom Teachers of Dallas, said many teachers suffer from stress and burnout from trying to deal with "a sense of lawlessness in the schools."

"I've got folks just walking wounded," he said. "I'm fighting to keep them in the profession. They're on anti-depressants and seeing psychiatrists."

Thirty-two teachers have been assaulted by students this year. Four more teachers suffered attacks by parents or campus intruders, according to DISD security reports.

The reports show that six principals have been assaulted by students, including one youth who fired gunshots during a foot chase in September. Five attacks against youth action officers also were reported.

Barbara Pausey, a teacher for 17 years at Kimball High School in Oak Cliff, said an attack on her earlier this year was "a total absurdity."

Ms. Pausey said she was lecturing to an algebra class when five students began shouting and banging on the door, demanding to talk to a student in the classroom.

"I asked my class to ignore it and not laugh," Ms. Pausey said. "Then, one of the girls came inside and said, 'I want to talk to *you*.' She bullied toward me and hit me, just slapped me up the side of my face."

The experience left Ms. Pausey anxious. She said she now is more likely to believe that students are capable of violence.

DISD psychologists say the students who lashed out are probably using violence to deal with problems unrelated to the individual teacher. The students also may be copying behavior they've seen at home.

"Maybe they're very angry at a situation at home, something they really have no control over, like mom and dad getting a divorce," said Virginia Wolforth, a district coordinator in psychological services. "A lot of times, kids who get physical don't have the words to get their true feelings and expressions out."

DISD policy requires that students who assault school staff be expelled for at least a semester. Also, teachers are supposed to refer students with persistent behavior problems to counselors. In more serious cases, students are sent to a special downtown school called the School Community Guidance Center. There they learn ways to control and express anger.

"We offer counseling on the source of anger," Ms. Wolforth said. "We don't want to teach them you can't show anger. It's just there are certain ways to do it."

Concern for teachers' safety is not confined to Dallas.

This year, two legislators in Florida proposed a law to allow teachers to carry stun guns for self-defense. The bill has not been adopted. This month, the school board of the Houston Independent School District authorized security officers to carry guns in school.

DISD security officers are not allowed to carry guns, but they work closely with Dallas police officers who do.

Mr. Woolery, the department superintendent, said the district is attempting to deal with an increase in school violence by adding security measures.

"We see an acceleration in the kinds of incidents that are very serious," Mr. Woolery said. "But we are apprehending more students with weapons than ever before."

On average, DISD confiscates 400 guns from students each year. An additional 100 weapons, such as knives and brass knuckles, also are found.

The district's $6 million security price tag includes fences for school parking lots, walkie-talkies for school staff members and salaries for school-based Dallas police officers and district security officers.

Southwest Airlines has donated 10 walk-through metal detectors, and Mr. Woolery said the district plans to buy one for every high school in the next few years.

The district also has a responsibility to provide psychological services to students with behavioral problems, he said.

"We have an endless referral system in human services," Mr. Woolery said. "We have a very sophisticated program, with crisis teams assigned to every single campus. We work closely with the courts, drug-intervention programs."

In addition to expelling students who assault school personnel, district officials call police and pursue charges, Mr. Woolery said.

But some educators say that can produce other problems. Students expelled for assault automatically are excluded from the district's

THESE STORIES REMIND ME OF THE POWER OF WORDS

Parts of each of the following four articles were used earlier in the book. One of the reviewers noted that he wished he could read the remainder of the article. So we're printing them here.

These special articles also help me remember the power of words. I hope they inspire you to report and write with passion. Your sources and fellow staff members will appreciate your hard work. Your readers will eagerly await stories with your byline. And you'll gain that special satisfaction of seeing your best efforts in print.

counseling program. When they return to school, after a semester or school year, their problems could be overlooked.

"The student who assaulted me needs to be getting help," Mr. Miller said. "I'm told that he'd been running from police but showed up to school one day. He needs to be put somewhere to be taught how to become a productive citizen."

In many cases, criminals are entering school grounds to prey on teachers.

School security reports daily tell of cars in the faculty parking lot that are stolen or burglarized, and teachers' purses are frequent targets.

Denise Pulliam said she was grading papers in her classroom at John Henry Brown Learning Center last fall when a woman attacked her and tried to steal her purse.

The woman came to the classroom door and asked about a child, and Ms. Pulliam referred her to the office.

"All of a sudden she ran toward my desk . . . grabbed my neck and mouth as if choking me," Ms. Pulliam said. "I tried to scream, bite her hand. She took one hand off me and reached for my purse under my desk. With that, I kicked her somewhere and scared her away."

The teacher said she does not believe that administrators have taken enough measures, such as locking side doors, to secure the South Dallas school.

But Louise Smith, an administrator who supervises Brown and other nearby schools, said all doors except the front entrance are kept locked. And she said security officers have been asked to patrol the school more often.

Security officers reported that Ms. Pulliam's attacker, who is believed to be a drug addict who roams the neighborhood, has entered the school several times and attempted to steal other teachers' purses, even after being arrested once.

The suspect, who is facing assault charges, was caught hiding in a girls' restroom, the teacher said.

Ms. Pulliam said she is seeking a transfer because she now gets verbal threats from her attacker passed along through her fourth-grade students.

"She says to the kids, 'Tell your teacher next time I won't just strangle her, I'll do her in,' " Ms. Pulliam said. "Now I'm very leery at school. I don't stay alone anymore. I lock my doors."

Mr. Castilla, the school board president, said that the district's security efforts will be more effective when parents become more involved.

Parents can participate in safety committees at every campus.

"This city has to realize that we cannot solve the problem by ourselves," Mr. Castilla said. "We need help. Many are psycho-socioeconomic problems.

"We can bring in more metal detectors, more police," Mr. Castilla said. "But as long as the community is not involved, we'll continue to have these problems. We need to reach the point that parents treat the schools with the same concern for security that they treat their own home." ★

New Kid in Class

So students find that first day real scary?
New teachers do too

By MARK MCDONALD
Dallas Morning News

IT'S THE SMALLEST of sounds, a door clicking shut. But two weeks from today, for new teachers all over Dallas, that sound might prove to be the most frightening thing they'll ever hear.

Their training is over, the degrees have been earned and theories digested. And when that classroom door swings shut for the first time, The Student of Teaching will suddenly become The Teacher, and there will be those 25 young faces— 25 chances for hope and joy and reward, 25 potential stab wounds in the new teacher's heart.

"In that first year you just get the feeling that you're all by yourself and you're all alone," says Laura Corman, a former teacher at Dunbar Elementary in South Dallas. "You're just out there, without any support."

"It's a very lonely experience," says Julie Bangle, a teacher at Rosemont Elementary in Oak Cliff. "Each person has to go in and reinvent the wheel because you're in there with the kids all by yourself."

All by yourself. That is how many teachers will feel during their first year in the Dallas Independent School District. *Here's the classroom, there are the kids, now get in there and teach.*

Almost none of them know what they are getting into.

"College doesn't teach you what you need to know," says Brent Vidrine, 25, who spent his first year of teaching at Rusk Middle School last year. "You can learn about Freud and dogs salivating and all that, but it doesn't mean anything. You've got to reach that certain place in each kid. It's there. You just have to find it."

Finding those places is hard enough even for the experienced teachers. The newcomers usually flounder along, learning as much in their first week of real-life teaching as they did in entire semesters back at dear old State U. Their classes will spin out of control, they will argue with their principals, they will be blitzed by paperwork.

"That first year you find out what you've learned and what you haven't," says John Crain, DISD assistant superintendent for staff development. "That's not unique to DISD or to the first year in any profession. You take all that book learning and put it into practice."

But how to practice counseling a pregnant 14-year-old? How to practice recognizing child abuse? How to practice field trips, detention hall and science fairs?

Vonn Oden, 25, was new to the DISD last year. She taught physical education at Kimball High School after having come from an elementary school in Longview.

"I had to teach in the gym (at Kimball), and that's where all the hooks (truants) hang out," she says. "There was class disruption constantly.

"At the first of the year, I really tried. I'd call parents at night and talk to them about their kids' problems. But the last semester, I was overwhelmed. I just wasn't expecting all the problems . . . . This year did me in."

Kimball principal Robert Payton approved Ms. Oden's request for a transfer to Polk Elementary.

"I understand her frustrations," he says. "Classroom management is our most common problem. She ended up with 17- and 18-year-olds, and it was just too different (from elementary school)."

The trip wires of failure are everywhere for the novice teacher. Every day fairly bristles with chances for some new despair. But the pull of the profession is ineluctable, as powerful as the call to medicine or athletics or poetry.

Laura Corman felt the tug of teaching early. "I decided when I was a little girl that I was going to be a teacher," says Ms. Corman, who attended Dallas' Greenhill School, "and everything I've done since then has been to prepare myself. Camp counseling every summer. I went to Peabody (College at Vanderbilt University) because it was the best education school in the country."

The early rewards were equal to her dreams, and her best moment came when she realized she had taught her first group of first-graders to read.

"It was a little book called *Come Out, Bear*," she says. "When they actually read it, I said, 'Dear God, they did it.'

"I cried, it was so special. It's just the most amazing feeling. It's better than *anything*. Plus, it was a total affirmation that I was doing the right thing with my life."

But her assignment to predominantly black Dunbar Elementary was causing her more than a little apprehension. It was, as she says, "a total culture shock."

"I had never spent much time in South Dallas, and I was put into that school with no support," says Ms. Corman. "I saw one black kid push another black kid up against a wall and call him a nigger. Now, I don't understand where you're expected to get the preparation to deal with a situation like that."

Annette Mitchell became the principal at Dunbar after Ms. Corman's first year.

"She didn't appear that frustrated to me," Ms. Mitchell says, "but you have to realize that things happen in the inner city. A child comes to school and says, 'My daddy was taken to jail last night' or 'They arrested my mother.' Those are things that even we (experienced educators) cannot be prepared for. . . . There's just no way to provide that on-site education for a person coming from North Dallas who's suffering from 'culture shock.'

"If the Laura Cormans and the others read magazines or a newspaper and watch the TV specials, why should they come in with these idealistic views? I mean, let's be realistic."

Ms. Corman got some realism—and help—from an experienced teacher who had the classroom next to hers. "If it hadn't been for my neighbor, I'd have quit within three weeks," she says.

Eventually, even the thrill of that first reading group was not enough to hold Laura Corman. She resigned after three years to work with a B'nai B'rith youth group in Memphis, Tennessee.

"Sept. 1 is going to roll around, and I know I'm going to miss it," she says. "It was such a hard decision. I love teaching and I love children, but my anger was getting in the way of my performance."

How to detour the anger and improve the performance? How to soften the culture shock? How to learn the intricacies of controlling a classroom? How to keep the Laura Cormans in the profession?

The DISD hopes it has the answer with a new teacher-mentor program, which is expected to be in place for the 1990-91 school year. The plan is to have each new teacher teamed with an experienced "mentor."

"Everyone recognizes that you need a mentor, and research has shown that it's extremely effective," says the DISD's Mr. Crain, whose program will be similar to one now in place in Houston.

Meanwhile, some DISD principals, like Cele Rodriguez at Rusk Middle School, have already made use of informal mentoring.

"I assigned a master teacher to be a buddy," says Mr. Rodriguez. "Some first-year teachers do have problems, especially with those who haven't had experience with minority children. They come in with the theories they learn in college (and) their first inclination is to say (about their kids), 'They can't learn.' "

Mr. Vidrine, one of two new teachers Mr. Rodriguez had at predominantly Hispanic Rusk last year, found just the opposite to be true:

"They're the wantingest-to-learn kids you'll ever see."

Still, Mr. Vidrine, who had managed a bowling alley before taking his teaching degree to Rusk, hit some rough spots. The most serious came when he yelled at and embarrassed one of his students—the leader of a youth gang—in front of his class of seventh-graders.

"I lost that kid, and that was a mistake," says Mr. Vidrine. "But I learned from that. I had this other kid, a tough little guy, the leader of the Love Field Rules gang. He had scars all over him. I took him aside after class one day and said, 'Just do your work and we'll get along.'

"By the third (grading period) he was making 95s. When we had a test, he'd give it to me, he'd make 100, and I'd throw it in the trash right away because he didn't want the other kids to see. He made the honor roll the last six weeks, and nobody knows except him and me."

Mr. Vidrine, 25, had reached that certain place with that certain kid. And it was exactly that kind of small victory that led him to pass up a promotion to W.T. White High School to remain at Rusk this year. Even the smallest victories count.

"These kids are brought up losers," he says in his singsong Cajun accent. "All their life they've been told they can't make it. But they really want to learn. They'll work hard, and they won't quit."

Lucky for them, neither has he. ★

Misery on the meatpacking line

For a time, safety improved. But the industry is once again the most hazardous in America

By WILLIAM GLABERSON
The New York Times

SIOUX FALLS, S.D.—Mary Tvedt had learned to live with the dirt and the danger of a meatpacking house. So she did not think much of it when the huge blade jammed in the bacon slicer where she was working. She turned off the power, opened the machine and began clearing out chunks of bacon the way she had a hundred times before in her years at John Morrell & Company's plant here.

After a minute or two, a co-worker thought the cleaning was finished. From where he was standing he could not see that Mary Tvedt was still working. Morrell had not supplied the most rudimentary of safety devices, a lock to keep the power supply off. He hit the switch. The four fingers of Mary Tvedt's right hand came off in one swift turn of the big blade.

It is 81 years since Upton Sinclair's *The Jungle* described the brutal working conditions of the Chicago slaughterhouses. But here in Sioux Falls—and in places like it throughout the Midwest—history is quietly repeating itself.

Modern machinery has changed the look and the sound of a packing house. But the meatpacking industry, which employs about 100,000 people, remains today the most hazardous industry in America. Meatpackers work in extreme heat or refrigerated cold, often standing shoulder to shoulder, wielding honed knives and power saws. Grease and blood make the floors and the tools slippery. The roar of the machines is constant. Occasionally, an overpowering stench from open bladders and stomachs fills the air.

The workers cut themselves. They cut each other. They wear out their insides doing repetitive-motion jobs. They are sliced and crushed by machines that were not even imagined when Sinclair published his book in 1906.

At one end of the plant are the yards teeming with livestock. At the other, boxed and processed meats emerge ready for market. In between, a chain carries hanging carcasses past workers who dismember the meat with a series of cuts, each person performing the same motion over and over, sometimes a thousand times an hour, tens of thousands of times a week.

A meatpacking house has always been a grisly place to work. But after years of improvements, life in the packing house has been getting worse again. Several forces have combined to make life tougher for meatpackers: weaker health and safety regulation, automation, intense competition in the industry and unions weakened by a fight for survival.

After her accident, Mary Tvedt went home, by way of the Mayo Clinic, to adapt to life with her mangled hand. The Occupational Safety and Health Administration cited Morrell because it had not supplied a lock to keep the power off.

But at the packing house, life went on as before. It is three years this month since Mary Tvedt's accident. In those years, 15 of Morrell's Sioux Falls workers have lost fingers or hands or feet, according to a union study of the company's safety logs. Last year, one out of every two of the 2,500 workers here had serious job-related medical problems.

This spring, after a union complaint, OSHA returned to John Morrell in Sioux Falls. After its inspection, the agency proposed the fourth largest fine in its history: $690,000. OSHA claimed Morrell routinely covered up the seriousness of worker injuries in its records. And OSHA charged that the company exposed its workers to 15 serious safety hazards. Morrell is contesting the sanctions. Among the OSHA charges was one that cited the company for willfully failing, still, to supply power shut-off locks for the machines. It was as if Mary Tvedt had never been hurt here.

Lewie G. Anderson, president of the packing-house workers' union, charges that cover-ups of safety problems are pervasive in the industry. Industry representatives say the charge is baseless. Last week, OSHA announced that it was expanding a major investigation, begun last fall, into charges that industry leader IBP Inc., a unit of the

Occidental Petroleum Corporation, underreported worker injuries. IBP, like Morrell, denies the allegations.

Neither Morrell nor its corporate parent, the United Brands Company, would discuss the OSHA charges or the safety record at the Sioux Falls plant. Through a secretary, the chairman of United Brands, Carl H. Lindner, said he would not answer questions. A Morrell vice president, E. Ted Steadman, declined a request to permit a reporter to visit the plant and interview company mangers here. But the OSHA citations and the Sioux Falls employees themselves tell a story of an industry that is using up its workers.

Richard D. Krier is a mechanic. He is a burly, black-haired 45-year-old, and he has worked at Morrell's since just after his 18th birthday. He and his wife have raised four children on his earnings, which have sometimes topped $25,000 a year. They have built a comfortable home in Hartford, 15 miles from Sioux Falls. These days, when he talks about his work, there are sometimes tears in his eyes.

When he signed up at the packing house on the edge of town, Morrell's was where working people went when they wanted to make it. The union was strong. The wages were the best in South Dakota. Working at the company meant security in a company town, where there were few choices.

Over the years, things began to change. The company went from family to corporate control, and the workers did not know who the bosses were anymore. All they heard from their supervisors was talk about competition in the industry and pressure from other meatpacking companies. Always, that meant that the people at Morrell's would have to work faster; they would have to cut more meat in less time.

When Richard Krier started, they were killing 365 hogs an hour at Morrell's. By the mid-1960s, when he was still a new kid working in the canned ham department, they were killing 640, without having added workers. Every time they got a chance, it seemed, the company managers cranked up the chain that carried the carcasses past the workers' stations. These days, according to the union, the hog chain at Morrell's moves at 1,065 heads an hour. Workers on the chain have 3.4 seconds to do their jobs before they must start again. And some of them have to make more than one cut as the pork whisks by.

Even those who are not ruled by the frenzied pace of the chain feel the pressure. When he first got off the line and became a mechanic, Mr. Krier said, everybody seemed to pay attention to safety concerns. But as the production kept getting faster, that would often get forgotten. There was no time for it.

One day four years ago Richard Drier was down in the pit of a freight elevator shaft doing repairs. In the past, he said, the elevator in the next shaft would have been shut down. But with the production line racing, there was no time. "They holler at you," he said. "'You get that thing going. It's costing us a lot of bucks to have that thing down.'"

On that day, the elevator in the next shaft kept going as Richard Krier worked. When the elevator went up, a 10,000 pound counterweight came down, inches away from him. A mesh guard that would have separated the two elevator shafts was missing.

As he worked, he kept watch on that counterweight. And then, on one trip, perhaps by a fraction of an inch, he misjudged it. The counterweight caught him and crushed his left arm on a steel beam. It kept pressing down, as though there were nothing in the way. Instinctively, he pushed at the weight with his other arm. It pinned that one into the beam as well.

Finally, the elevator went down and the weight went up and Richard Krier crawled out of the elevator pit, somehow pulling himself out with his two crushed arms.

It took months for him to recover, and even now, he said, there are still not five minutes a day when he does not think about his left arm because of the ache. When he looked down in that pit three and a half months after the accident, the company had not yet put a guard on the counterweight.

The meatpacking companies acknowledge safety deficiencies in their plants. "No one ought to think we are callous about it," said C. Manly Molpus, president of the American Meat Institute. "It's a problem that is being addressed."

The industry group is planning a safety task force and will soon hold a national seminar, the first on the subject, Mr. Molpus said.

Those measured steps come after the meatpacking industry has topped the Bureau of Labor Statistics' most-hazardous-industries list for five years in a row. For more than a decade it has been in the top 10.

In 1985, the most recent year for which statistics are complete, for every 100 packing-house workers, there were 30.4 work-related injuries and illnesses that required more than first-aid. That is nearly four times the average of 7.9 in all private industry.

Even at companies that say they have aggressive safety programs, the injury rates are high. Last year at George A. Hormel & Company's state-of-the-art plant in Austin, Minnesota, the rate of work-related medical problems was 30.1 per 100 workers, the company said. At Oscar Meyer & Company's Perry, Iowa, slaughterhouse, the company said, the rate was higher than 40 per 100 workers.

Marrianne Sudenga is a meat loader in Morrell's sausage department. She is 57 and single. For 36 years she has supported herself by lifting and loading boxes that weigh up to 90 pounds in a room where the temperature is 32 degrees.

There was a time, she said, when "people used to say, 'What do you do, Marrianne?' I'd say, 'I work for Morrell's,' and I was proud of it. But now it's more of a drudgery to get up and go to work."

One day in November, 1983 a sausage-packing machine malfunctioned and started itself while she was fixing the plastic wrapping at its base. It clamped down on her hand. She had to watch as the packer completed its cycle the way it would have it had been wrapping a pile of meat. She lost the ends of her two fingers.

Last year, she slipped on a greasy floor and broke her leg. Morrell, as it usually does, sent her to see doctors who are under contract to the company. The Central Plains Clinic is across town from the plant, and its doctors say they treat the Morrell employees the way they treat everyone else. But when the workers are sent to the clinic, they say they are "going to Morrell's."

Three days after Marrianne Sudenga broke her leg, the company's doctors said she could go back to work. To keep her job, she went into the packing plant every day on her crutches. There were many days when she could not get an elevator in time to get to her station and she climbed the steps to the light-duty job she had been assigned on the eighth floor of the rambling plant.

Marrianne Sudenga's leg is healed, and she is back at the packing house on her old job. She says she worries about another accident. She has another worry too: money.

In 1982, the union here made a sobering decision. Other companies were closing plants and winning wage rollbacks from their unions.

Morrell told the union local that its time had come. In the end, the Sioux Falls workers agreed to have their pay cut to $8.25 an hour from $10.69.

To keep their jobs, the Morrell workers agreed to change their lives. For Marrianne Sudenga, the concession meant that working at Morrell's would no longer be enough. Her father died after a long illness several years ago. He did not have insurance so she is helping her aging mother slowly pay back the thousands of dollars in bills. Five nights a week, when she is finished at the packing house, Marrianne Sudenga cleans offices at night for $3.55 an hour.

The wage concessions in Sioux Falls came during a period of disruptive change in the industry. A number of packers, led by IBP, built modern, highly automated plants that turned plants like Morrell's ancient Sioux Falls facility into expensive dinosaurs. These "new line" packers also managed to use nonunion labor in many of their plants; in others, they negotiated pay rates that were lower than those prevailing at the old-line processors. Softening of consumer demand for meat in the early 1980s increased the competitive pressures.

The old-line packers had to cut costs and increase production or they would not survive. Between 1969 and 1979, one third of the pork packers in the country closed. Several major old companies went out of the beef business entirely. In 1983, Wilson Foods, one of the largest companies in the industry, filed for bankruptcy protection and slashed wages for thousands of union workers overnight. At almost every plant, the United Food and Commercial Workers union agreed to concessions to keep plants open.

In 1985, the Sioux Falls union negotiated a new contract with a $1-an-hour increase. But the peace was short-lived. This spring, Morrell advanced a plan for a $1-an-hour cut at its 800-worker plant in Sioux City, Iowa, 90 miles away. A strike followed. The Sioux City workers set up a picket line at the Sioux Falls plant on May 1. Since then, the Sioux Falls workers have been on a sympathy strike, honoring the picket lines.

The company says that during the strike it has hired about 1,000 replacement workers here. The union says the accidents are continuing in the plant, as always.

Tim Denherder worked on the kill floor before the strike. He is one of the smart, tough young men who handle the most demanding of the jobs in the packing house. He and a partner share a wobbly hydraulic bench that travels up and down with them as they split 175 beef carcasses every hour. Dick Brown, the head of the union's safety committee, said that the beef chain moves 84 percent faster than it did in 1979. In that time, he said, the injury rate has increased by 76 percent.

Tim Denherder and his partner each hold a heavy bandsaw suspended from the ceiling and each runs the 19 inches of exposed blade down the center of every other carcass on the chain.

If he had grown up somewhere else, Tim Denherder might have been a carpenter or a car mechanic. He would have been good at it. He is a quick study, and he has an easy smile that makes people trust him.

Eight years ago he became a packing-house worker because the packing house offered the best money around. It is a decision he regrets.

At 28, he already has the hands of a packing-house worker. They call what he has carpal tunnel syndrome, and he has had two operations for it. It is a blockage of the channel that carries the nerve to the hand. It comes from moving parts of the human body repetitively, at the pace of a machine. In many departments at Morrell's, half the workers say they have carpal tunnel syndrome.

Long before the doctors were calling it a syndrome, the packing-house workers knew about their hands. On the chain, workers say, it is not unusual to see people forcing their fingers open in the morning and then forcing them back to grip the handle of a knife or saw for the day.

Even after an operation, the weakness and the pain often return. Already, Tim Denherder's grip is so weak that he cannot pick up his children and carry them up to bed. At night, he said, he feels as if something sharp is digging into his wrist. He cannot open his hands all the way and, though he is a strong man who has worked all his life, his handshake has the grip of a boy.

"I think, what's going to happen to me 20 years from now when I can't do anything with my hands?" he said. "I'll be a cripple."

He has looked for other work, but no one will hire him, he said, because his hands are weak. So he goes back and stands next to his partner on the bench splitting cattle all day, every day. There are no breaks except when the chain stops. And it only stops for a 30-minute dinner break at noon, a 10-minute break in the morning and a 10-minute break in the afternoon. With every cut, he knows, his hands get worse. "I've got a high tolerance for pain," he said. "You get used to your hands hurting all the time."

Even when a saw blade snaps, which it does as many as six times a day when the cattle are old and tough, the chain doesn't stop. The man whose blade has broken sits down and changes it right there on the bench and his partner cuts twice as fast.

In the summer on the kill floor it is hot and there are special dangers. The heat of the day combines with the heat that pours out of the carcasses. Once, Tim Denherder took a kitchen thermometer to work. "That day it was 136 degrees in my pocket," he said. With the steam and the sweat, there is more chance of a slip. Time Denherder knows how close he has come. The bottom of his apron and the top of his right boot are in shreds from the saw.

Not long ago, Tim Denherder said, he told his 7-year-old son never to go to work in a packing house.

No one ever told that to Mary Tvedt. Her father had worked at Morrell's, and, she said, from the time she was 5 she always knew that was where she would go.

For a while before the accident, it was a good life. She worked six days a week, often nine hours a day. But she earned more than $25,000 a year, more than she could have hoped for anywhere else in Sioux Falls. She bought a house in the middle-class southwest section of the city. And, like Richard Krier, Marrianne Sudenga and Tim Denherder, she built her life around the packing house.

When she was 29, she decided to face a problem she had always had. She had been vastly overweight. With the help of special surgery, she lost 100 pounds.

"Then," Mary Tvedt said, "this accident happened, and it threw me back in the closet. I was stepping out of one person and becoming a totally new one—and they deformed me."

Mary Tvedt has few visitors now. She will not go out where she might see old co-workers from Morrell's.

But she agreed to tell a reporter about her experience, although she said it was very difficult. "I know it has to be told," she said. "I don't want anyone else to end up like I am." ★

Never too late to make a spare

Madness goes into the 'whee' hours for Dallas' after-midnight hours

By STEVE LEVINE
Dallas Morning News

THE APPEAL IS NOT immediately apparent when you walk past the Camaros and vans in the parking lot and reach the front door where teenage boys smoke cigarettes *and try to impress the girls.*

Inside, it's not the too-bright fluorescent lights blinding you to young love at the shoe counter, not the dull chorus of balls rumbling down the lanes and the resulting explosion of pins. It's not even the great expanse of carpet, Formica and multicolored shoes with numbers on the back. Everything is just as it should be until you glance at a clock and see that it's past midnight.

And then glance at the lanes and see that they're all full. And glance at the shoe counter and see that all the size 9s are gone. Don't glance at your favorite video game. It probably has a waiting line.

Welcome to midnight bowling: Haven for insomniac bowlers, home for *lonely singles searching for a different kind of score* and hangout for people just looking

Midnight bowling, where you can dress up silly, act foolish and be considered normal. Where the guys slug their beer like it's the last one of this lifetime. Where foreigners test their English on teenage girls and harried waitresses. Where gambling—bowling for dollars—is part of lane life. It is, says one alley aficionado, "very, very different."

At least five area bowling alleys regularly offer after-midnight bowling: the two Don Carter's All Star Lanes, which are open 24 hours; Bronco Bowl, open until 3 a.m. on weekends; Jupiter Lanes, open until 2 a.m. on weekends. The Forum Bowl in Grand Prairie is open until about 1 a.m. on weekends.

But why after midnight? One reason is that most bowling centers cater only to league players from about 6 p.m. to midnight every weeknight. Late-night hours give non-league bowlers another option, besides the morning and afternoon, to play their game. In addition, some people are looking for fun that's not necessarily on Greenville Avenue or at the bottom of a pitcher of margaritas.

Yet others are drawn to bowling alleys to be voyeurs of a lifestyle light years away from the Galleria and Sakowitz village—monogrammed bowling bags, rock 'n' roll T-shirts, high-teased hairdos, greasy chili dogs.

"We probably would never date anyone we met at the bowling alley," Sherry Coleman is saying. Miss Coleman, 22, is bowling this Friday night away with two girlfriends at Don Carter's All Star Lanes on Northwest Highway at Skillman. It's their first time out midnight bowling.

Of bowling alley men, Miss Coleman says bluntly, "They're just not the kind of people I want to go out with."

When pressed to explain, she points to the lane at her immediate left where nine guys are drinking and bowling. One of them is wearing a Darth Vader mask and dipping snuff; another has on a clear plastic hat with a feather and is bolting beer.

"Would you go out with them?" Miss Coleman asks.

"Them" includes Jack Hood, the human beneath the Darth Vader mask. Basking in the attention, Hood breaks into a bowling stance he calls "The Launch." He rolls up both pants legs, takes a big pinch of Copenhagen and puts one foot flush on the foot of a friend sprawled on the floor.

When he yells "Takeoff!" he gets a kick start from his friend, runs at top speed toward the foul line and throws the ball as hard as he can.

"It's kind of a good place to be kind of crazy," says Andy Maddox, who admits to being a friend of Hood's. "We're not out here to meet women.

Most guys have their girlfriends with them. We come out for the thrill of competition, for the thrill . . ." Maddox pauses as Hood screams "Takeoff!" and picks up a spare ". . . of victory. but you do find a lot of weirdos out here."

Soon, Maddox and Hood and their seven buddies have forsaken "The Launch" and have begun "Rapid Bowl," where, Hood explains, "you bowl as fast as you can." Miss Coleman and her two friends gamely bowl on.

Jo Jennings, assistant manager of the bowling center, indicates that "Rapid Bowl" and dressing strange are the gutter sports of midnight bowling. She says people used to dress more formally for midnight bowling when she started working at Don Carter's seven years ago, but that was when older people made up the crowd. Now, they have given way to a crowd dominated by college-age kids.

"Most people here are well-behaved," she says, surveying the crowd from her spot behind The Cove bar at Don Carter's. "It's according to how many they've had to drink. When we close the bar, they become a little more testy because they think we shouldn't close. Beer and bowling just seem to go together."

Bob Cruson, president of the Tarrant County Bowling Centers Association and owner of the Forum Bowl in Grand Prairie, says that midnight bowling "has its cycles. Bowling centers do it to generate a certain amount of traffic."

Different alleys use different ploys to draw midnight bowlers. Some offer special rates. Others dim the lights, something that Cruson says "brings people closer together."

"We're always looking for something new," he says.

Something old that Cruson admits has always been popular with bowling is the gambling, "only we don't like to use the world 'gamble,' " he says. "We use the world 'chance.' It's just like golf. Everybody does it. You see the same people in here time after time after time."

Cruson says bowlers normally bet an amount on each game. Several midnight bowlers asked about this admitted they bet "some friendly money" on their games but declined to say how much. City ordinances prohibit gambling in public areas such as bowling alleys.

However, across town at Jupiter Lanes, the weekly special "9 Pin No-Tap Crossover Carnival" brings out more amateur chance-takers than a cheap flight to Las Vegas. Actually, it's not gambling—it's a legal promotional contest.

Bowlers are awarded prize money ranging from $1 to $1,000 depending on which specially marked pins they drop. For instance, a 7-10 split with a colored pin is worth $500 if the bowler picks it up; 4-6, 8-10 or 7-9 colored pins splits are worth $100.

Roger James, manager of Jupiter Lanes, says that "some of the people here live and die with their shots," because many make private bets on the side. "People out here are betting their house rent, their car payments, you name it. And a lot of them have got no business doing that."

During Carnival time, which usually lasts from 8 p.m. to 12:30, the lanes are plunged into an eerie darkness. While people bowl, James strolls around with a cordless microphone shouting encouragement to some and harassing others, even blocking the lanes of the better bowlers trying to win big money. Sometimes he wears masks and sheets to destroy bowlers' concentration.

"It takes a lot of guts to get out there in front of somebody you don't know who's holding a bowling ball," James says.

People enjoy coming out for Carnival time, he says, because they have a chance to win money instead of just spend it. Plus, James says with a grin, "Everybody likes to gamble. I don't care what they say."

"A man and wife can come out here, spend $20 and win half of it back as opposed to going out to dinner and to a movie. That $20 is gone, and they can't get it back. At least here, you've got that chance to get it back."

But not everyone who goes to midnight bowling actually bowls. At Don Carter's East at 1 a.m. on a recent Friday night, there was a 1 1/2-hour wait for lanes so people amused themselves at the video games or pool tables.

And then there's Bronco Bowl, the family entertainment center on Fort Worth Avenue. Here, there is almost too much to do: archery, an indoor batting range, an indoor golf-driving range; 31 billiard tables, a private club and even a 2,500-seat Bronco Auditorium. Oh yes, there also are 72 lanes for bowling.

Kelly Kendrick, the night manager of Bronco Bowl during the late-night bowling hours on the weekend, says that the place becomes a menagerie then.

"That's quite a variety of people when you get archers, baseball players, bowlers and then billiard players all in the same place and then people partying in the club," he says. "It's quite a night."

The majority of midnight bowlers at Bronco Bowl arrive in groups of four to six, grab two or three lanes (there is a reservation system for lanes at Bronco) and "they just party down and drink quite a bit," Kendrick says with a laugh.

Be forewarned though. Bowling at midnight takes its toll. If you figure that you throw a 12-pound ball an average of 20 times a game and you bowl three games, that's 720 pounds of effort. Now add in about two beers per game, a chili dog and several cigarettes. Let's get physical.

"The crowd starts dying out around two o'clock," Kendrick says. "It starts dropping off rather drastically. It is physical. But it's a lot of fun. It's good, clean entertainment." ★